REVISED AND ENLARGED EDITION

SUCCESSFUL
A ☆ R ☆ T ☆ I ☆ S ☆ T
MANAGEMENT

Xavier M. Frascogna, Jr.

H. Lee Hetherington

P9-CFF-652

BILLBOARD BOOKS
An imprint of Watson-Guptill Publications/New York

Revised and enlarged edition first published 1990 by Billboard Books, an imprint of Watson-Guptill Publications, a division of BPI Communications, Inc., 1515 Broadway, New York, NY 10036

Library of Congress Cataloging-in-Publication Data
Frascogna, Xavier M., 1946–
   Successful artist management / Xavier M. Frascogna, Jr., and H. Lee Hetherington.—Rev. and enl. ed.
     p.   cm.
   Includes bibliographical references (p. 278)
   ISBN 0-8230-7689-X
   1. Performing arts—Vocational guidance.   I. Hetherington, H. Lee, 1948– . II. Title.
PN1580.F7   1990
791'.0068—dc20

                              89-18521
                                CIP

Manufactured in the United States of America

First printing, 1990

5 6 7 8 9/99 98 97 96 95

To Fran, Bernadean, and Frank

About the Authors

Xavier M. Frascogna, Jr. is a partner in the law firm of Frascogna & Courtney in Jackson, Mississippi. Frascogna received a B.S. in business and an M.A. in liberal arts from Mississippi State University, as well as a J.D. (with distinction), an M.B.A. and an M.S.S. from Mississippi College. He is a member of the American Bar Association, the Mississippi State Bar, the American Trial Lawyers Association, and numerous other professional and business organizations. He also serves as an Adjunct Professor of Law at Mississippi College School of Law teaching courses in negotiation. Frascogna has served as a member of the board of directors for recording studios and music publishing and production companies. He is coauthor of *Negotiation Strategy for Lawyers*.

H. Lee Hetherington is a Professor of Law at Mississippi College School of Law teaching courses in intellectual property and negotiation. Hetherington received his B.A. from Millsaps College, J.D. from the University of Mississippi School of Law, and LL.M. in Trade Regulation from the New York University School of Law. He is a member of the bar in Mississippi and New York, and a member of the American Bar Association, the A.B.A. Patent, Trademark and Copyright Section, and the Country Music Association. Hetherington is a former Group Vice President of Columbia Pictures Television in Los Angeles, and has been engaged in the private practice of law representing clients in the entertainment industry. He began his career as Legal Counsel and Assistant to the President of Peer International Corporation/Southern Music Publishing Company, Inc. in New York City. Prior to becoming an attorney and law professor, Hetherington was a recording artist and performer under contract to United Artists Records. He is a frequent lecturer and the coauthor of *Negotiation Strategy for Lawyers*.

Acknowledgments

Thanks to Paul Adler, Buddy Allen, Steve Allen, Robert Altshuler, Billy Arnell, Larry Baunach, Sid Bernstein, Marty Blackman, Lorraine Bobruk, Woody Bowles, Nat Burgess, Buzz Cason, Terry Cline, Mario Conti, Ezra Cook, Paul Corbin, Marilyn Craig, Mike Daniel, Stewart Fine, Jim Foglesong, Greg Frascogna, Steve Gatlin, Gina Gaylord, Mark Goldstein, Juanita Elefante Gordon, Cathy Gurley, Gail Hamilton, Mike Hightower, Frank Jones, C.W. Kendall, Barry Knittel, Al Kugler, Judy Libow, Steve Loeb, David Ludwick, Kathryn Lumpkin, David Maddox, Bill Martin, Brad McCuen, Jim Morey, Tom Noonan, Max Okun, Chip Peay, Ralph Peer II, Diane Petty, Judi Pfosky, Michael J. Pollack, Frances Preston, Bob Reno, Emma Sansing, Ed Shea, David Skepner, Debbie Smith, Doyle Smith, Roy Smith, Jimmy Walker, Josh Wattles, Larry Welch, Gerry Wood, and Rolland Yancey.

American Federation of Musicians, Arista Records, American Society of Composers, Authors & Publishers, *Billboard* magazine, Broadcast Music, Inc., Conference of Personal Managers, Harry Fox Agency, the law firm of Maddox & Hicks, Peermusic, SESAC, the Songwriters Guild of America, and Warner Brothers Records.

Special thanks to Tad Lathrop, John Istel, Kay Collier, Mary Bevill, Tracy Graves, Myrna Lea, Alisa Ravenstein, and Toula Zouboukas.

Contents

Foreword
1

PART ONE   ESTABLISHING THE ARTIST-MANAGER RELATIONSHIP

1. Artist Management: What Is It?
7
2. The First Step
15
3. Finding a Manager/Finding an Artist
22
4. The Preliminary Exploratory Conference
34
5. The Management Contract
44

PART TWO   PLANNING THE ARTIST'S CAREER

6. Taking Care of Business
61
7. Attorneys, Accountants, and Business Advisors
72
8. Artist Evaluation and Image Formulation
77
9. The Career Plan
88

PART THREE   MAKING THE PLAN WORK

10. Making Your Own Breaks
97
11. The Artist's Development Team
104
12. The Record Deal
122
13. Music Publishing
129
14. Music Videos, Television, Radio, and Motion Pictures
142
15. Personal Appearances
152
16. Merchandising, Commercials, and Corporate
Sponsorships
163
17. International Considerations
172

PART FOUR   CAREER MAINTENANCE AND CONTROL

18. The Manager's Juggling Act
181
19. Helping the Record Company Help You
187
20. The Road
196
21. Re-evaluation and Critique
205

PART FIVE MASTERING SUCCESS

22. Coping With Fame   215
23. Money Management   221
24. Superstardom: What's Next?   228

APPENDIXES

Appendix 1. American Federation of Musicians
              (AF of M) Agent-Musician Agreement   235
Appendix 2. AF of M Performance Contract (Local
              Engagements)   239
Appendix 3. AF of M Performance Contract (Touring)   241
Appendix 4. American Society of Composers, Authors
              and Publishers (ASCAP) Writer Agreement   243
Appendix 5. Broadcast Music, Inc. (BMI) Writer
              Agreement   245
Appendix 6. Songwriters Guild of America Writer-
              Publisher Contract   249
Appendix 7. Popular Songwriters Contract   254
Appendix 8. Exclusive Songwriter Contract   256
Appendix 9. Management Agreement A   258
Appendix 10. Management Agreement B   263
Appendix 11. Recording Contract (excerpts)   268
Appendix 12. Organizations, Unions, and Guilds   276
Appendix 13. Suggested Further Reading   278

Index   279

Foreword

To say that good artists need good managers is as sublime a statement as saying that the Titanic needed a port in a hurry.

During my years with the American Society of Composers, Authors, and Publishers (ASCAP), when signing up songwriters and publishers, I was amazed at the numbers of both who would sign contracts with other organizations without considering ultimate ramifications—because they received a few dollars more in advance money than what we offered, even though we were offering a one-year contract and they were offering a three-year contract.

Likewise, I'm sure that our counterparts at BMI and SESAC also scratched their heads in disbelief when writers whom they'd nurtured from the early high-risk years defected to ASCAP for a few advanced dollars more.

To many creative types—those folks who like to decry commerciality and the trappings of materialism—the manager represents either an unnecessary, dollar-gulping extravagance or a necessary dollar-gulping extravagance. Neither is completely true, though the latter category comes closer to reality.

One of my friends in this creative cosmos even went so far as to write a song stating, "I'm not making my music for money. I'm making my music for me."

But the same artist became somewhat disjointed when I told him essentially the same thing: Having advanced him several thousand dollars beyond what he had recouped, I, in effect, told him that, for the present, he wasn't making his music for money, but was making it for himself.

He grew furious. He turned red. He called me the Devil.

He stalked out of my office.

So much for my relations with artists.

Let's try managers.

Somewhere, deep in the heart of Texas, a well-known manager invited me up on stage to view the proceedings at an open-air concert. I left the stage voluntarily after he strong-armed a female friend of mine while she was trying to do her best job as head of publicity for CBS Records/Nashville.

Simply stated, I don't like bad artists or bad managers.

But, conversely, I like good artists and good managers. They make the best teams. Whether it's Bruce Springsteen with Jon Landau, Kenny Rogers with Ken Kragen, or Jerry Jeff Walker managed by his wife Susan—not always a recommended pairing, but it works in this case—an artist/manager-combo that's working is one of the most beautiful, and profitable, relationships in show business.

Each feeds off the other's virtues, wallows in the other's weaknesses, and longs for the other's vices. Creative and business intellects seldom merge in the same brain. When they do, it's sometimes more dangerous than advantageous.

"I handle all my business affairs myself," boasts one artist, not knowing that the time and effort he spends in dealing with business matters, if concentrated on his proven creative output, would return dividends ten times that amount.

I treat that artist with the same degree of disrespect that I show any manager who asserts, "I'm learning to play the guitar so I can relate to my clients."

The complexities of both the music side and the business side of the music business are staggering. While one artist shifts some of his energies to tangle with contracts, guarantees, or advances, some upstart Elvis with a lot of talent and a good manager will steal his thunder, top billing, and ticket to the heart of America in a minute. While one manager learns G, D, and E perfunctorily on the guitar, some ace talent-broker will have his clients in a second.

Let's let creators create and managers manage.

Which brings us to this book.

Though "Frascogna and Hetherington" sounds like a Sicilian/Southern combo, I'm here to say that I've known them both—and they're an intelligent and honest team that knows the intricacies of both music and management. That's a rare coupling.

This book holds interest for those artists within and without the music industry. It's flexible enough to give a how-to course in self-management for those foolish enough to try it, perceptive enough to urge career re-evaluation and critique, pragmatic enough to assume that money and fame don't cure all ills, and blunt enough to recognize that there are such pitfalls as drugs, alcohol, and complacency that can torpedo the most well-endowed talents.

It also addresses itself to the unique problems wrought by "the elite few who have reached the level of superstardom" (few) and the "new artists and managers who believe they will achieve this height" (all).

The artist/manager relationship can be the most frustrating, or the most endearing, valuable relationship for both. This book will give you guidance in how to make it the latter. Long live the latter.

Gerry Wood
General Manager/Nashville
Billboard

[PART ONE]

ESTABLISHING THE ARTIST-MANAGER RELATIONSHIP

Artist Management: What Is It?

Artist Management is a familiar term to anyone associated with the entertainment industry. But what exactly does it mean? Usually we think of a manager as the artist's personal representative. While this is generally true, it still doesn't tell us what managers do or how they do it. More importantly, it provides little information on how you can make better decisions on behalf of your clients, if you are already a manager, or how you can make better decisions about your career, if you are an artist trying to make it in the music business. That's what this book is all about.

THE ROLE OF THE MANAGER

Actually, artist management consists of anything that will help enhance or further an artist's career. This can range from comprehensive career planning or complex contract negotiation to suggesting a lyric change in a song or commenting on a new recording. The personal manager is the alter ego of the artist, the part of the artist the audience never sees.

An artist's manager is a planner, adviser, organizer, strategist, overseer, manipulator, coordinator, detail person, traveling companion, and friend. The manager's involvement in an artist's career is total in scope and crucial to its success. In fact, the manager is the only other individual, besides the artist, who gets to see and touch all the jigsaw puzzle pieces that fit together to create the artist's career.

Certain types of managers have narrowly defined duties. A business manager, for example, will ordinarily not be involved in creative decisions or day-to-day details. Rather, it's his function to take care of the books, make sure the bills are paid, and be responsible for making other business-related decisions. In other instances, the manager might be totally involved in every detail of his client's career from both a business and creative standpoint. In the final analysis, the role a manager plays in an artist's career is directly dependent on the needs of the artist, the capabilities of the manager, and what both of them are willing and able to bring to the relationship. Probably the closest analogy is that of a good marriage. To succeed it takes a lot of hard work along with a willingness to communicate, compromise, and change as the relationship grows and new challenges are presented. Above all, a good marriage requires a strong sense of mutual trust and the ability to see things as they are and not necessarily as we would like them to be.

WHO NEEDS MANAGEMENT?

"Why do I need a manager?" It's a question often posed by artists, especially those inexperienced in the realities of the music business who would prefer to avoid paying a management commission. The answer might indeed be, "Maybe you don't." However, the rest of the answer is certainly, "but you sure need management."

The two aren't necessarily the same thing.

Not every artist's career is complex enough to merit a full-time manager, but every artist's career demands at least as much management as there is talent if the artist is to have any kind of chance at making it. If you don't believe that, just stop and take a long-range look at the music business. What pops out at you is that today, more than ever before, the music business is a lot more business than music. Just look at who owns the major record, publishing, and media companies. Warner Communications, Sony Inc., General Electric, and MCA are a few that come quickly to mind. These familiar names conjure up images of earnings per share, return on investment, quarterly earnings, and unfriendly takeovers. Rest assured that these and other major entertainment industry players are in it for the money.

If you still have doubts, just ask any record executive who has been fired for not meeting his corporation's growth projections. It happens all too often despite their being acclaimed for having a great ear or the sensitivity for knowing what makes an artist comfortable in the studio. Sure, all that's important, but if the bottom line isn't there, that executive becomes expendable in favor of someone who can get the job done. And that job is making money.

As an artist or manager, it is that record executive that you have to impress to get a deal. Today, that can mean a commitment by the record company of a half million dollars and up to cover recording costs, video production, tour support, promotion budget, etc., etc., etc. Have no doubt that the executive who green-lights your deal expects to recoup all of that and a whole lot more in gross profit that will allow the company to meet its quarterly income targets and provide a healthy bonus and a little extra job security. If the exec harbors any serious doubt about you and your ability to recoup the company's investment, he or she will likely look elsewhere. Getting the picture?

The high-stakes risks associated with breaking a new artist or keeping an established artist on top is precisely why talent alone is never enough. That record executive has a lot of talent to choose from, but never enough artists and managers capable of doing all the big and little things that spell Successful Artist Management. Specifically, that record executive wants an artist who sets goals, who plans, who executes, who follows up. He or she wants someone capable of interacting effectively with a seemingly unending stream of producers, agents, publishers, promoters, publicists, program directors, roadies, lawyers, bankers, accountants, and fans—all competing for a few minutes of the artist's time. That record exec wants someone with enough drive and discipline to return phone calls, sign autographs, do interviews, and deal with the ongoing pressure of endless details that won't wait until next week and still have enough energy left to put on a killer concert or do as many studio takes as are necessary to get a recording right. That's management or at least part of management. Without it, the reaction to your demo will most likely be "Pass." Can you blame them?

If you, the artist, can effectively handle these management-related responsibilities, then by all means, do so and save the commission. There's no sense in paying someone else to do what you can do just as well for yourself. However, if you can't, then maybe you do need a manager.

MANAGEMENT IS MORE THAN TAKING CARE OF THE DETAILS

If you think you're starting to get a handle on the what and how of management, consider a few more essentials to fold into the equation. The best managers, just like the best business executives, are planners. They are also catalysts that make things happen: movers, motivators, and communicators who work with record companies, producers, agents, promoters, publicists, and anyone else with a stake in the artist's career. The objective is simple: to make sure everyone pulls together with effectiveness and enthusiasm to make the artist shine. If that sounds like a tough order, just know that the reality of doing it consistently is so much tougher.

Jim Morey, who guides the careers of such diverse artists as Neil Diamond, the Pointer Sisters, and Dolly Parton summed it up best: "The artist is the corporation; the manager is the CEO." If you need any more parallels, take a look at successful corporations and their chief executives. The process is the same; only the product is different.

THE QUALIFICATIONS OF A MANAGER

Now that you have a better idea of what management is, let's turn to the next obvious question, "Who can be a manager?" The answer is simple: "Anybody." There are no universities offering degrees in artist management, although there are several very good commercial music programs located in music centers such as Belmont College in Nashville. Aside from a few states, the most notable being California, there are few if any requirements or qualifications a manager must meet. On the whole, artist management is wide open to anyone who wants to get involved. Relatively easy access to the field coupled with little or no regulation can potentially open the door to well-meaning incompetents as well as unscrupulous con men who earn their livelihoods victimizing unsuspecting artists. Chapters Three and Four discuss techniques for recognizing and avoiding both types of would-be managers.

Many persons earn their livelihood exclusively from the personal or business management of artists. They may manage as individuals or as part of a corporate management team. Other very successful and competent managers have dual professions as practicing attorneys, accountants, or financial consultants. Because of their special qualifications or skills, they may be able to offer an artist more versatility. By the same measure, the artist should be certain that these dual-role individuals are as capable as managers as they are in their primary professions. A basic requirement is practical experience in *entertainment* management. Booking agents, record producers, and music publishers may also double as artist managers, though the artist should guard against possible conflict-of-interest problems. These problems will be discussed in more depth in later chapters.

In addition to these traditional categories, friends and relatives may also serve as managers by virtue of their close personal relationship to the artist. When selecting a manager, a new artist may often tend to choose a friend or relative, rather than seeking a professional with whom he has had no prior relationship. This is natural and understandable, but it may not be the best career decision. Often a friend or relative, while being well-meaning, will not possess the knowledge, experience, or contacts necessary to further the artist's career beyond a limited point. There's also the danger that, because of this close personal relationship, a friend or relative will not stand up to the artist and say "no" when firmness and objectivity are required. A "yes man" may be an asset to an artist's ego, but he's certainly of no value to meaningful career development. This is not to say that a friend or relative may not prove to be the right manager for a particular artist, we're only suggesting that the artist should make a special effort to view a friend or relative objectively when assessing his strengths and weaknesses. If you find your judgement beginning to cloud, just remember that record executive working overtime to hit the parent corporation's profit projections. It's business first for him; it should be for you, too.

WHAT A MANAGER IS NOT

While a manager seems to have more duties and responsibilities than any dozen neurotic overachievers, there are certain things he or she should not be expected to do to earn a management fee, unless specifically agreed to by the parties. For instance, a manager is not a booking or theatrical agent. In California, such a dual role is prohibited by statute. In those states where there is no such law, it is traditionally not the manager's responsibility to seek employment for the artist. This is the function of an agent specializing in this type of work who collects a fee that is separate and distinct from the manager's compensation. It is, however, the manager's responsibility to locate agents willing to seek employment for the artist. It is also the manager's responsibility to accept or reject dates and coordinate the artist's schedule with those agents. This isn't to say that a manager may not be directly responsible for a booking now and then, subject to state law, because of certain opportunities or contacts, but the artist should remember that the manager is generally under no obligation to do this.

Likewise, a manager is not normally a record producer. If he does fill this dual role by virtue of special expertise and experience, the artist and manager should work out provisions in the management contract for fair compensation for these additional duties.

A manager shouldn't be expected to promote, exploit, and administer copyrighted musical compositions written by the artist. This is the function of a music publisher. As in the case of dual record production and management arrangements, there are usually separate forms of compensation to cover these added duties.

In certain situations, an attorney or accountant who also serves as a manager will command a higher percentage or fee because of his added dimension of expertise and additional services rendered. This doesn't mean that an artist's manager is required to also act as his attorney or accountant merely because he possesses this special expertise. This is a matter to be resolved in the management contract under the section dealing with definition of duties and manager's compensation.

In addition to the foregoing major overlap areas, the manager should also be distinguished from a publicist, graphics specialist, choreographer, recording engineer, studio musician, side man, road manager, or songwriting partner.

As in many other aspects of life, the final substantive area of overlap and conflict involving artist's managers has to do with money. As a general rule, the manager is not a banker. He shouldn't be expected to make loans or gifts to the artists or to pay for business or personal expenses. However, there are exceptions. There have been and will continue to be instances of wealthy and not so wealthy managers who sink a great deal of their own money into an artist's career. As with any investment, there are some dazzling success stories and probably a lot more tax write-offs.

There is certainly nothing wrong with a manager investing more than just time in an artist, provided both parties go into such an arrangement with their eyes wide open. One potential down-side consideration for the artist is the likelihood that he or she will be expected to give up a much greater percentage of future income in the form of a higher management commission where cash from the manager is involved. One only needs to review some of the sad examples from professional boxing where a kid with a hard left jab sold 125 percent of himself for some easy front money. The best advice here is for both parties to be represented by counsel and to spell out any such arrangement fully and completely in the management agreement. If there is a subsequent change in practice or policy, put it in writing. And finally, to artists tempted by generous offers of advances, remember that loans are just that. Those checks are easy to cash and a whole lot tougher to pay back.

THE THREE SIMPLE BUT PROFOUND
PRINCIPLES OF SUCCESSFUL ARTIST MANAGEMENT

Other than applying honesty, diligence, and time-tested principles of interpersonal relations, there is no one right or wrong way to manage a show business career. This conclusion is supported by interviews we conducted with artist managers and other music professionals in Los Angeles, Nashville, New York, and places in between. These music pros have collectively experienced all the highs and lows the music business has to offer, from the frustration of trying to get that first record deal to the challenge of turning an unknown artist into a national phenomenon to guiding the multi-faceted careers of music legends. Besides providing valuable information, their insights and comments confirmed what we suspected to still be the case ten years after publication of the first edition of this book. We have distilled this wisdom into The Three Simple But Profound Principles of Successful Artist Management, which in the final analysis sum up the basics of effective career management.

1. Talk is substantially more plentiful and less effective than action.
2. You can never know enough people in the business, unless they have a bad opinion of you—then one is too many.
3. No one has yet come up with a satisfactory substitute for hard work, imagination, and persistence.

SUMMARY

It's the manager's responsibility to work with all the various persons enumerated above in the coordination of their respective functions as they relate to the artist. The manager should be viewed as the artist's personal representative, authorized to act in his behalf when dealing with these and others in the entertainment industry.

When the artist negotiates with prospective managers, it's important to discuss exactly what the manager is and is not expected to do. Each party to the artist-manager relationship must understand the role of the artist and manager and the expectations shared by both. A clear understanding of these points is an absolute necessity to any meaningful professional relationship.

║ 2 ║

The First Step

The first step for any artist striving toward a successful career in the music business is to evaluate and recognize his particular management needs. We have already established that every act needs some form of management. The next questions should be: What type? To what degree? What are my alternatives? The answers can only be supplied by the artist himself after careful examination of his goals, resources, and circumstances, yet too rarely do artists ever get around to doing this, or if they do, the analysis is not as complete as it should be. The purpose of this chapter is to help the artist take a good, hard look at what his or her career needs are in terms of artist management.

"HOW SERIOUS AM I?"

The key to constructive self-appraisal is honesty. When you're looking at beating the tremendously long odds against financial success as an artist and, to a lesser extent, an artist's manager, that honesty has to be absolutely brutal. For every singer/songwriter or group who makes it to the charts, there are a lot more who end up doing their tour of duty in L.A. or New York before finally giving up and moving to something that will do more than just pay the rent on a dream that is destined to never be realized.

There is nothing wrong with deciding not to bet all the marbles on something as elusive and potentially unrewarding as a career in show business. Any number of talented individuals lead extremely interesting and rewarding lives after having made an honest acknowledgment that singing, dancing, acting, or playing a musical instrument is an avocation or hobby. If this is the case, you need not read beyond this page. However, there is no penalty for changing your mind, so maybe you will want to continue after all, if just for curiosity's sake.

Whether or not an individual or group is really serious about a career in show business is a difficult question to answer honestly. The gut reaction of most 19-year-olds who can sing and play guitar is likely to be, "What do you mean, am I serious?" That's certainly understandable. The dream of wealth and fame touches us all. But before we accept rock and roll as a ready-made ticket out of the nine-to-five world of adult reality and into the dream world of money and fame, it is helpful for any would-be artist and essential for artist managers to ask three questions:

1. Is the talent there?
2. Is the desire there?
3. Is the belief there?

Talent

The best way we've heard it put came from David Skepner, a long-time manager in Nashville who for many years guided the career of Loretta Lynn. He described the talent necessary to make a career happen as simply being "It." You can't describe "it" but you sure know it when you hear or see it. Don't confuse talent with perfect pitch or technical vocal mastery. Bob Dylan, Rod Stewart, or Mick Jagger wouldn't win an award from the local college music department, but they all had "it" when it came time to make and sell records.

Finding, developing, and exploiting talent is the life blood of the music industry, and while most record company A&R men can tell you what clearly is and is not talent, their collective track record over the years has been severely tainted. For example, several record companies passed on the Beatles before they were eventually signed to Capitol Records. The Grand Ole Opry told Elvis to go back to driving trucks. So much for experts, huh?

The only practical advice we're willing to give on the subject of talent is this:

1. Your competition is whoever is currently on the charts. You had better be a little bit better than they are.
2. Records and concert tickets are expensive. You had better give a

potential fan some real good reasons to lay down their hard cash to see and hear you.

Desire

We have already alluded to the personal sacrifice, the long, thankless hours of hard work, and the years of rejection and frustration that go into making it to the top and staying there. Only the most naive haven't heard the horror stories. Every record company in (New York, L.A., Nashville—choose at least one) passed on _____. (You fill in the name and you'll probably be right.) But even assuming that an artist is willing to give the effort and make the necessary sacrifices and put up with the rejection, there's no guarantee that years of dues paying will finally pay off. Thousands of talented Never Weres have struggled for a lifetime, only to live permanently in the shadow of obscurity. Imagine a contemporary music business version of Vincent van Gogh. They are out there right now, beating their brains out to make it. In fact, one of them might be you. This is the reality of show business.

Even for the few who do make it, how long does it last and at what cost? Decades of the *Billboard* Hot 100 bear witness to more forgotten "one-hit" acts than is humane to recall. Even hard-won success achieved against fantastic odds can still have the potential to destroy performers as artists and as persons. We all know the stories behind Janis Joplin, Jim Morrison, Jimi Hendrix, and Elvis. And then there is the danger always lurking on the road: Buddy Holly, Patsy Cline, Otis Redding, Jim Croce. This list is there for anyone who cares to risk the pain of remembering.

Anyone considering entertainment and especially the music business as a career should balance this aspect of the industry along with the undeniable potential for rewards.

Belief

You think you (or your potential artist-client) have the talent to make it. You say you have the desire to go the distance. Belief is what separates stars from talents. It draws the line between wanting and getting. Belief transcends desire and goes beyond persistence. It is the intangible, inner quality that every act with staying power shares. Without it, an artist and manager may achieve a measure of success, but will never sustain it at the highest levels. There isn't enough talent in the world to make that happen. You've got to want it that bad.

WHAT ABOUT YOUR CAREER COMMITMENT?

The degree of commitment to a show-business career is a factor that can only be controlled by the artist. Some are willing and able to throw themselves totally into a full-time career. But many more artists are unable to financially support themselves from their entertainment-oriented income, especially at the outset. As a result, they often hold part-time jobs or pursue dual careers while working toward their career development goals. The management principles contained in this book are equally applicable to both types of artists and may be applied regardless of financial resources. What's important is not a person's financial status, but rather his talent and desire and belief in both to make it. Without this, management principles are worthless.

Once an artist has decided to seriously pursue entertainment as a profession, he or she need only make a determination of the type and degree of management suitable to his particular circumstances. Regardless of the artist's talent or specific goals, he'll need to employ management principles to fully develop that talent and to realize those goals. For those not yet convinced of the need for some form of management, let's consider the alternative of no management. "No management" means no planning, no organization, and no attention to the day-to-day details relating to the artist's career. The result of this "let's see what happens" approach is an inevitable aimless drift of one's career from one haphazard encounter to the next. The up side of no management is that it's cheap and anybody can do it. Unfortunately, no artist can have a realistic chance at success by taking this approach, unless of course, the lead singer's rich uncle owns controlling interest in the corporation that owns a record label or booking agency. Not great odds, but we imagine it's happened.

MANAGEMENT ALTERNATIVES

What are the management alternatives available to an artist? Basically, there are three: Self-Management, Limited Management, and Total Management. The particular needs of the artist, coupled with his or her financial and creative goals and circumstances, will provide the answer to which alternative should be adopted.

Self-Management

Self-management simply means that the artist will function as manager of his own career rather than retain the services of a separate individual or firm. Every artist should practice self-management if he doesn't intend to seek outside help.

Self-management may often be the most suitable alternative to a new artist who is in the "break-in" phase of his career. Often, his management needs are not sufficiently demanding to require a full-time manager. This is also a very attractive alternative for the artist not financially able to pursue his career on a full-time basis. Another obvious advantage to self-management is that it's less expensive than hiring someone else to provide the same service. It also provides the artist with more decision-making freedom that might not otherwise be present. Self-management avoids the need for interplay and communication between artist and manager closing the gap between planning and execution.

Probably the greatest disadvantage of self-management is that many artists simply don't have the experience and expertise needed to effectively manage their own careers. This is especially true of new artists in the breaking in phase who need an experienced hand to organize and develop their careers. Many costly mistakes can be avoided and a great deal of time saved by taking the advice of a seasoned manager who has faced the same problems before and probably has some innovative solutions to offer.

Another problem is time. It takes a great deal of time to properly organize and map out long- and short-term career strategy, as well as to attend to day-to-day activities. When the artist is already spending much of his time in rehearsal or personal appearances, his management needs often suffer.

A third problem of self-management is the lack of meaningful contacts in the business. A significant part of a manager's value is the ability to obtain exposure for the artist, which is often done through contacts with others in the industry. The new artist usually doesn't have these contacts.

Even though self-management isn't always the best approach, it's always preferable to no management. The principles contained in this book provide the self-manager with a basis for developing his own particular program. As his career develops, he may eventually abandon or modify the self-management approach by utilizing a form of limited management or securing the services of a full-time personal manager.

Limited Management

A second alternative available to the artist is that of limited management. This approach involves retention of a person other than the artist to provide certain specific management services. The artist performs all other management functions not delegated to the manager.

The most prevalent example of limited management is the business manager. This person or firm is usually concerned only with business or financially-oriented matters. The business manager, in most instances, has no input into creative decisions or day-to-day operations. His role is restricted to that of a business advisor and consultant. Usually he is responsible for payment of salaries and expenses, insurance, banking relations, and other business-related functions. In short, it's his responsibility to manage the income generated by the artist. In some cases, depending on his qualifications and relationship to the artist, he'll also advise the artist on tax planning and personal investments. Since the business manager's activities are more restricted than those of a personal manager, he will be paid less. Compensation is normally based on a percentage of earnings or a flat hourly, monthly, or annual fee.

There are other applications of limited management that can prove beneficial to the artist, while stopping short of a total management involvement. An example is a consultation arrangement with an established manager at a fixed hourly rate. This permits the artist to benefit from the manager's knowledge and experience through periodic consultation sessions while not having to pay a percentage of his earnings as a fee. Because of the limited nature of the relationship, the manager wouldn't be involved in the day-to-day details of the artist's career. He'd only serve as an advisor and counselor, much like an attorney rendering advice to a client.

Limited management relationships can be structured to fit the particular needs of artist and manager. This approach is often an effective bridge between the two extremes of self- and total management. It should be considered by the artist as a potential solution to his individual management needs.

Total Management

The third major management category is the total management concept. This approach to artist management usually involves an individual or management firm that is completely involved in the creative and business development and maintenance of an artist's career. This type of manager, often referred to as the artist's personal manager, is concerned with the total picture. His responsibilities usually include ultimate decision-making authority with regard to every aspect of the artist's professional life. The personal manager is in charge of day-to-day operations ranging from major policy decisions to seemingly trivial details.

Obviously, total management is preferable to other management forms previously discussed, provided that the artist's career requires this type of full-time attention and that the artist has the means to pay for it. Clearly, the established artist is the type of performer most in need of total management; however, any artist whose career is sufficiently complex can benefit from the total management approach.

3

Finding a Manager/ Finding an Artist

In many respects, the biggest problem confronting artists is making the decision to get their careers moving with some form of management. Many never do, somehow hoping that talent and luck alone will get them that record deal, producer, booking agent, and all the other ingredients they know are necessary for success. A quick survey of any major- to medium-sized city's music scene will reveal a lot of talented musicians spinning their wheels in small clubs or rehearsal halls waiting for lightning to strike. Most of them are still waiting.

We don't mean to suggest that merely making the decision to approach music as a business solves all your problems. It's only the first step toward building a career, but it is a step many talented people never get around to making. Of course, if you just happen to have a top-10 record, or have half a dozen major labels bidding to sign you to a guaranteed, multi-album release, you will have the luxury of choosing from any number of heavyweight managers on the lookout for the next Michael Jackson or Madonna. But we all know that scenario is a fairy tale. Reality says that it is up to the artist to seek out and sell his or her act to a manager who has the contacts and know-how to put their careers in gear. For the unknown act it's not easy. In fact its an uphill struggle that could take years, but then it's not impossible either. If an artist has the talent, desire, and belief he or she can make it, then there is simply no choice—you go out and do it. The alternative is either to quit or wait on a fairy tale. Not much of a choice, is it?

FINDING A MANAGER:
THE ARTIST'S PERSPECTIVE

We've already alluded to the two courses available to the artist in search of management. He or she can either take the initiative or, in the alternative, sit back and wait to be "discovered."

Before we get into specifics of how to find a manager, it is important to spend a little more time on what to do if a manager does indeed discover you. The odds of a top manager, agent, or A&R man finding you are slim indeed, although if you have been able to book yourself onto the stage of a showcase club in L.A., New York, Nashville, or some other influential music center, your chances have increased. But more on that later. For now, let's say you are playing a medium-sized club in Charlotte or Dayton or Sacramento or any of a hundred other places boasting an active entertainment scene. Assuming you have talent and energy, your chances of being discovered have gone up dramatically. In fact, it happens every night of the week in clubs and lounges all over the country. Unfortunately, being "discovered" under these circumstances could be the worst thing that could happen to a young artist's career. The following true example illustrates the point. Names aren't important, but the lesson is.

A good local rock group that has been together for about a year has finally started to create some excitement locally. All the group members are either freshmen in college or seniors in high school. As musicians, they're better than average, having played in smaller bands in high school. Over the past few months they've become a hot attraction. For the first time since any of them started playing professionally, they're making some money.

The scene focuses on one of the top local clubs, where the group is playing to a packed house. The band is having a good set. The music is tight, their stage show has finally come around, the audience is enthusiastic. The group has never been better. On their first break, they're surrounded by admiring fans. Suddenly, they're approached by a man who looks older and a little more "hip" than the rest of the audience. He introduces himself, telling them that he's a personal manager who just happened to be in the club. He thinks the group is one of the best he's ever heard. The manager is positive that a friend of his at a major record company would be interested in them if he heard their original material. In fact, if they'd sign a management contract with him, he could guarantee a recording contract and a concert tour as an opening act for a "major" artist. Throughout the conversation, he makes reference to all the different record companies and booking agencies he's worked for and all his contacts with entertainment industry executives in California and New York. One thing leads to another and before the night is over, the group has signed a seven-year management contract that they can barely read, much less understand.

For the next couple of weeks, things are fine with the group. They're sure that in a few more months they'll be the hottest new act in the country. But this optimism begins to fade when the group finds out their manager's friend that was to sign them to a recording contract is no longer with the record company. Their prospects continue to dim when the manager tells them they're not quite ready for concerts yet and need more work in clubs.

Little by little, they find out that the manager who was to make them stars actually knows less about managing their career than they do themselves. Loss of enthusiasm is replaced by total disillusionment. The manager has lost interest in the group, but refuses to give them a release from their contract. All the while he eagerly collects his management commission on dates that were already booked, even though he has done nothing on behalf of his clients. Within a year, the group that had so much potential and high hopes breaks up because of dissension and mistrust brought on by this unfortunate situation. The group members go their own ways, cynical and hurt. They're turned off to the music business and to anyone that even mentions the word "contract." Does any of this sound familiar? It should, because it has happened too many times, and will surely happen again.

While there are many honest, capable young managers who approach artists in clubs or recording studios and go on to establish long and successful relationships, there are many more would-be managers who fit the mold of the fast-talking, over-promising con man in our example. This is indeed unfortunate for the legitimate manager because it makes his job more difficult.

The moral of the story is simple: be careful. Never make impulse decisions on a matter as serious as the management of a career. If an artist is approached by someone claiming to be a manager who says he's interested in him and his career, he or she should look for telltale signs of a con man. Does he want to sign the artist on the spot even though artist and manager are total strangers? Does he offer the artist instant fame and success? Is he unrealistic in his promises? Does he make success sound easy? If this is the approach, the artist should beware.

A legitimate professional will never offer to sign a total stranger. He'll want to know as much about the artist's background as the artist would want to know about the prospective manager. If the prospective manager is for real, he'll want to set a meeting away from the club or studio to get to know the artist better and to discuss the artist's needs and his ideas on development of his career. He shouldn't mind giving the artist some background information about himself that can be verified. A legitimate manager won't offer to make an artist an instant success, but will instead offer to work toward achieving success together. A legitimate professional won't ask an artist to sign a contract until he or she has had a chance to discuss the terms with a lawyer. These are things any artist should consider and look for in a potential manager. If the would-be manager doesn't pass these basic requirements, chances are that he's a fraud or a well-meaning incompetent.

One very effective technique available to the artist who has been approached by a fast-talking, big promiser is to simply ask the question, "How?" "How are you going to secure a recording contract for me? How are you going to get me a major concert tour? How are you going to make me a star?" A professional's response would be, "I can't guarantee you any of that, but from what I've seen and heard, I think you have potential and I'd like to explore the possibility of working together toward realizing that potential."

Remember, all the professional should be trying to do when he approaches a new artist is to open the door to establishing a relationship. The con man, on the other hand, is trying to pressure the artist into signing a contract without doing any research or advancing any realistic plan for achieving career goals. Most of the time, this type of manager won't even know or care what the artist's goals are. All the artist represents is a quick commission or the chance to get rich if the artist does get lucky and happens to make it through his own efforts. The best advice in this situation is to take a good look before jumping on someone else's bandwagon. Anyone else's bandwagon.

Taking Action

The alternate path to a sound and successful management relationship is through a well-planned program of action. We assume that, at this point, the artist has recognized that he has management needs, but isn't sure what the next move should be.

Before doing anything else, the artist must first determine what his or her specific needs are. Do I need total management or is my weakness in business management? An artist may not need a manager at all, but rather an attorney, accountant, banker, or business advisor.

A big part of this process is to define career goals and objectives with questions such as: "Where do I want to go with my career? Do I want to place more emphasis on recording? Do I want to concentrate on personal appearances? Do I want to spend my time writing songs? Do I want to do all of these things?" The answers to these questions will further define the type of help the artist needs. This self-analysis may indicate that the artist needs a record producer, booking agent, or music publisher instead of a manager. Likewise, these career goals may indicate the artist needs a manager in addition to these other persons. Yet another conclusion might be that building a complete artist's development team is premature. Perhaps the short-term emphasis should be on building a tighter stage show or writing more and better original songs. Real music pros seldom give an act more than one shot at an audition. If the artist isn't ready, a premature move to impress the right management team can spell failure over more than just the immediate future. The key to success in the quest for the right management situation does not only extend to being ready, but also in knowing when you're not ready.

Selecting a Manager

Once an artist determines where he or she wants their career to go and precisely what is needed to get there, it is time to target potential managers.

This brings us to a brief discussion of geography. There is an old maxim which applies to just about everything, but especially to the music business: "People in business do business where business is being done." As far as the music business goes, that means go to Los Angeles, New York, or Nashville if you are serious about making it big. That's where the people are; that's where the deals are.

Of course all of this is easy for us to say and substantially more difficult for aspiring artists to do, but it's also the truth. Circumstances may dictate a delay in making the move, but eventually you will have to do it if you are serious about taking a shot at the big time. When you get there, make it a point to meet as many people as you can and learn as much about the music scene as you can. It won't be long before you'll know who the players are, from managers to record people to lawyers to agents. It's also your best chance for visibility and exposure. Contrary to conventional wisdom, music people still go to clubs and showcases, provided it's convenient and potentially worth their while. If you are an artist trying to break in, this is your best and quickest opportunity to find a manager with contacts, savvy, and clout.

All of this is not intended to denigrate other cities or music centers outside the Big Three. It is also not to suggest that there are not competent, experienced managers in these cities. But as far as making a serious run at the world of high stakes record deals and songwriting, it's going to be a lot tougher in Oklahoma City or just about anywhere other than where deals are being made. Making that decision to go and seeing if you can compete head-to-head with the best is when an artist's talent, desire, and belief are really tested.

Maybe you aren't ready to make the big step or your career goals are more modest. Fine. We didn't say putting the house up for sale and striking out for Hollywood or Nashville's Music Row was the only way to find quality management or earn your living in music. There are plenty of other avenues which should be utilized no matter where you live. One of the best sources of information regarding potential managers are entertainment industry professionals such as record company executives, booking agents, music publishers, entertainment attorneys, and accountants. These people possess knowledge of and contacts with successful managers and are in a position to recommend potential managers to the artist. In some instances, depending on the circumstances, they may even offer to make personal introductions or set up appointments between the artist and manager. For this reason, the artist should make an effort to get acquainted with those persons involved in the business aspect of entertainment. They are easier to get to know if you live in the same town, but if you can't do that, you can still spend time in one of the major music centers and make friends without having a permanent address. A lot of very productive relationships began through a friend of a friend of a friend.

Another source that may be of some help are organizations such as the Conference of Personal Managers that will provide information on member managers as well as instructions as to how and where they can be contacted.

There are also a number of directories and listings of personal managers, such as *Billboard's International Talent and Touring Directory*. These directories are usually published annually and contain valuable information regarding managers and management companies. They may also contain other types of information. For instance, *Billboard's Talent and Touring Directory* publishes a section devoted to artists. Under each artist listed, there will usually be a notation of the artist's personal manager or management firm. An artist in search of management can tell a great deal from analyzing a manager's clientele, such as how many artists he represents, what type of artists he represents, the field of entertainment in which he specializes, and how effective he is based on the track records of his clients.

These directories, while helpful, don't tell the full story. Many successful managers aren't listed because of personal preference, especially those who aren't seeking new artists because of commitments to their present artist roster. Attorneys or accountants who also serve as managers may, for professional reasons, not be listed. Artists should also note that a listing in such a directory isn't necessarily an endorsement or assurance of a manager's competence. Most of these publications merely publish the names and addresses that are sent to them.

A directory is just a compilation of information and should only be used as a point of departure. An artist should investigate the people he may be interested in and never assume they're competent professionals just because they have a listing. And never assume they're the only managers available.

Getting the Appointment

With this preliminary information in hand, it's now possible to narrow the list of prospective managers the artist will want to pursue. Unfortunately, getting a name and phone number from a directory and getting an appointment are two very different exercises. As with any other successful businessperson, a manager with a track record and a stable of established, income producing artists will most likely be surrounded by secretaries and assistants whose job it is to screen out everybody who wants 15 minutes of his or her time. In a nutshell, that's why "cold calls" seldom work. The challenge facing the new artist, then, is to find ways to make the initial contact something other than just a cold call.

Because the music business is built on personal relationships, the best way to break the ice is through a mutual friend, preferably another entertainment professional whose opinion the prospective manager respects. This sets the stage for the artist by putting the manager in a receptive mood before the first meeting. However, this method of "getting in the door" is generally not going to be available to new artists unless, for instance, they're already under contract to a major record company, booking agency, or publisher who has a direct interest in helping him or her obtain a quality management situation.

Another method that has gained in popularity over the past decade is the "hired gun" approach. Many influential entertainment attorneys may be hired by new artists to make introductions and set up appointments and auditions with people in the business. Most charge an hourly fee for their services, though there are other forms of compensation, including percentage arrangements if their efforts lead to a deal. The word here is to ask around about fees and integrity. While lawyers are bound by a code of professional ethics, there is still the potential for abuse.

Before you start flipping through the yellow pages, a word of caution is in order regarding the hired gun approach. Attorneys are no different from the influential people they introduce their clients to. Their reputations and credibility are their stock in trade. No reputable, connected attorney will risk that by taking on a client they are convinced cannot make it. Top managers rely on their judgement. This means you had better be prepared to sell yourself to the lawyer as if he or she were a manager or record company. If you aren't absolutely convinced you can do that, you're not ready yet.

If the friend of a friend and hired gun approaches aren't workable options, the next best and about the only other approach is for the artist to go directly to the manager through letters or phone calls. But, be prepared for disappointment. Rarely will the switchboard put an artist through to the top on the first try. The artist will often have to convince a subordinate that the boss should talk to him personally. This can become an art form in itself. It can also pay big dividends. In the music business as in most fast-paced industries, never underestimate the power of the secretary or personal assistant. Oftentimes, they can get you in the door if they want to. The key here is sincere persistence without becoming a pest. If every unknown artist gave up trying just because someone told him "no" or put him off, there would be very few stars around today.

On the subject of getting in the door, a high percentage of decision makers we talked to confided that they consider the barriers they throw up to be a test of persistence and self confidence. "The people with the drive to make it will find a way to see you," was the way the President of a large and successful agency put it.

One last word on getting that all-important appointment: the more activity an artist can create, the better the chance he or she has of coming to the attention of people that can open the right doors. Country singer Dwight Yoakam is a good case in point. The Los Angeles-based singer had developed a loyal following of fans, radio, and press people in L.A. by releasing his own record and playing top showcase clubs like the Palomino in North Hollywood long before he was finally signed by Warner Brothers. He had created so much activity on his own that the music establishment could no longer ignore him.

Assuming you have secured the initial appointment, remember that the purpose is merely to introduce yourself to the manager and lay the groundwork that will lead to a more detailed exploratory conference. Be brief and to the point, and don't waste the manager's time. The object at this stage is to make a good first impression and create curiosity in yourself as an artist. That means being organized, concise, and businesslike. Above all, be prepared.

The Sales Kit

Before initial contact is made with any prospective manager, the artist should prepare a kit that includes a cover letter stating who he is and his purpose. It's important that the artist convey to the manager how he came to select him. If the artist was referred by a friend of the manager or another industry professional, he should mention that fact in the letter. At the very least, the artist should cite recommendations or references from within the industry. He should mention the names of the individuals making the recommendations, especially if they are well known and respected. Do not mention a name if it would be meaningless. The cover letter should list the artist's name, address, and telephone number, and should make reference to the enclosed kit.

The kit should contain pictures and information about the artist, including at least one 8 x 10" (20 x 25 cm) photograph of the artist, a brief one- or two-page biography setting forth the nature of his act, his past experience, and other relevant information (e.g., does the artist write his own material, has he been associated with other name acts, and so forth), and a brief statement of the artist's goals and management needs. Other items that could be included are trade press or newspaper clippings, a list of important past appearances, and information on future bookings, especially those the manager could attend. Another must for the kit is a tape of three or four of the artist's best songs or routines. The tape should be as professional as possible. Remember, the manager will be making his all-important first impression of you based on what he hears and sees. An artist rarely gets a second chance to make a favorable impression.

This type of professional presentation, combined with the artist's ability to conduct the first phone conversation or personal interview in an organized, articulate, and businesslike manner will improve the chances of the manager becoming interested in the artist. The manager will appreciate the fact that the artist is professional in his approach to the entertainment business, has at least a basic understanding of the importance of management and organization and, above all, is realistic about what a manager can and cannot do for an artist.

All of this may seem like common sense to you, but you would be surprised how few artists go to the trouble of doing it. Believe us, it makes an impression on a manager, indicating that here is a potential long-term artist and not just another thrill-seeker or somebody with a pretty good voice and little else. Of course, all the slick presentations in the world won't compensate for lack of talent, but if the talent is there, this type of presentation will probably rate you a closer look by a pro. Face it, everybody is looking for talented, intelligent, persistent people. This kind of presentation is your best bet for communicating those qualities.

Every artist should be cautioned that the all-important first impression can cut two ways. An artist can cause himself immense harm in the initial interview by making certain fundamental mistakes. For instance, never be rude or arrogant, make demands for large advances, or voice unrealistic goals. Know when to talk and when to listen. Remember what has been emphasized before—talent alone is never enough. Attitude, cooperation, self-confidence, persistence, and drive are just as important if not more so. Talent is everywhere; these other qualities aren't. An experienced manager can usually tell a great deal about the artist's attitude from the first meeting. If it's bad, there won't be a second meeting.

Trying Again

If you've managed to get a foot in the door and sell yourself effectively, things should begin to happen for you. If not, don't quit. Resourcefulness, ingenuity, and persistence comprise the only formula that will finally pay dividends for you. Nothing is going to happen unless you make it happen.

If you succeeded in making initial contact but failed to make the sale, seek the manager's advice as to how you can strengthen your weak points. An artist can obtain priceless information by listening to what an experienced manager has to say. If the manager feels the talent is there, but that he personally doesn't have adequate time to devote to your career, ask him to refer you to other managers or music business figures.

Regardless of the outcome of the meeting, strive to establish and maintain a good rapport with him. Often, this initial contact can be the first in a series of "breaks" that will lead to the realization of your goals. It's also possible that a manager who may not be interested today may very well be interested at some point down the road. Things change; never close the door.

FINDING AN ARTIST:
THE MANAGER'S PERSPECTIVE

Managers, especially younger and less experienced ones, have many of the same problems as new artists. Finding a promising artist who possesses talent, a realistic view of the industry, and a willingness to take advice and work hard is not easy. It's even more difficult when a manager doesn't have the same level of reputation and track record as more seasoned managers.

Getting Started

The question is often posed: "I want to get into management, where do I start?" Just as in any other profession, there are dues to be paid and contacts to be made. In this respect, an aspiring manager bears a close resemblance to a new artist. One should gain as much practical experience in the entertainment business as possible before trying to pay the bills managing careers. Because good managers oversee the big picture of their client's careers, any experience in the business is valuable, whether it be in management, booking, recording, engineering, producing, music publishing, public relations, or any of a number of other capacities. All of these training grounds provide a feel for the environment in which you'll be operating. They also allow you to make contacts that are essential to effectiveness.

Another form of dues paying is education. To be effective, the manager will be expected to understand or at least be aware of many complex financial and legally-based subject areas. He must be able to make important business decisions and deal knowledgeably with attorneys, accountants, and bankers. The manager must be able to communicate with others, to express himself orally and in writing on numerous levels. For these reasons, a college degree as well as some form of advanced professional training in law or business can provide a tremendous edge.

Attracting Clients

Aside from developing qualifications and gaining experience, the more direct question is, "How can I attract clients?" Probably the best way is through referrals from others in the business such as label executives, publishers, booking agents, producers, entertainment lawyers, or accountants. These people have the inside line on promising new artists. Through personal contact with these people, a young manager can gain valuable information on these emerging artists.

Another method of attracting clients is through existing clients or other artists with whom the manager is acquainted. Artists frequently count other artists as their friends. The unknown manager's best calling card is his own artist-client. An artist who believes in his manager and is satisfied with the job he is doing for him will spread the word. The artist grapevine is an effective business attracter.

A third method of finding new artist-clients is the direct or discovery approach. This means personally scouting talent in clubs or recording studios hoping to find artists with the talent and personality that would merit an investment of time and effort to develop their careers. The problems inherent in this type of approach have already been discussed from the artist's point of view. Many artists will mistrust managers taking this type of approach for the reasons mentioned previously. The young manager should not over promise or make bold statements that he may not later be able to back up. The initial approach should be businesslike and reserved, inviting the artist to meet at a later time, preferably at the manager's office.

The manager should be extremely cautious as to the type of artist he approaches. Many artists don't have the willpower, maturity, or ability to make it. This type of artist can become a drain on the manager. Although problems are possible with any new artist, the likelihood is probably greater with artists discovered through the scouting method. In order to guard against this happening with any artist, the manager should conduct a very thorough preliminary exploratory conference in order to increase the prospects for success of the artist-manager relationship. There are so many aspects that go into career development and management and only a limited amount of time to get it done.

[4]

The Preliminary Exploratory Conference

Probably the most influential force behind an artist is his manager. He is concerned with the day-to-day planning, control, and development of the artist's career. As discussed in Chapter One, the function of a total manager includes a multitude of duties, with the focus of attention being the artist-client.

The most important factor in establishing and maintaining a truly rewarding artist-manager relationship is mutual trust. The artist must have total confidence in the manager's motives and abilities. Conversely, the manager must be committed to the artist and his art form. We have previously suggested that a strong artist-manager relationship is a partnership analogous to a stable marriage. Research indicates that the longer couples date prior to entering into a marital relationship, the greater the probability for a lasting marriage. We believe this theory is applicable to a successful artist-manager relationship. A long "courtship" offers both artist and manager the opportunity to evaluate the other, hopefully resulting in mutual trust and respect. Without these qualities, problems will undoubtedly surface at some point. Although the luxury of time is not always possible given the fast pace of the entertainment industry, both parties to a prospective artist-manager relationship should nonetheless be very sure about each other before undertaking an obligation of this magnitude. The key to ensuring a strong working relationship between the parties is the preliminary exploratory conference.

The purpose of the preliminary exploratory conference is to afford both artist and manager the opportunity to accumulate the various bits of information necessary to make an intelligent decision regarding formation of an artist-manager relationship. The information exchanged at the preliminary exploratory conference will also help to determine the type of management relationship that is actually needed. Furthermore, this information will aid the attorneys in the preparation of the final management agreement.

The purpose of the preliminary exploratory conference is not to negotiate the management contract, but rather to assemble data helpful to both artist and manager in evaluating whether to set up a formal relationship.

THE PRELIMINARY EXPLORATORY CONFERENCE—THE ARTIST'S VIEWPOINT

Assuming sufficient interest has been indicated by a prospective manager, the artist should request a conference to explore the advisability of representation. Prior to this conference, the artist should have formulated the answers to three key questions:

How did I get involved with this particular manager? Was it by recommendation or referral from someone else in the business? What is this person's track record? Who are his or her clients? Too often a manager is retained because it "just happens," or because the person has been a long-time friend or because he is a "yes" man that will tell the artist what he or she wants to hear. Being a close friend or relative should not necessarily exclude a person from being considered as a potential manager, but they should be subject to the same objective scrutiny as any other potential manager. Because of the profound effect that a manager has on an artist's career, it's absolutely essential that the artist investigate the potential manager as thoroughly as possible.

Where do I want my career to go and how can this person help get me there? If the artist doesn't have some idea about his future, it's difficult to expect a manager to read his mind. Even more dangerous is the artist who turns over his career to a manager who might have divergent ideas or conflicting philosophies of career development. Sooner or later there will be trouble with a lot of wasted time in between. The artist can be specific in his request for managerial help only if he first has formulated his goals.

Although the artist may generally know where he wants to go with his career, how to get there may be a puzzle. This is where a good manager earns his or her percentage. Once the goal has been established by the artist, and the manager has acknowledged that it is both realistic based on the artist's talent and within the manager's range of expertise, the discussion should turn to "how" the goal can be reached. This can include a preliminary timetable for action and the formulation of sub-goals and proposed strategies for meeting them.

The parties shouldn't try to map out an artist's career for the next five years at this preliminary stage, but the approach does provide a framework for substantive talks aimed at fleshing out goals, philosophies, and capabilities. It's a great way to find out if the prospective artist and manager are on the same wavelength.

Beware of a manager who has no answer to the "how" question. A lack of ideas regarding the preliminary construction of an artist's career plan could indicate a lack of interest in the artist, or a deficiency in expertise necessary to help that artist take his or her career in the desired direction.

What specifically do I want a manager to do for me?   The answer to this question will enable the artist to compare the services offered by the manager to the artist's preconceived needs. While deviation from these management needs does not necessarily indicate the manager can't do the job, it does give the artist some conception of his own needs for purpose of discussion during the initial conference. This provides a starting point for preliminary discussions. Objectives and needs might change, or the artist might discover what he really needs is a lawyer, banker, producer or what have you. It is much more productive to discuss specifics than have a conversation that goes something like this:

MANAGER: "How can I help you?"
ARTIST: "I need a manager."
MANAGER: "Fine, where would you like to see your career go?"
ARTIST: "I want to be a star."
MANAGER: "Good."

Tells you a lot, doesn't it?

During the actual conference phase, the artist should discuss his goals and needs in detail and invite the manager to scrutinize them objectively and aggressively. If there is going to be a personality conflict or just a failure to connect, the preliminary conference is the time to find out. Likewise, if the manager's ideas are off the wall or just not meshing with those of the artist, it's better to know that before a deal is struck.

What is this manager's background?   As another key topic during the preliminary exploratory conference, the artist should inquire about the manager's credentials and track record. While a prospective manager may know a lot about record production or booking, this doesn't necessarily give him the credentials or background to do the job in other areas. Unless a manager's reputation is well-known, the artist should inquire directly, but tactfully, into the manager's capabilities and past experience.

Another often overlooked qualification in a manager is his level of formal education. Although it isn't essential that a manager have a college degree in order to be qualified for artist management, it would certainly be a valuable credential. This is true not only in the entertainment industry, but in any business. Moreover, if the manager's degree is in business or psychology, the credential is potentially worth even more to the artist. And if the manager holds graduate or professional degrees, the value is higher still.

Probably the most critical factor in determining a prospective manager's credentials is his reputation. This can be easily determined, first, by asking others in the industry. Is he respected for his ability? What about honesty, integrity, and fairness? Because the manager is an extension of the artist, these are critical questions. Reputation can also be determined by finding out who his clients are. Having highly successful clients speaks for itself, although it doesn't always provide an accurate measure of integrity and honesty. That question should always be asked separately and verified to the artist's satisfaction without regard to track record.

Another method of measuring a manager's value is by observing his involvement in various organizations. Is he a member of the Conference of Personal Managers or other important trade organizations or associations? Does he serve or participate as a panelist at music industry forums and seminars? Although not always dispositive of the question, it will provide some indication of how plugged-in to the industry the manager is.

What does the manager want for his services?   An obvious issue of importance to the artist that should be confronted at the preliminary exploratory phase is money. Depending on the relative bargaining position of the parties, several alternatives are available. The percentage arrangement, whereby the manager is paid a percentage of the gross earnings of the artist, is the most common. The percentage will vary from 10 to 25 percent of gross earnings, with some managers taking an even higher percentage. A refinement of this approach is to base the percentage on net income with the problem being a definition of the term "net."

Another approach is to set the manager's percentage at an escalating rate, depending on the amount of total gross income. As gross income goes up, so does the percentage. Alternatively, depending on the status and negotiating position of the parties, a management percentage could decrease as gross earnings increase. Each particular arrangement is as unique as the parties themselves.

Sometimes a young artist may be in a very weak financial position, incapable of paying any management percentage, but in desperate need of a manager. A possible solution here is the retainer method of compensation. Instead of paying the manager a percentage of all monies received, a flat or fixed sum is paid on a weekly or monthly basis. Although the retainer may be much less than a set percentage of gross earnings, it might be a vehicle to bridge the gap between artist and manager during the artist's early, struggling years. Hopefully, with the help of an effective manager, the artist's earnings will increase to a sufficient level to allow conversion to a percentage-of-gross-earnings arrangement.

In some cases, a manager might offer his services for no compensation at all until the artist's earnings reach a certain level, and thereafter take a higher percentage than normal to make up for the earlier deficit. The attraction is obvious, but the artist should consider the down side as well. While it may appear the artist is getting a "great deal," the actual net cost to him could be substantially higher. Another pitfall in the nonpayment situation is a lack of commitment of both parties. An unsatisfied artist is in a weak position to voice complaints.

What are some other areas of doubt or potential conflict?   Another question that should be raised during the preliminary exploratory conference pertains to a manager's potential conflict of interest. Simply stated, he should be asked, "Do you have any conflict of interest that might have a detrimental effect on your ability to manage my career?" For example, a manager may also be a producer or publisher. Although various state statutes and musicians' union and management association guidelines prohibit overlap of a manager's involvement in other areas such as booking, such overlap does take place. While the artist should be cautious in defining such areas, they shouldn't necessarily be construed as negative in themselves. Many times, the fact that a manager owns or has an interest in a recording studio or production company can be beneficial to the artist-client. The artist should be aware of any overlap and take appropriate steps to guard against potential problems arising out of any such conflicts of interest.

Another question to ask is, "How inquisitive is the potential manager during the preliminary exploratory conference?" An experienced manager will want to know all that he or she can about an artist. There should be a multitude of questions, aimed at accumulating personal and business data in order to construct the preliminary career plan. Beware of the manager who doesn't seek information about the artist. Without it, a plan cannot be formulated and without a plan, there's no management.

Specifically, an astute manager will want to know about the artist's career history and financial condition, both professionally and personally. Does the artist have a lawyer or accountant? Does he or she have life insurance, equipment-vehicle insurance, and so forth? Are there any outstanding contractual commitments with record companies, publishers, agents or other managers? What about debts or other financial obligations?

Once the artist has been through the preliminary exploratory conference stage, he or she should have a great deal of information coupled with a strong first impression with which to evaluate a prospective management relationship. The artist should take a couple of weeks, if possible, to reflect on the preliminary exploratory conference meetings. He should objectively review the manager's ideas, proposals, and suggestions, especially if they are at odds with those of the artist. Careful consideration should be given to the personal chemistry between the two as well as the manager's credentials and reputation in the business. It's also important that an artist reconsider his or her own goals and preconceived ideas about the role a manager should play in career development and direction. If there are any major areas of doubt or conflict, clear them up before going forward. If this can't be done, the artist would do well to keep looking.

THE PRELIMINARY EXPLORATORY
CONFERENCE—THE MANAGER'S VIEWPOINT

The formation of a good artist-manager relationship is a two-way street. This is why the preliminary exploratory conference is just as important for the manager as it is for the artist. Basically, the manager's questions during the preliminary exploratory conference should center around certain key areas which correspond to concerns of the artist. As in the case of the artist, the manager should ask himself, "Why did the artist come to me? Was he recommended or referred by one of my clients or by an associate or friend within the industry?" Quite possibly, the artist and manager may have been working together in another capacity (e.g., publisher-songwriter). Whatever avenue the artist has traveled to reach the manager, the specifics are important.

First of all, the prospective manager will want to know where the artist stands in his or her career. If the referral came from the head of a major label who had just committed to a multi-record guarantee, the manager would be in a much stronger posture to assess the advisability of getting involved and the kind of competition he or she might face. If, on the other hand, the artist was brand new or had just been dropped by a record company or booking agency, the manager would want to know that as well. In any event, one of the first calls a manager would make would be to people who could provide reliable information on the artist seeking career help.

The manager should next evaluate his managerial style, philosophy, and current client obligations to see if the potential for a compatible match exists. For example, if the manager's strengths are in the country music market, he would be extremely cautious of signing a hard-rock attraction unless the artist sought to make a change in direction. Even then, a manager would be well advised to pass if he or she concluded such a reversal was too much of a stretch. Unless the manager has the requisite knowledge of the music industry segment required by the artist, he or she cannot adequately represent that client. A manager capable of wearing several "hats" is certainly not impossible to find; however, such versatility is not common. In short, the manager must be aware of his own capabilities and limitations when considering signing a new client.

In addition to other considerations, the manager's perception of the artist and art form must be analyzed. The manager must be on the same artistic wavelength as the artist. Each must be in clear agreement on the career direction of the artist and be committed to taking that path. If, for example, a manager views his client as Prince with subtle country overtones while the artist envisions himself as hard country in the vein of a Randy Travis, there has been a serious lack of consensus on image and direction. This kind of fundamental difference in image perception can only lead to problems. It is very important to devote time to a detailed discussion of artistic goals and direction.

Management compensation is obviously another important consideration for discussion. As noted in the artist's view of the preliminary exploratory conference, management compensation can take many forms. The primary point here is for the manager to know and understand his or her bargaining position. The same general considerations discussed earlier are equally applicable.

In addition, if a manager is inclined to sign the artist, the goals and time requirements for accomplishing these objectives must be analyzed. Especially if the manager has several other clients, time availability can be crucially important. Also, the financial arrangement must be equitable in terms of time expenditure versus compensation. Ideally, from a business standpoint, a manager should view his clients like an investment portfolio, some being current revenue producers, others on the brink of financial maturity, while still others are advancing through a building and growth stage with little expectation for immediate return. A mixed portfolio of clients can be a strong determining factor as to the flexibility a manager has in setting the amount and method of compensation.

A MANAGER'S CHECKLIST

In order for the manager to suggest a preliminary career plan for the artist, a wide range of business-oriented questions must be answered. This checklist of fundamental questions provides a suggested framework which you will want to supplement as circumstances dictate.

1. What legal entity is the artist doing business as: sole proprietor, partnership or corporation, or joint venture? An ownership entity must be established, especially where the artist is a duo or group.
2. Are there any existing management, booking, recording, or publishing agreements in effect? If so, what are the terms of these agreements and what is the status of the artist with regard to the parties to those contracts? If there were previous agreements that are allegedly inoperative, are there proper releases evidencing such?
3. What are the artist's professional assets?
4. Is the artist a member of the proper union organization? If so, but not in good standing, why?
5. What is the artist's personal and business debt structure?
6. Does the artist own a registered servicemark, and what about other legal safeguards relative to the Right of Publicity, Unfair

Competition, and other applicable doctrines designed to protect one's name, likeness, and identity?

7. What is the artist's earning history over the past five years, broken down into amount and source?

8. Does the artist keep proper financial records?

9. Does the artist have good banking relations?

10. Has the artist filed proper federal and state income tax returns for the last five years?

11. Does the artist have proper insurance coverage?

12. What is the artist's reputation and present image?

13. Does the artist write his own material? If so, is he a member of a performing rights society? Who controls and administers his copyrighted musical compositions?

14. Does the artist have any affiliate companies (e.g., publishing, production)?

15. What is the artist's past recording experience?

16. What has been the artist's exposure, both live and recorded?

17. What current industry trends might influence the artist's career?

As stated earlier, these questions are fundamental. While they don't indicate the entire spectrum of inquiry a manager could delve into relative to business planning, they do provide the basics. As each question is raised, additional questions will undoubtedly be suggested. Prior to drafting a final management agreement, the expertise of an attorney and accountant will probably be required, depending on the training and background of the manager.

Finally, but probably most important, is the personal aspect of the potential management relationship. The manager must determine what kind of personal relationship he'll have with the artist. He must ask himself, "Are we compatible? Is the artist willing to work toward his goals or does he expect me to do everything? Is the artist realistic? Does he or she have the ability and discipline to face the hard times as well as the good? Is this artist dependable? What is his or her reputation in the industry?" Answers to all the questions related to talent, potential, and business considerations may be positive, but unless the same can be said of the personal dimension, the manager should seriously question any decision to proceed. The real-life stories of personal problems wrecking a promising career have been amply documented. Be careful that the opportunities aren't outweighed by the potential problems, and act accordingly.

EVALUATING THE PRELIMINARY EXPLORATORY CONFERENCE

The formal vehicle of the preliminary exploratory conference provides both artist and manager with a comprehensive tool to evaluate each other's talent and personality. At this stage, the manager should have enough data to begin to design a career plan for the artist, should a management relationship result, while the artist should have a much better understanding of his or her management needs. No matter how long the preliminary exploratory phase takes, whether it be several days or several weeks, it should be complete.

Once the questions have been asked and answered, approaches and ideas shared, both manager and artist have a decision to make. Procrastination doesn't enhance a good artist-manager relationship. If both agree on goals, direction, and methods, and most importantly, on each other, they should be eager to begin. If the answer is yes, then go to work. If it's no, on either side and for whatever reason, then keep looking.

[5]

The Management Contract

Assuming the preliminary exploratory conference results in a decision to proceed with an artist-management relationship, the next step is to define and formally structure the business and legal details. The end result of this process is the management contract.

It's often difficult for an artist and new manager to sit down and address delicate areas relative to financial and legal rights and responsibilities that flow out of their newly created relationship. Both parties are eager to get started on more creative matters, and neither wants to jeopardize the fledgling relationship by bringing in lawyers and legal jargon. Regardless of this understandable reluctance, it's absolutely essential that a formal management contract be negotiated and finalized before anything else is done. Handshake management deals, despite their good intentions, are nothing more than open-armed invitations to disaster.

The first step in negotiation of the management agreement lies with the parties themselves. The preliminary exploratory phase should have provided the forum in which to exchange viewpoints on how each envisions the relationship, including the respective roles each will play. There should also have been a treatment of the specific subject areas relating to financial, business, and legal aspects of the management relationship. Depending on the depth of those discussions, the parties should move to finalize the basic areas of their agreement. Undoubtedly, many unanswered questions and new areas for discussion will surface. Listed below are several broad subject areas on which the parties should focus during their initial discussions:

- Manager's duties
- The artist's role

- Length of the agreement
- Manager's compensation
- Manager's expenses and accounting procedures
- Prior contracts that may still be in force

Once the parties have reached a general understanding of what they want their relationship to be, the next step is for each to seek separate legal counsel. When choosing an attorney, each party should make sure his lawyer has experience in the entertainment industry. Law has its specialties like everything else. A good entertainment lawyer will save you time and be able to anticipate issues and potential problem areas that an attorney without a background in the field might overlook or fail to fully appreciate. The standard method of billing for negotiation and contract drafting is to compute charges on an hourly basis. Be sure to ask your lawyer to provide his or her hourly rate along with an estimate of the number of hours anticipated for completion of the project.

The artist or manager shouldn't be concerned if every point is not worked out before counsel is retained or that there may be unanswered questions or differences of opinion as to specific provisions of the agreement. Part of what you are paying for is advice and help in negotiating the specific aspects of the management agreement. Your lawyer will have some very good ideas along these lines, especially regarding some of the trickier or more sensitive provisions.

After artist and manager have reached a basic agreement on the major points, they should turn negotiations over to the attorneys. The biggest mistakes one can make is attempting to completely negotiate and draft a management agreement without assistance of counsel. There are several reasons for this.

The most important is that an experienced entertainment lawyer will make sure all necessary points of the contract have been addressed and included in the final document. He or she will be able to counsel and advise the client on the merits of all relevant subject areas, whether previously discussed or yet to be considered. Secondly, the lawyer is able to act as a negotiator, sparing artist and manager any direct confrontation over delicate matters, thus allowing the parties to preserve their close personal and aesthetic relationship while still ensuring that essential points are covered. Finally, the entertainment attorney has the ability to draft the final agreement in clear, concise language that will help avoid ambiguities that could lead to disagreements while ensuring that the parties have a legally enforceable document.

We can't stress enough that one should never adopt a "do it yourself" approach when it comes to legal matters. It will be tempting, especially when an artist or manager is trying to save money and one of them has access to a form management agreement. However, every artist-management relationship has its own unique aspects or special twists that a form may not be capable of fully expressing. It's worth a little extra money at the outset of the relationship to insure that the management contract accurately reflects the true intent and complete agreement of the parties.

The unique nature of each management relationship makes it difficult to draw generalizations regarding specific legal provisions. However, there are certain subject areas common to all management agreements. We have outlined and discussed these topics in order to give the artist and manager a better understanding of the scope of the management agreement and to serve as a point of reference as to subjects that should be dealt with in the preliminary negotiation phase. Moreover, a better understanding of the terms, provisions, and intent of the management agreement by the parties will assist the attorneys in drafting an instrument capable of accomplishing their objectives.

Most management agreements can be divided into nine major subject areas:

1. Appointment of authority
2. Manager's compensation
3. Exclusivity
4. Term
5. Disputes
6. Artist warranties
7. Accounting and trusts
8. General legal clauses
9. Definitions

APPOINTMENT OF AUTHORITY

Generally speaking, there are four basic areas to look for in the management agreement regarding this topic: appointment, manager's duties, power of attorney, and employment agency disclaimer.

Appointment

The appointment provision usually does just what it states, appointing the manager to perform certain specified acts. It is important that the appointment language be clear and specific. This provision can be used to specify the type of management relationship the parties desire, i.e., personal management, business management, consultant, and so forth. Also, the issue of an exclusivity or nonexclusivity of management services can be dealt with under this section.

Manager's Duties

The manager's duties should be spelled out under the Appointment of Authority topic. The general phraseology used in many management agreements sets forth a number of specific duties. Traditionally, these are: to represent the artist as an adviser in all business negotiations and other matters relating to his entertainment career; to supervise professional engagements, and to consult with employers in the entertainment and literary fields; to cooperate with and supervise relations with any booking and literary agents whom the manager may from time to time employ with the artist's consent; to be available at reasonable times at the manager's office to confer with the artist on all matters concerning his artistic career, including but not limited to publicity and promotion; to use best efforts to arrange interviews, auditions, and tryouts designed to further the artist's career; to perform, wherever and whenever possible and whenever called upon such other functions as may be consistent with any of these duties.

It must be emphasized that these subject areas are generalizations. The duties of a manager can be made more or less specific depending on the desire of the parties. The needs of the artist or the manager's capability may totally alter the sample language just cited. Nevertheless, reference is made to them to help stress the importance of specifying duties and responsibilities of the manager.

Power of Attorney

A power of attorney is an instrument authorizing another to act as one's agent or attorney. The power of attorney clause can be styled to fit the needs of the parties. It can be general or specific in its form. For example, in most cases, the artist rarely signs personal performance contracts, endorses checks received in the course of business, deals directly with union organizations, or corresponds with royalty collection societies. These are normally the duties of a manager. However, in order to make the documents the manager signs on behalf of the artist binding, it's necessary to have a power of attorney authorization in the management agreement.

As stated previously, such a clause can be general, that is, pertaining to all business matters of the artist, or specific, relating to a narrow segment of the artist's business affairs. The artist can limit the power of the manager by restricting or omitting the power of attorney clause.

Employment Agency Disclaimer

Most management agreements clearly disclaim any duty to obtain employment for the artist. While the American Federation of Musicians has lifted its regulation against agents acting as managers, other professional management organizations still oppose the dual function.

The duties of a manager and agent are separate. However, during the span of an artist's career, the manager may find himself devoting a substantial amount of his or her time to developing agency outlets for the client or, if necessary, seeking engagements directly with promoters or purchasers of entertainment where permitted by law. So, while the functions of manager and agent are distinct, there can be overlap. This is an important point that must be carefully studied by the manager prior to entering an agreement with an artist who needs help in obtaining engagements. The artist should clearly understand that the manager has no obligation to seek employment directly if his efforts in motivating agents to book the client fail. Of course, if the manager is also acting as an agent pursuant to another agreement, then an obligation would exist.

It should be reemphasized at this point that certain states, the most notable being California, restrict and regulate this dual function. The manager should therefore consult an attorney to determine the legal consequences of acting as a manager and agent. He or she should also inquire into any licensing requirements of the particular state in which he or she is a resident or is doing business.

MANAGEMENT COMPENSATION

Once the artist and manager have agreed on the amount of compensation to be paid for the manager's services, there are still certain issues to be resolved. These include: establishing the percentage base, time of payment, renewals and extensions, reduction of fee in the event of the manager's death or disability, and reimbursement of expenses.

Establishing the Percentage Base

Once the management percentage has been established, assuming this is the form of compensation utilized, the parties will need to determine the base to which the percentage will apply. Will the manager receive a fee on gross or net earnings? Will the fee be calculated only on personal performance income and record royalties or will endorsements and songwriter income also be included? In short, on what sources of income will the manager's percentage be based? Although managers normally charge a fee ranging from 10 to 25 percent, the areas of income to which this fee applies will vary. To some artists, the compensation clauses won't be as important as the manager's authority and designated duties or some other pertinent provisions of the agreement.

Special attention should be given to the artist-manager relationship when the artist desires to utilize an affiliated firm in which the manager has an interest, such as a booking agency, record label, or music publishing company. The manager may voluntarily waive his management fee from incomes derived by the artist from his affiliated company, since he will already be receiving indirect compensation from those firms. Alternatively, the manager may argue that the incomes earned by these companies should be treated as any other income and therefore be commissionable to the manager.

In discussing the compensation provisions of a management agreement, the artist must not only consider the percentage to be charged, but the areas of his income to be affected. Many artists are overly concerned with the percentage, while ignoring those provisions that could substantially reduce the significance of a higher percentage. An artist should always consider the percentage and the base to which it applies simultaneously.

Although common in the industry, management compensation certainly need not be limited to a percentage of income. In some instances, the artist may want to retain the manager on a fee arrangement, that is, a guaranteed amount payable at predetermined times. Such an arrangement may be more economically feasible or advantageous to the artist (or manager) than a percentage of the artist's income. Again, different circumstances will influence the final arrangement.

Time of Payment

Another important consideration is determining when the management percentage will be paid: monthly, quarterly, or semiannually.

When attempting to resolve this question, attention should be given to the artist's type of work. For example, an artist performing primarily on the nightclub circuit would have regular cash flow capable of paying management fees on a monthly or even weekly basis. However, an artist playing one-nighters may elect to perform only during certain months, making it hard to maintain a monthly payment schedule. In addition, the accounting problems associated with a popular one-nighter attraction may necessitate payment of all management fees at the end of the quarter or at the end of a tour. For a recording artist/writer, the bulk of income is paid in record and songwriter royalties usually twice a year. All of these considerations, along with the tax consequences attached to each, should be examined before a final decision is made on when commissions are paid. It may be advisable to consult an accountant on this particular issue.

Renewals and Extensions

One provision somewhat misunderstood by many artists deals with renewals and extensions. Simply put, the typical provision states that if a manager negotiates a contract for the artist and revenue from that contract is received beyond the term of the artist-management agreement, the manager is still entitled to a commission on that portion of the artist's income. For example, let's assume that an artist wants to secure employment in a major hotel in Las Vegas. He contacts a manager specializing in that market and requests an audition. After the audition, the manager informs the artist his act is not suitable for the Las Vegas market. However, the manager is interested in working with the artist and believes Las Vegas dates could be secured by using their joint business and creative talents. They enter into a three-year management agreement calling for the artist to pay a 15 percent management commission. One year later, the artist and manager have developed a show suitable for the Las Vegas market. The manager utilizes his contacts and secures a one-month engagement for his client in a major hotel. The artist does well and the Las Vegas employer books a return engagement the next year. The second engagement is so successful the employer now wants to book the artist for periods of 16 weeks a year for three years. The manager would obviously be entitled to his commission for the engagement played during the final year of the management agreement. But what about the two additional sixteen-week engagements following the termination of the agreement? The manager could argue that he is entitled to his fee on the monies received by the artist for the dates played after termination of the management agreement.

There are various ways to control, compromise, or limit the extension and renewal clauses. An attorney familiar with the repercussions of these types of provisions will seek to obtain the most favorable wording possible for his client. Both manager and artist can advance strong arguments for removing or retaining these types of provisions. However, unless this potential problem is dealt with in the agreement, a costly lawsuit could ensue, especially if manager and artist parted under strained circumstances. This is just another example of why a clear, complete management agreement should be welcomed by the parties rather than avoided.

Reduction of Fee in the Event of the Manager's Death or Disability

Another provision often included in the management agreement involves the amount of commission paid in the event of the manager's death or disability. If the management agreement is with a partnership or corporate entity, this clause probably will not be included unless other circumstances dictate. Assuming, however, that the agreement is with an individual, language is often included to protect the manager or his estate from a total loss of all income on contracts made on behalf of his client prior to death or disability. For example, a clause is often inserted whereby the estate of the deceased manager would receive a reduced percentage of management compensation derived from contracts negotiated by the deceased manager for the artist. Similar clauses can also be added to cover disability. These types of clauses can be used in conjunction with the provisions previously discussed regarding contractual extensions and renewals.

Reimbursement of Expenses

Normally a manager is reimbursed for all direct expenses relative to a particular artist in addition to his management commission. However, this area can be structured in many ways.

Where it is the artist's money at stake, he or she might want to incorporate controls over the manager's discretion to incur reimbursable expenses. Amount, type, time, and geographic limitations are just a few of the many ways to control spending by the manager. For instance, the manager may have the authority to spend up to a certain amount without the artist's approval—for example, any expenditure less than $500. Alternatively, the manager may be granted the right to spend any amount necessary for certain purposes. Yet another approach allows the manager to spend up to a certain amount each month in artist-related expenses without artist approval. This approach is normally used after a budget has been established and usually becomes a matter of simply paying the regular monthly bills.

Still another approach provides that the manager be reimbursed for expenses incurred only beyond a certain radius of operation. By way of illustration, let's assume artist and manager are based in New York City, but that it's necessary for the manager to spend time in Los Angeles. All expenses associated with Los Angeles trips could be recoverable, but trips within a 250-mile radius of New York, representing the majority of the manager's travel activities, are not recoverable from artist earnings. These are just a few of the many alternatives that could be incorporated into the reimbursement clause under the compensation provisions. Certainly, trust is at issue here. The manager's hands shouldn't be unduly tied, nor should the artist be subjected to unduly expensive surprises.

EXCLUSIVITY

In most management agreements, the artist grants the manager an exclusive right of representation. However, the manager is normally not obligated to the same exclusivity provisions as the artist. Although this type of practice is standard within the industry, it can still, in some instances, be the subject of negotiation.

The basic premise supporting this one-way exclusivity is the unique talent of the artist. It's virtually impossible to duplicate the style and personality of an artist, especially one who is established with a loyal following. On the other hand, the manager's talents are normally business-oriented, which can be more easily duplicated or substituted. Of course, this is a generalized statement. Certainly there are managers who are stars in their own right due to unique image and talents. But generally speaking, it's the artist who has the unique characteristics. Therefore, the manager will normally insist that the artist be the one exclusively bound in the agreement.

Of course, there have been some notable exceptions to this, with a manager committing himself to one artist. Colonel Tom Parker always maintained that managing Elvis Presley was a full-time job and thus chose to devote all of his time to his famous client. But such one-to-one relationships are rare, with the trend being toward full-service management firms which operate much like major booking agencies such as William Morris or ICM.

Another frequent argument supporting the manager's right to represent other clients is that his or her compensation represents only a fraction of what is earned by his clients. To be competitive, it is necessary to have several clients. In addition, many artists are not income producers when they first seek artist management. So unless the manager is deriving income from other sources, it might be impossible for him to represent a young, inexperienced artist. Of course, some of the most successful managers don't represent newcomers at all, because they don't have to.

From a practical standpoint, the manager must have the ability to make important career decisions with the assurance that others having a stake in the artist's career won't have the power to countermand or interfere in the process. While agents, publishers, producers, and publicists are empowered to make decisions affecting the artist's career, they are usually made within certain boundaries established by the manager, or with his or her direct approval. Any other approach to final decision-making would result in confusion, if not catastrophe. Everyone with a stake in the artist knows this to be the case and depends on a strong manager to act as the glue to an artist's career—thus the exclusive representation clause.

While it will be difficult for any artist to compel a manager to devote full time to his or her career, there should certainly be a demand that adequate time be spent on their behalf. Special care should be taken by the artist to ensure a manager is both willing and able to do the kind of job that needs to be done. A manager who is extremely successful might not have the time to spend on a new addition to the artist roster. This is precisely why it might be a good idea to consider a manager who might not have the track record or client list of the competition, but does have the time and dedication to do the job for his newest client.

Another approach is to insert a "best efforts" clause and reduce the term of the agreement if there are doubts about a busy manager's time constraints or level of commitment. Better yet, if doubts are that strong, the artist should reexamine the advisability of the entire relationship.

TERM

The term or length of the management agreement is one of its most important points. Because there are numerous advantages and disadvantages attached to this provision, special attention should be devoted to coming up with the right formula for both parties.

From the manager's viewpoint, a long-term agreement is beneficial in protecting his or her investment, especially when dealing with a new artist requiring a long development phase. A manager usually won't be inclined to invest substantial amounts of time to develop an artist, only to lose him once results are achieved. Conversely, a manager may be wary of a protracted development phase and may seek a short-term agreement with option provisions exercisable only on one side.

The artist, however, may not want to be bound for an extended period with a new manager. On the other hand, the artist may want to enter into a long-term agreement with a well-known manager who is capable of developing the artist to his or her maximum potential.

The term of most management agreements ranges from one to three years with options. The option term usually consists of one to six consecutive one-year periods. An option provision means that at the conclusion of a stated time, the agreement will continue if one party, normally the manager, exercises his option. Options are often tied to certain levels of performance by the artist and/or manager. Options exercisable by the artist are recommended as a way to insure performance by the manager, especially where he or she may represent a full roster of other artists. Options, likewise, are advisable for the manager as an effective control device.

The artist should be wary of committing his career to a manager for a term longer than three years. Time changes people and circumstances. Regardless of the strong belief an artist may have in a particular manager, it is always advisable to maximize flexibility by limiting the agreement to a three-year span. If the artist is successful, a contract of short duration will allow a renegotiation with the manager on more favorable terms. If the management relationship is not successful, the shorter term will allow the artist to terminate the agreement and seek alternative management representation. In reality, term option provisions are based on bargaining power of which new artists have little and powerful managers have plenty.

But there are always compromise positions. Use of a short-term agreement with mutually exercisable options or option terms based on performance of the parties is an approach that potentially provides artist and manager with a workable middle ground that affords sufficient protection to each.

DISPUTES

It's good practice to include a clause in the management agreement whereby, if either party has a grievance against the other, written notification must be given and then a certain time period allowed for rectifying the dispute before the offending party can be held in default. This is often referred to as a "cure" provision.

In the event a controversy does arise between artist and manager that can't be settled, then it may be wise to insert an arbitration clause. Arbitration is a procedure for resolving disputes without having to resort to litigation in a court of law. The person conducting the arbitration hearing is not a judge, but rather someone knowledgeable of the subject matter in controversy. The arbitrator is usually chosen by mutual agreement of the parties from a list submitted by organizations such as the American Arbitration Association. Once the arbitrator takes jurisdiction, he or she has wide discretion to conduct a hearing and make any ruling deemed appropriate under the circumstances. The arbitration clause will normally grant the prevailing party the right to recover any and all reasonable costs including attorney fees. Depending on the wording of the arbitration clause and governing state law, the arbitration award may or may not be subject to appeal. Given the unique character of the entertainment industry and the crowded court dockets across the country, the arbitration clause may be beneficial to both artist and manager as a speedy, inexpensive manner of resolving disputes.

ARTIST WARRANTIES

A blanket indemnification clause is usually included in the management agreement whereby the artist guarantees certain facts. For instance, let's assume that an artist, believing himself to be fully released from a previous management agreement, when in fact he really is not, enters into an agreement with a new manager. Assume further that this new management contract happens to contain a clause that warrants that the artist was free to enter into this new agreement. A short time later, a major recording contract is secured. The previous manager believes that his efforts on behalf of the artist was the reason the contract was obtained, while the new manager strongly contends that his efforts alone resulted in the contract. The result is a lawsuit between the two managers. Regardless of the outcome, under the indemnification clause contained in the second management agreement, the new manager would still be entitled to be reimbursed by the artist for any losses incurred by him as a result of the artist's breach of warranty. This is because the artist has guaranteed that he was free to contract with the new manager and has agreed to protect him from any loss if the manager relies on his warranty. This type of clause makes it important for an artist to understand the full implications of any prior contractual commitments. More than one potentially rewarding artist-manager relationship has failed because of previous legal entanglements.

ACCOUNTING AND TRUSTS

The artist should always include an audit provision in the management agreement giving him or her the right to examine the books of account kept by the manager. Conversely, if the artist or his representative keeps the accounting records, then obviously the manager would want the same privilege. The management contract should contain a specific provision stating exactly whose obligation it shall be to keep the books of account. As a regulatory provision to the right of examination, the audit clause should provide for a written notification and a time period for the examination (e.g., within 10 days from notification during normal office hours). To avoid unnecessary or vexatious examinations, the party to be audited will often seek to limit such examinations to no more than one per year.

A trust provision places a duty on the artist or manager to hold and preserve monies that might be collected by one but belong to the other. The party in possession of these funds is obligated to protect said monies until the other party is paid. Legally, this establishes a trust or fiduciary relationship which carries a greater degree of accountability between the parties to a contract than is normally the case. Over the last decade, the trend in state law is to regard the entire management agreement as creating a fiduciary relationship much like attorney-client. This imposes upon the parties the duty of utmost good faith, fair dealing, and full disclosure of all matters materially affecting the relationship. Here as with any legal matter, an attorney can provide in-depth advice appropriate to the situation at hand.

GENERAL LEGAL CLAUSES

All formal management agreements contain various general legal clauses characteristic of all contracts. For instance, a *jurisdiction* provision sets forth an agreement by the parties that the contract will be construed under the laws of a particular state or country. A *modification* clause states that once the agreement is reduced to writing and signed, then all subsequent changes must be reduced to writing and signed by both parties in order to be enforceable. An *assignment and delegation* clause may be found in the agreement regulating transfer of rights and duties under the contract. Many other general legal clauses may be contained, depending on the desires of the parties and their attorneys. While these clauses may not appear to be important to a layman, they can be of great importance with regard to legal interpretation and construction of the agreement should the need arise. This is one more compelling reason to retain an attorney rather than take a do-it-yourself approach to legal matters.

DEFINITIONS

Some management agreements contain definitions of specific words and terms used in the body of the agreement. This is done to guard against an ambiguous meaning being attached to a frequently employed word or phrase. If the parties to the agreement are unclear as to the meaning of any word or phrase, then it should be defined. As with the other provisions of the contract, care in drafting of the document can alleviate greater problems later on.

SUMMING UP THE MANAGEMENT CONTRACT

Different things are important to different people. Consequently, each artist and manager will be motivated by different needs when negotiating the management agreement. Much of the final product will be determined by the parties' mutual desire for a positive, workable relationship, though some of it will be the result of hard bargaining and the respective levels of bargaining power. The delicate balance of maintaining a good personal relationship in the midst of hard-nosed bargaining is where the services of a good entertainment attorney can be invaluable. While the artist and manager should both feel comfortable about the management contract, neither party should be timid about having it tailored to meet their needs. In a successful negotiation, everybody wins, but sometimes one party wins a little more than the other. Consequently, both parties must be prepared to give, take, and compromise to make the final agreement acceptable to both artist and manager. If it's not, then what you might think is a legal blueprint to success is really a time bomb bound to explode. When that happens, nobody wins.

[PART TWO]

PLANNING THE ARTIST'S CAREER

6

Taking Care
of Business

Once the formal management agreement has been finalized, the manager begins the actual formulation of the artist's career plan. The first matter of concern is to determine where the artist's career presently stands. This means the manager, in effect, must take inventory of the client's business and creative assets. For those employing principles of self-management, the same is true. It's impossible to plot a course to the future if you don't have a clear grasp of where you are. This chapter is devoted to the business portion of this evaluation.

Generally, the manager's analysis should cover the following: form of doing business, employment agreements, service mark, banking, insurance, bookkeeping/tax planning, budgeting, and legal overview.

FORM OF BUSINESS

The starting point of any business evaluation is the question, "What form of business is my client currently working under?" Next, one should ask, "What form of business *should* my client be working under?" Basically, there are three types of business entities available. They are: proprietorship, partnership, and the corporation.

Each form has its distinct characteristics, advantages, and drawbacks. The manager should analyze the various entities in view of the artist's circumstances and needs before making the appropriate selection. Often the advice of an attorney or accountant will be necessary to make a proper determination of which form to select. As we've advocated before, if the manager has any questions regarding the selection of a particular business entity, he or she shouldn't hesitate to seek appropriate counsel or even recommend the use of a business manager, provided the artist's income and business warrant such a move.

Let's briefly review the advantages and disadvantages of the three basic entities.

Proprietorship

A proprietorship is an unincorporated business operation owned by an individual. The advantages of the proprietorship form of doing business are numerous. The primary advantage is that the owner is the boss. He makes all decisions regarding the operation of the business without having to consult with others, such as a Board of Directors, which is associated with the corporate entity. There's little formality or cost associated with the formation of a proprietorship. The business is free to trade and operate anywhere without having to comply with various qualification statutes in each state where it does business. The proprietor is not subject to liability for the actions of others, which is inherent in partnerships and with officers of a corporation. Moreover, the individual proprietor is not subject to as many regulatory and reporting requirements as are other forms of business enterprise. Finally, a proprietorship may be granted borrowing power beyond the value of the business to the extent of the owner's assets outside the proprietorship.

A primary disadvantage of the one-person business is that no one other than the owner can act on behalf of the enterprise, except as an agent. Consequently, the business has limited decision-making capability and expertise. More disturbing is the fact that the owner is subject to unlimited personal liability for all the obligations of the business. Furthermore, the amount of the investment in the business is limited to the resources of the owner. Another distinct disadvantage is that the proprietorship is subject to termination upon the death or incapacity of the owner. In addition, the other entities provide certain tax advantages not found in the one-person business structure.

Partnership

A partnership is created when two or more people agree to combine their property, talent, or other resources to establish a business in which each is to be an owner sharing the profits or losses of the enterprise. While the characteristics of a partnership are similar to the proprietorship, there are major distinctions, the foremost being the general agency feature of the partnership. Every partner can act on behalf of the business, therefore rendering the enterprise liable for any partner's action within the scope of the firm's operation. Therefore, it's extremely important that each partner have the utmost confidence in the integrity and ability of his associates. Generally, the partners are liable not only collectively, but individually, for all the obligations of the business including liability resulting from wrongful acts of the other partners.

The growth of a partnership can be restricted because all its members must consent before any additional members are included. However, termination of the partnership takes place upon the withdrawal of any one party. If the withdrawal is in violation of the partnership agreement, it may give rise to an action against the withdrawing party, but the partnership is nevertheless terminated. Dissolution of the partnership also occurs upon the death or incapacity of one of the partners. The effect of the death or incapacity of a partner can be minimized by various provisions either embodied in the partnership agreement or by a collateral agreement between the parties. Nonetheless, if some provision has not been made, then the death or incapacity of a partner terminates the business.

Corporation

The corporate form of doing business is more complex than the proprietorship or partnership. The formation of an incorporated business creates a new entity capable of doing business in its own name.

The major positive characteristic of the corporation is freedom of the shareholder (owner of the corporation) from personal liability for the obligations of the business. The ease in transferring ownership through exchange of stock shares is another desirable aspect of the corporate entity as is its ability to exist for a set period of time without being impaired by the death or incompetency of individual shareholders. Another major benefit is the ability of the corporation to raise large amounts of capital through investments of many shareholders.

On the negative side, the corporation is more costly to form compared to proprietorships and partnerships. In addition, corporations are subject to more governmental regulation, such as requirements of periodic filing of reports and various statements. The fact that minority shareholders are subject to the control of the majority shareholders in the corporation can also be an impeding factor. Also, the credit available to a corporation is limited to its own assets, and not those of the individual shareholders without some form of personal guarantee.

Other Business Entities

As stated at the outset, the proprietorship, partnership, and corporation are the three basic business vehicles available to an artist. It should be noted, however, that there are other business entities available that are derivatives of the three basic forms, including the limited partnership and joint venture. Since their use is rather limited and extremely complex, these business arrangements are beyond the scope of this discussion.

To aid and assist the proper selection and formation of any of these entities, the advice of an attorney and accountant is recommended. It should also be noted that the corporation will normally require the services of an attorney to ensure that proper records are being maintained and reports required by law are being filed. The use of one of the derivatives of the major entities also requires counsel in its formation.

SELECTING THE FORM OF BUSINESS

The manager can recommend selection of any one of the various business entities available. The choice will depend on the circumstances of his client and the advice of professional counsel. For example, a young artist recently signed to a major recording contract would probably select the sole proprietorship form of business. However, as an artist's career develops, the need may arise to transform the proprietorship into a corporate entity depending on increased exposure to liability, tax consequences, and other considerations.

For another example, let's assume we're dealing with a four-man rock group. On first glance, this would seem to suggest the creation of a partnership arrangement. However, after investigation, it's revealed that one member is the financial strength of the entire group while another member possesses all the creative, writing, and vocal talents. Given this situation, the best arrangement might not be a partnership between all four members. Instead, those members with the financial and artistic strengths may want to consider the formation of a partnership between themselves and employ the other two members. Of course, this example could be altered drastically if we assume that all four members contributed equally to the group's financial strength and artistic output, or because of pre-existing personal considerations which might suggest a partnership among all four members as the most desirable arrangement. In short, the manager must assess the artist, or the group as a whole, to determine if a partnership arrangement is the appropriate alternative for a given situation. One should never just assume that a partnership is warranted just because two or more individuals are involved.

EMPLOYMENT AGREEMENTS

Once the manager has assessed the artist's business entity, consulted counsel, made the appropriate recommendations, and has taken measures to set up the appropriate form of business, the first step is completed. Next comes a review of the personnel requirements of the artist. For instance, if the artist is a single act, will he or she require a full-time backup group? If the artist tours regularly, will a road crew be required? Does the artist need a road manager? Regardless of specific career objectives, he or she will require the services of other people on either a regular or irregular recurring basis. These people might be regular employees or contract personnel.

Certainly, the creative and economic circumstances of the artist along with the adopted career plan will greatly affect the number of people the artist will have to employ. The manager must analyze the existing situation in view of how many people are presently employed and how many are contemplated for future projects. Are all employees necessary? Does the artist have employment contracts with them?

Making personnel recommendations to the client and subsequently negotiating employment contracts can be a big job. It can also spell the difference between annual profit and loss given the spiraling costs of hiring backup and studio musicians, musical directors, backup vocalists, arrangers, road manager and crew, sound engineers, stage directors, wardrobe designers, lighting technicians, drivers, pilots, bodyguards, promotion men, publicists, and all the other supporting cast that help get an artist to the top and keep him there. Only through this type of coordinated approach to personnel management can an artist track overhead, which is one of the keys to controlling profit and loss.

SERVICE MARK

An often overlooked aspect of the business inventory is the value of an artist's or group's trade name. There are many nightmarish stories about the hit group who found out they didn't have full right to use their own name. Even more common is a situation in which no partnership agreement has been executed between members of a group, and the group subsequently breaks up. When the former members create new groups and utilize the original trade name, the result is often protracted, expensive litigation.

The way to avoid problems related to trade name is to seek federal service mark protection by registration of the proper application with the Commissioner of Patents in Washington, D.C. The artist should simultaneously file for state service mark protection or its equivalent, if available.

The advantages are numerous. A service mark indicates the origin of the artist's services. It's a vehicle for building and valuing goodwill in the artist's business. It can be included on the artist's financial statement as an asset. It also helps protect the artist from mistake, confusion, or deceit fostered by other artists who may subsequently adopt the same or similar name. It provides insurance that the artist may exclusively perform under his professional name. In addition, it's a potentially marketable commodity. The only disadvantage is the out-of-pocket cost associated with the filing. The manager should consult an attorney with regard to securing service mark protection at the same time he seeks advice as to the various forms of doing business.

At the same time, the artist should specify the ownership of the name and what happens in the event of a breakup. This is especially important in the case of groups. The partnership agreement or a corporate resolution is the appropriate vehicle for clarifying this potential problem.

BANKING

When examining the condition of the artist's business, the manager needs to ascertain his client's borrowing power. The artist's relationship with lending institutions will either be good, bad, or nonexistent. Given the last two situations, the manager must convert his client into a good risk in order to establish a solid banking connection.

If the artist has never dealt with a bank before, the manager can arrange for his client to meet the proper banking officer, not only to establish a business relationship, but to insure that the artist's personal banking needs are fulfilled. On the other hand, if the artist has a poor record with a particular bank, the manager should attempt to clear up the problem, if possible, or embark on a new relationship with another institution. As a last resort, the manager may choose to utilize his own borrowing capacity to assist his client in starting a bank relationship.

If the artist has maintained a good banking relationship in the past, then the manager should seek to build on the existing financial base. A sure way to solidify the relationship is to meet with the artist's banker and explain the direction of the artist's career, his goals and objectives, strategies for getting there, and the artist's contracts, budgets, and forecasts.

Some progressive banks in music centers have special departments to deal with the needs of entertainment clients. But even when it is unnecessary to explain the high profile and often unstable environment in which your client operates, it's still essential that you do your homework and present the artist for what he is—a business. The banker will be the first person to recognize professional business management.

Immediate benefit can be derived from presenting an artist to a banker in a businesslike fashion. Beyond performing the normal function of moving money for routine transactions, the bank can provide a host of additional services once the artist's career advances past the breaking-in stage. These include pre-approved lines of credit, open-note signature loans, credit cards, foreign exchange, long-term equipment or vehicle financing, mortgages, and so on. Banking is a fact of life; it's important not to overlook it or take it for granted. Being organized and talking the bank's language is at least half the battle.

INSURANCE

Like it or not, insurance is another fact of life in the business world. Any well-managed business maintains a variety of insurance policies as a hedge against personal or economic disaster. The artist's business is no different. The manager should examine the areas of vehicle, liability, equipment, and life insurance.

Vehicle Insurance

The bank will normally require insurance protection if it has financed a vehicle. From a financial standpoint, it's simply good business. But the need doesn't stop with the bank. If an artist or group has invested substantial amounts in vehicles, a total loss could have catastrophic financial consequences. Replacement problems are magnified considerably if the artist is in the middle of a tour and suddenly finds him or herself without vehicles or the cash to purchase new ones.

Liability Insurance

Liability insurance protection is a necessity. Just as vehicle insurance protects a property value, liability coverage insures against negligent acts of the driver of the vehicle.

The possible consequences of operating an uninsured vehicle are obvious. They are multiplied if the artist is doing business as a proprietorship or partnership, with personal exposure to the negligent acts of employees and, in some cases, independent contractors. And while the shareholders of a corporation would be protected from personal liability, the assets of the corporation are vulnerable to a lawsuit stemming from negligent operation of a vehicle owned by the corporation. To put the problem in perspective, if it is a stretch to make payments on a used Greyhound Bus, how much tougher would it be to come up with a million dollars to satisfy a wrongful death judgement? Unfortunately, it's happened. All too often.

Equipment Insurance

Artists must invest substantial sums of money in their musical equipment, sound, lighting, and staging to remain competitive in today's entertainment market. Substantial equipment investments require insurance protection from fire, theft, and other potential damage or loss. The artist must have the assurance that in the event of equipment damage or destruction he or she can resume activities as soon as possible without financial disaster. The cost of equipment along with high annual premiums can be a good reason to rent or lease equipment on an as-needed basis, but the artist can still expect to pay the insurance premium, either directly albeit for a shorter period, or indirectly as part of the agreed upon rental charge.

Life Insurance

Life insurance coverage is another protective device that should be used by the artist. As an artist's career develops, his or her income usually increases. The manager and other group members (if the artist is in a partnership) become vulnerable to substantial loss of income in the event of the death of the artist or other group member. In order to insure against this contingency, life insurance can be maintained on the artist or other key members of the group. Such a policy would normally name the manager or the other members of the group as beneficiaries. This coverage would be in addition to life insurance in order to provide for the artist's family in the event of his death. The amount of life insurance carried can be adjusted from year to year to provide sufficient protection.

Insurance companies offer an assortment of business coverage. The manager should seek the advice of an insurance expert in formulating a plan to protect all the various areas of the artist's business exposed to potentially crippling loss. Insurance premiums are no fun, but they are certainly preferable to losing everything.

BOOKKEEPING/TAX PLANNING

Is the artist maintaining a set of financial records? Have books been kept in the past? It's very important that the manager ascertain the adequacy of the artist's record-keeping system. Not only does the manager have to be concerned with the current bookkeeping system, but he or she should also review the artist's records for at least two previous years. This will help prevent any unannounced surprises from the IRS or the state tax commission.

Knowledge of a client's haphazard bookkeeping practices or of his failure to file certain tax reports doesn't mean that the manager can necessarily wave a magic wand over these problems if the tax officials raise questions. The manager can, however, help avoid problems in the future while taking steps to rectify past problems.

An accountant should be retained to help the manager install a new bookkeeping system or review the adequacy of an old one unless the manager has special expertise in this area. The accountant is usually responsible for filing all state and federal income tax forms and corporate franchise and income tax returns. An accountant will also be helpful in reviewing the artist's business as it grows to determine whether a new business form is desirable. One of the primary motivations for changing the legal structure of a business is to conform to the most favorable tax configuration. The accountant will be the first to recognize the tax ramifications of a particular business entity. As the artist's career progresses and income increases, the tax consequences become more of a factor in the overall career plan.

BUDGETING

A budget is a financial road map. Just as the road manager plots the route for an upcoming tour, the manager must map out his client's financial route.

The first step in budgeting is to prepare an income forecast. The manager must attempt to project the artist's earnings for a given year by studying the previous year's income. Once the manager has an idea of what was earned the previous year, when it was received, and what contracts are in effect for the upcoming year, he or she is in a position to forecast. Given the objectives of the artist, in view of the earnings forecast, the manager can determine the amount of money that will have to be generated during the year. The manager then starts balancing the various factors (i.e., banks, agents, record companies, budget) in an attempt to provide the desired effect. For example, let's say that an artist grossed $500,000 from personal appearances and desires to increase his earnings by $100,000 for the upcoming year. The manager would have to analyze several factors. Can my client command an increased performance fee? Can the agent deliver higher priced dates? As an alternative, should the client's overhead be reduced? Should the artist shift markets? Based upon his findings, the manager will attempt to formulate an economic plan capable of fulfilling the artist's wishes.

For another example, let's assume that an artist earned $200,000 the previous year by performing in the nightclub market. For the upcoming year, the artist would like to reduce the number of nightclub performances in order to devote more time to songwriting and recording. However, he wants to maintain his previous year's income. The manager has to answer several questions in designing a budget for his client. Can the artist maintain his previous year's income by working less? Should the artist cut overhead? Can the artist afford to pay the increased studio bills? Just exactly how is the manager going to help the artist accomplish his objective? Can he?

The first step is to formulate a financial plan based on a forecast and budget. The manager must be able to look into his client's economic future. From this point, he can then juggle the figures and usually structure a plan to achieve the artist's objective. But if he determines that the artist's goal can't be reached, the process he undertook to reach his conclusion will be helpful in explaining to the artist why the goal is not currently attainable. In this case, some options immediately come to mind. Cut fixed overhead by reducing the size of the backup band or non-stage personnel; raise the asking price to clubs knowing that it will probably result in approximately the same amount of income on fewer dates; help offset the income deficit by seeking an advance from a record company, music publisher or performing rights society; sell equipment or vehicles to raise money and then rent or lease on an as-needed basis.

All of these solutions rest on the premise that the artist's talents and abilities can command these options. If not, the answer might be that such a reduction in dates isn't presently possible. The focus then shifts to finding ways to create those options in the months ahead.

Artists are like everyone else in that they have personal and business financial needs. It's the manager's responsibility to help fulfill those needs, or at least explain convincingly why the artist's desires cannot be fulfilled. It's also the manager's job to help the artist spend his money wisely in order to insure that he has something to show for his efforts once his popularity wanes.

LEGAL OVERVIEW

We've previously discussed the importance of attorneys during negotiation and preparation of the management contract. During the business inventory stage, any legal question regarding the artist's business status should be reviewed by legal counsel. The artist's manager and attorney need to be aware of all business planning, pending litigation, existing contractual obligations, and all other pertinent legal data. The manager should consult the attorney on any matter of which he's unsure.

Once the manager has taken financial inventory of the artist's business, he or she should be ready to take creative inventory, which is followed by preparing the career plan. The specifics of the career plan will be discussed in subsequent chapters.

The final result of the business inventory phase should be a well-organized, efficient business vehicle, complete with all the protection that contracts and insurance can offer. Artist and manager should have a clear understanding of where they are financially and exactly where they're going in the future.

7

Attorneys, Accountants, and Business Advisors

While the manager is instrumental in structuring and administering the artist's business organization, many aspects of the artist's business will require the expertise of the professional support team. The professional support team normally consists of attorneys, accountants, and business advisors.

We have already alluded to the important role these professionals play in the initial stages of defining the management relationship and in business planning. The same is true in most other phases of the artist's career as well. The entertainment industry is a highly sophisticated and complex system. As the level of investment and corporate participation continues to increase, so does the complexity. A manager and artist can expect to be confronted with a wide range of legal and financial decisions over the span of a career. Just from a legal standpoint, a successful artist will probably be involved in contractual relationships with his manager, booking agents, record company and producer, music publishers, corporate sponsors, product endorsements, and possibly motion picture, television and video producers, and book publishers. Often, successful, multi-faceted artists will own all or part of some of these entities. The artist will certainly be involved with the protection and licensing use of his name and likeness as well as the exploitation and administration of copyrighted musical compositions and other literary and intellectual properties. As if that weren't enough, there is the seemingly endless entourage of musicians, road managers, drivers, roadies, wardrobe personnel, and publicists. There is also the matter of ownership or leasing of sound and lighting equipment, musical instruments, vehicles, props, and wardrobe. Besides business responsibilities, the artist will also be concerned with the administration of his personal finances and ownership of personal property. Sound complicated? It certainly is, and that's only a quick overview of routine matters requiring a good lawyer. This doesn't even include lawsuits, but that will be discussed later.

ATTORNEYS

The preceding two chapters brought up ways that an attorney can be very helpful during the initial stages of the artist-manager relationship. General legal counsel, contract expertise, and negotiation skills are all staples of a successful career, but that only begins to explain the role of a top-flight attorney.

When selecting an attorney, the artist and manager should seek a person with experience in the entertainment field. They shouldn't assume that all attorneys possess the special knowledge and training to adequately handle their particular legal requirements. The trend today is toward greater legal specialization than ever before because of the increased complexity of our commercial society. The entertainment world is no exception. In fact, music law is a sub-specialty as distinguished from motion pictures and television or sports law. Unless a lawyer regularly deals with management, recording, and music publishing contracts; copyright protection and administration; and licensing of intellectual and artistic property, chances are he or she won't sufficiently understand or appreciate the industry and its peculiar legal problems.

When seeking a qualified entertainment lawyer, other managers and industry professionals are good sources for recommendations. Professional directories such as Martindale-Hubbel may also be consulted as a starting point if the artist or manager is totally unfamiliar with members of the legal profession and their qualifications. This directory is found in most law libraries. The librarian will be glad to show how to use it.

Because of the high degree of specialization in entertainment law, the majority of practitioners are located in industry centers such as New York, Los Angeles, or Nashville. However, they may be found in other cities throughout the country, too.

Artists and managers should be cautioned against the natural inclination to use a friend, relative, or family lawyer to fill their entertainment law needs. This is fine if they're qualified. However, the manager could be doing his artist client a great disservice by retaining such an attorney without an entertainment background.

When contacting an attorney for the first time, the manager or artist should discuss the fee at the outset to avoid any misunderstanding. Often, the attorney will schedule an initial conference to discuss the artist's particular legal needs or problems on either a flat fee or an hourly rate basis. During this initial meeting, the artist or his manager and the attorney should discuss their financial arrangement, which will usually be based on an hourly rate which can range from as little as $75 an hour up to hundreds of dollars for each sixty minutes of billable time. In some cases, attorney's charges are based on a percentage of the artist's income, depending on the circumstances of the artist and the preference of the parties involved. In certain instances, attorneys will charge a flat fee for specified assignments such as drafting contracts or other legal instruments.

While it's understandable that a new artist must necessarily be cost-conscious, he or she shouldn't neglect seeking competent, experienced legal counsel because of price. Our advice is to shop around for legal representation just as you would for any other service. Attorney's fees vary with the experience and client load of individual lawyers. Often, a younger, less experienced, though competent, entertainment attorney may be just the right choice for the new artist or manager. Cost aside, it's important to find an attorney with whom you feel comfortable.

Whatever the final decision, the artist or his manager should never try to be his own lawyer just to save money. This is a guaranteed path to trouble which can result in having to hire an attorney for substantially more money later to deal with what should have been a routine matter. That's where suing and getting sued comes in. Either way, you lose. It is infinitely better to avoid litigation and concentrate on more productive pursuits. For this reason alone, it is worth digging into your pocket at the outset to pay for quality legal talent that can help you avoid an expensive mess later on.

ACCOUNTANTS

Just as an artist will require the services of an attorney, so will he or she need an accountant. One of the worst things that can happen to an artist is to experience financial success without being properly prepared for it from an accounting standpoint. There are many sad stories of artists who made fortunes, only to lose everything as a result of ineffective income management, failure to keep records, nonexistent tax planning, and failure to save and make proper investments. A good accountant can help avoid this unfortunate state of affairs.

We've already discussed the importance of the accountant in helping to select the artist's business entity and in reviewing and developing a workable bookkeeping system. As the artist's income increases, the need for professional accounting and tax planning becomes more important. Of special importance to a recording artist and songwriter is the ability of the accountant to interpret and verify royalty statements. Equally essential is the preparation and filing of income tax returns with the Internal Revenue Service as well as state and local governments. As with the attorney, the value of the accountant increases dramatically if he's familiar with the ongoing developments in the artist's business. Therefore, the manager should keep the accountant regularly informed of the artist's financial activities.

The same general rules regarding selection and compensation of an attorney also apply to accountants, with some exceptions. While it's helpful for the accountant to have a background in the entertainment industry, especially with regard to audits and royalty accounting, it's not generally as crucial as with attorneys.

Compensation varies with the expertise and experience of the accountant. A Certified Public Accountant usually commands a larger fee due to his special training and wider range of knowledge and expertise. Compensation is usually set on either a flat fee or retainer basis. As with attorneys, don't be shy about the subject of fees and don't hesitate to shop around for the right person as well as the right price.

BUSINESS ADVISORS

We'll refer to bankers, estate planners, and insurance professionals under the heading of business advisors. Their services are essential in maintaining an efficient business.

As we've mentioned before, the banker can play a central role in the development of a young artist's career. Finding the right personal banking connection should not be overlooked when time comes to put together the professional support team.

The estate planner is a highly specialized professional whose function is to plan the most efficient distribution of his client's assets at death. While most artists are not concerned with this aspect of business planning at the outset of their career, it does become important later. An artist must exercise caution when choosing an estate planner. There are many firms and individuals who profess to have such skills. Attorneys, Certified Public Accountants, and Chartered Life Underwriters are generally qualified to render this important service. Whoever is chosen, the artist and manager must be certain they select a well-qualified professional.

8

Artist Evaluation and Image Formulation

Having taken inventory of the artist's business, the manager should now turn to a detailed creative assessment of the artist. Despite a given artist's talent and abilities, there are going to be weaknesses. It's the manager's function to identify and become familiar with all of the artist's traits. This will enable him to help shape the artist's image and direction in such a way as to play to strengths while de-emphasizing and improving on the weaknesses.

A meaningful artistic evaluation requires the manager and artist to be totally honest with each other. It suggests not only praise from the manager, but criticism where deserved. This is no time for the artist to get his or her feelings hurt or let ego stand in the way of a process that will ultimately prove beneficial. Because this is a touchy subject, the manager should take steps to sufficiently prepare the artist. The artist should be reminded that any criticism is meant to be constructive in nature. The manager should point out that he or she wouldn't be involved with the artist if there wasn't a strong belief and dedication in the artist's talent and ability to succeed. Finally, the manager should stress the need for complete honesty and mutual trust. In many instances, this will be the first juncture in the relationship where there's the possibility of confrontation and friction. Both parties should know that and be ready.

ARTIST EVALUATION

The first level of inquiry by the manager should be a personal assessment of the artist. The same general types of questions will apply to both individuals and groups.

The process should begin with basic questions involving the particular talent or talents of the artist. Is he or she a singer? Instrumentalist? Dancer? Comic? Actor? While these questions may appear obvious and simplistic, they're not. Many artists who are ostensibly vocalists often possess other talents that can be developed and incorporated into the overall image. For example, Michael Jackson is a successful recording artist who has sold millions of records. But a large part of his appeal is an electrifying stage show built around his dancing ability. Michael Jackson's legendary stage show has been directly responsible for a large percentage of record sales along with additional revenues from music videos and touring. Michael Jackson is a classic example of combining multiple talents into a unique and successful act.

Another important factor for multi-talented artists and their managers to consider is career flexibility. During the decade of the '80s the career crossover artist became prominent as never before. Cher is an excellent example of a multidimensional artist who has achieved success on the screen, TV, and even in product retailing in addition to her traditional sources of income in record sales and concert tickets. Eddie Murphy is another example: starting as a stand-up comedian, he parlayed his talents into a phenomenal television, movie, and music career. As more avenues for talent exploitation continue to open up in the 1990s, there will be an increased demand for the rare artist that can cross the boundaries that define traditional entertainment career categories. The smart artist and manager will take this into consideration when taking creative inventory.

There are many potential areas of investigation. In the case of a singer, does he or she have a unique vocal style, or is the sound reminiscent of other well-known recording artists? No record company wants another Tom Petty, Whitney Houston, or Reba McEntire, because record buyers don't want imitations. Of course there is a difference between influences and clones. It's up to the manager to help the artist see the difference.

Another critically important factor for singers has to do with material. Does the artist write his or her own songs? If so, chances for a long-term record deal are greatly enhanced. First of all, an artist/writer is more likely to have a distinct sound or style by virtue of songs that are custom-tailored to his own performing abilities. Secondly, an artist/

writer is assured of a stable source of material. This enhances longevity and in the eyes of the record company reduces the risk of signing the artist. Of course there are many notable exceptions: Elvis Presley depended on other writers for material; Dionne Warwick was a pure singer who teamed with songwriters Burt Bacharach and Hal David for a steady stream of classic hits. Many country acts have sustained careers for a decade or more while depending almost exclusively on Nashville songwriters for material. But even this is changing. The conclusion is clear. If an artist doesn't write, it's time to start.

Physical appearance is another important factor in career success. Clearly, if your goal is to make it in television or motion pictures as a lead player, you had better be great looking or very, very interesting, physically. Fortunately, the music business is less demanding in this area. A survey of managers, publicists, and record people evoked the following responses to our question, "What kind of physical appearance must an artist have to enjoy success in the music industry?" Pleasing, different, and interesting were the top answers. However, almost all agreed that the odds were against someone who was physically unattractive. Fortunately, the miracles of diet, wardrobe, and cosmetic enhancement can work wonders with almost anybody. The key is finding the right look and doing what is necessary to maintain it.

While physical appearance is certainly important, it's really only one element in the total image. How someone speaks, moves, projects, and photographs are all part of being an artist. Because this can turn into a 24-hour-a-day job, it's important for the artist to adopt an image that is both comfortable and consistent with one's personality and set of values. Playing the part of someone else, especially a role with which the artist isn't comfortable, just for the benefit of fans, will backfire sooner or later. Once the image has been adopted, it's important to be consistent in presenting it. Publicity photographs, video clips, interviews, and even wardrobe all combine to tell the public who the artist is and what they are about. The image and how it's projected shouldn't be left to chance.

The artist should be viewed as a total package, with both artist and manager trying to objectively determine the overall impression the artist makes on an audience both on and off the stage. Even though an artist may seem to be weak in a vital area, this may work to his advantage by making him different or unique. A wonderful example is George Burns, who turned advanced age into a distinguishing factor that allowed him to enjoy some of his greatest successes. A resourceful manager will be able to recognize weaknesses or points of distinctiveness and capitalize on them. If that's not feasible, steps can be taken to disguise or hide them if need be. More than one sex symbol has dazzled audiences with capped smiles that would never betray the secrets of stage corsets, lift shoes, and tinted hair.

The next area of inquiry in the artistic evaluation should be a look at the history of the artist. The artist and manager will want to structure their career planning to take maximum advantage of the artist's past successes and experience. They'll also want to avoid repeating past mistakes and failures. For this reason, it's necessary for the manager to know in detail where the artist has been, both professionally and personally, including triumphs, failures, and the motivations behind both. Insight into personal and psychological makeup of the artist can be very helpful in selecting goals and structuring a plan for career development. For instance, singer/songwriter Merle Haggard's now well-chronicled experience with prison, as well as his love for the traditional country music of Bob Wills and Jimmie Rodgers, played a big part in shaping his image when his career was in the breakthrough period. Emphasis on these factors combined with good timing helped give him a unique identity that the public embraced, thus launching a legendary career. Obviously, sensitivity is required in this phase of the artistic evaluation process.

Specific areas of information that should be dealt with include the artist's present status and past history with regard to personal appearances. This includes the type and amount of experience; a list of the artist's contacts with agents, promoters, and club owners; and the present status of bookings. All of this information is useful in helping the manager structure an immediate network of contacts and possible return engagements that could be turned into immediate income for the artist.

The same types of questions should be asked in the area of recording, beginning with a review of the artist's present status, i.e., current producer, recorded material in the can, and affiliations with record companies and record executives. Previously released material, sales and airplay history, and contacts with radio program directors and disc jockeys should also be thoroughly discussed and noted. The parties should touch on anything relevant to furthering the artist's career as a recording artist, ranging from a discussion of producers, A&R (Artist and Repertoire) men, and other record executives who have previously expressed interest in the artist. In addition, the parties should review and critique all of the artist's previously recorded material, both released and unreleased, in order to determine a future strategy.

As with personal appearances and recording, the process of evaluating the present status and past history of the artist should be repeated in every substantive area of the artist's career. Other subject areas include songwriting, music publishing, television and motion pictures, commercials, and merchandising and endorsements. The detailed information concerning the artist and his career compiled in the artistic evaluation should enable the manager to begin the formulation of the artist's image.

IMAGE FORMULATION

We've already touched on the issue of "image" in the preceding material on artistic evaluation. It refers to the way the artist is perceived by the public both in a professional and personal setting. The concept isn't hard to understand, but the reality of shaping, projecting, and maintaining an image that will play with the public and still allow the artist to remain a person is among the most difficult tasks confronting the artist-management team. Here are some suggestions for going about it.

Generally, the image will be determined in light of the artist's goals, abilities, values, resources, and the existing commercial setting. Based on an analysis of the information gleaned from the artistic evaluation, the place to start is setting some basic goals.

Goals

Every artist must decide what direction they want to follow with their career. That sounds rather obvious, but an alarming number of very talented people only know that they want to be "stars" or have a driving desire to "make it" in the business. Those aren't goals, they are wishes, and rather abstract ones at that. Goals can be both long- and short-range, but they must be specific, such as aiming to be a major rock recording artist or a top concert draw on the country music circuit. These goals are concrete enough to suggest shorter-term objectives which in turn help the artist move toward achieving the long-term aims.

As a general rule, an artist's image must be consistent with what will sell in the career area he or she has chosen or run the risk of losing credibility with fans. It must also comport with one's personal lifestyle and values. Moreover, the image must be both original and commercial. If an artist is merely a clone of someone else there is little chance of a major breakthrough. If an artist is too trend-conscious, there is a risk that the public will forsake the artist later, when the trend passes.

Anybody can count the examples of long-extinct careers that failed to survive disco, urban cowboy, and new wave. The answer seems to lie in a balancing act between being original and somewhat flexible. Trends shouldn't control image, but neither should they be completely ignored. Easy, isn't it?

Present Image

Aside from the artist's professional and personal goals, a major consideration is existing image. The manager should ask the question, "How is my artist presently perceived by the public as well as by others in the entertainment industry?" If an artist is new or relatively unknown, this won't present a problem, because there is no established perception. However, present image can be much more of a problem for an established artist who wants to renew a slipping career with an image change. The veteran artist runs the risk of alienating those fans that he or she already has. Then there's the additional danger that a radical change simply won't be accepted by the public. This can be especially true of an artist long known for a particular style of recording or performing.

Everybody is obsessed with labels—the trade press and industry decision makers as well as fans. There is nothing malevolent involved. Labels are just an effective short reference that allow us to categorize and deal with a complicated world. And once accepted, labels are difficult to change. Consider how long it took Sally Field to shake the Flying Nun, or how difficult it was for people to accept the fact that a former Monkee, Mike Nesmith, could produce serious music videos. This should illustrate why an artist and manager should pay careful attention to formulation and development of image. Flexibility should be built-in to allow for shifts in direction or development of an artist's art or music that will be accepted by the public without alienating hard-won fans. Walking this fine line requires a great deal of management dexterity.

Finding the Right Image

Beyond these fundamental considerations, manager and artist must develop an image that will complement the talent, appearance, and personality of the artist, while still being commercially viable. For instance, let's assume that an artist's songs and style are compatible with the image of an early 1960s Greenwich Village folksinger. Projecting and perpetuating such an image would be a blunder if there's no substantial market for that particular style of music. Yet by taking some basic elements of folk music, such as "message" songs with contemporary social themes and a basic acoustic guitar accompaniment, and blending them with a unique voice and a striking, contemporary personal appearance, you have innovation. We have just described Tracy Chapman, who used these basic ingredients to become a Grammy Award winner in 1989. This demonstrates the important role played by image. It also illustrates the fine line between recycling a trend or genre that is long since passé versus true innovation that seizes on time-tested elements that can succeed again.

The lesson here is that nothing ever actually repeats itself to the letter, yet almost everything hailed as an innovation is a hybrid of styles and influences that have gone before. Elvis, Jerry Lee Lewis, Chuck Berry, Little Richard, and the rest of the rock and roll pioneers didn't just sit down and invent the genre; they had influences and role models to draw from just as the Rolling Stones, the Beatles, and the rest of the British Invasion drew from those rock pioneers.

One of the most striking examples in the late '80s is the obvious influence that the early James Brown shows, which were a staple on the all-black nightclub circuit, had on the current musical and live performance styles of Michael Jackson and Prince. Very few fans of these two mega-entertainers ever sat in a black nightclub in South Carolina or Mississippi in the early '60s, yet today they are witnessing many of the same approaches and styles that the "hardest working man in show business," as Brown was known in his early days, pioneered. Despite Brown's strong influence, Jackson and Prince are rightfully hailed as true innovators.

This just underscores the fact that the artist who leads the field by carving a truly unique niche is usually a perceptive student of recent music history. The gift of innovation is to add a personalized touch that strikes a chord with a target audience. These lessons should not be lost when it comes time to assess artistic strength and create an image that projects star quality, musical innovation, and all those other intangibles that translate into gold and platinum records and SRO concert appearances.

Because image is so important to the success of an artist, the manager must constantly be aware of the various factors that comprise it. They include the artist's recording style and sound; selection of material; songwriting; the content and style of his personal appearances; mode and style of dress, speech, and physical appearance; the types of interviews he grants; the television and radio shows on which he appears; and even the way he or she conducts himself offstage. These are all components of image that must constantly be monitored, reviewed, refined, and kept current and consistent by the manager.

Charisma

A prime ingredient in an effective, commercially viable image is the element of charisma. Charisma is best described as an exceptional quality or magnetic power generated by an individual that allows him to stand out in a crowd or draw followers or fans to him. Charismatic qualities are often intangible in nature, yet they can spell the difference between just another artist and a superstar.

Although charisma is difficult to manufacture, managers should try to distinguish their artists from others by developing or maximizing any unique characteristics they might possess. For instance, if an artist is from a distinctive region of the country, such as parts of the Deep South or Texas, emphasizing this may create curiosity about the regional characteristics of the artist which might, in turn, result in increasing his appeal. The same principle can be used by artists from foreign countries or by artists that tour countries other than their own. Another example of a possible charismatic trait is a slight imperfection. Here a manager can use an apparent handicap, such as blindness or a scar, to advantage. A personality trait may also furnish a form of charismatic appeal, as with a reclusive artist who refuses to be interviewed or photographed. All of these are characteristics that a manager can use in image formulation and projection.

What's in a Name?

Even the names that roll easily off the tongues of record buyers and concert goers are often touched up to reinforce the image an artist seeks to project. While there is not as much of it in the music business, stage names are an obsession in Hollywood. Groups really don't have a choice. They have the often difficult responsibility of finding a name that will project and promote the collective identity of its members and their music. Individuals enjoy the same option, but often choose not to adopt a stage name.

The key is to make sure that a good fit exists between name and image. If it doesn't, a change may be in order. Considering the images of the following artists, which name sounds better to you? Conway Twitty or Harold Lloyd Jenkins; Elvis Costello or Declan McManus? As with everything else, use proper judgement. Recognize what works and what doesn't.

A successful manager will carefully evaluate all of the elements we've discussed that affect the artist's image and coordinate them to create a consistent and credible pattern. An artist's image should never be left to chance. Neglect in this area could lead to public confusion about who the artist is or what he's trying to do. Another possibility is that the artist may develop a bad public image as a result of unfavorable press or a distorted perception of him or his actions. The manager and artist should always be on guard to protect against this type of situation.

PROJECTING AND MARKETING THE IMAGE

Once the image is formulated, the next step is to project and market it. This process never stops. Given the heightened sophistication of marketing techniques and greater competition for coveted chart positions, coupled with an increased number of avenues through which to promote an artist's career, the task of image projection has become a very complex, full-time job. Record labels, full-service booking agencies, corporate sponsors, and even music publishers are all involved in the process. However, the artist still has primary responsibility for promoting the image that has been so carefully crafted.

Clearly, the first step is to hire a publicist whose sole job is to promote the artist in the media. The down side is cost. Depending on reputation and range of services, a publicist can cost $400 to $4,000 per month. Over the past decade, the publicist has become a fixture in any established artist's career. Because this comprises so much of what artist management has become, we will deal with the role of the publicist at length in our discussion of the Artist's Development Team.

For now, let's focus on a new artist who doesn't have an extra $400 to $4,000 lying around. There is still plenty the artist can do and indeed *must* do before getting to the point when the giant publicity and promotion machines of the record labels and booking agencies become part of the career equation. It is crucial that the artist make enough noise to get noticed and signed. Here are some basic image projection techniques any artist can put to work immediately.

The Press Kit

This kit should contain at least two 8" × 10" (20 × 25 cm) black-and-white glossy photographs of the artist, a professionally written biography, some reviews, a copy of the artist's latest recording or demo cassette, and other pertinent information or quotes regarding the artist. Do not use color photographs, although it is a good idea to have some color slides available on request for certain kinds of duplication. While it can be expensive, a short video bio can be a great help when it comes to pitching television shows, major magazines, and top-rated showcases. Optimum time for a video bio is seven minutes. Even if financial limitations preclude a video component, a well-written, professionally produced press kit is a relatively inexpensive image projection tool that is both essential and highly effective in presenting the artist in the most positive light possible.

Personal Appearances

One of the most effective methods of image projection is through live personal appearances at concerts, clubs, or showcases. This means arranging for the artist to appear in the right market at the right venue before the right audience, and that his dress, speech, actions, material, and onstage performance all come together to reinforce the image that has been formulated. The same considerations apply to radio or television appearances. At the breaking-in stage, exposure should take precedence over all else, and certainly over money.

If you are an artist in the breaking-in phase or if you've ever been there, you are probably laughing, or should be. How many times have you heard, "Son, it doesn't pay much (if anything), but it's great exposure." The trick here is to know the difference between valuable exposure and charity. It doesn't take half a brain to calculate what an appearance on "The Tonight Show" or "Late Night with David Letterman" can do for a career even if the AFTRA scale that a performer receives barely makes a dent in expenses. It is much tougher to decide how much to invest in showcases or how much of a financial hole to go into for the right club appearance.

The other word of caution here is to be ready once the financial sacrifices of an exposure appearance have been resolved. New artists seldom get a second chance to impress the "right" people, whether it be a live performance or demo tape. Make sure the image is right and that all the pieces for putting the artist across are coordinated. If there is any doubt, don't take the risk.

Do-It-Yourself Promotion Campaigns

Another valuable and effective means of image projection for new artists is the do-it-yourself promotion campaign. Popular and effective examples include the artist-released recordings, fan clubs, newsletters, even organized word of mouth insuring a club owner a guaranteed audience for a personal appearance. These techniques have proved successful in focusing attention on artists who were then able to parlay that attention into a record deal, an agency contract, and even representation by a name manager.

Any contact an artist has with the public, either personally or through record sales, print, or the electronic media, is a method of image projection. Maximizing public exposure while avoiding the dangers of overexposure should be a key agenda item on the artist's career plan at all levels, but especially during the breaking-in stage. Much is at stake in terms of financial reward and career development. Take the time and find the money to do it right.

9

The Career Plan

We've made reference to the career plan on numerous occasions in previous chapters. Now, in this chapter, we'll discuss fundamental concepts of business and creative planning and some of the considerations in formulating the plan. All the preliminary matters—negotiation of the management contract, business organization, artistic evaluation, image formulation—are undertaken with the objective of enhancing the successful completion of the career plan.

The career plan is the artist's and manager's blueprint for attaining the success they both seek. In an earlier chapter, reference was made to a young group who was approached by a manager wanting to represent the act. This would-be manager was full of promises and illusions of great things. However, the group made a key mistake when they failed to ask that all important question, "How will you make us a success?" The career plan is the "how" to successful artist management.

In order to fully understand the career plan, it helps to be aware of the many components that are involved in its makeup. The primary element to any plan is the planner. The personal characteristics, vision, and abilities of the planner are always reflected in the plan. Whether an individual sets high or low goals in a plan is usually a reflection of his approach to life. Is the planner a success-oriented person or is he negative or defensive in his approach to life? Whether the planner is an enthusiastic, freewheeling optimist, or a cautious, steady type will obviously affect the formulation and execution of the career plan just as those personality traits will be indicative of management style. No matter how sound a plan may be, it will encounter problems, obstacles, and delays. It is here that the qualities of persistence, discipline, and follow-through will pay off. The planner with those qualities will surely have incorporated them into the plan as contingencies and backup devices.

ANALYZING THE PLANNER

One of the first steps in the career-planning process is to learn about the planner. For purposes of our discussion, the career planner is both the manager and artist; the personalities of both are important and should be factored into the planning process. The preliminary exploratory conference, contract negotiation, business and artistic evaluation, and other meetings and discussions obviously will give manager and artist an insight into each other's personalities. Both the artist and manager should conduct a self-examination of their own success chemistry. Each should ask, "Am I a positive-minded person? Do I totally believe in this artist-management relationship? What do I want from this relationship? What are my personal strengths and weaknesses?" This self-appraisal will assist the planner in formulating the career plan, or it may add new insight and perspective into an existing plan.

If both manager and artist are formulating the career plan, a better self-awareness may prevent one of them from objecting to the high-goal aspirations advanced by the other, especially if either artist or manager is conscious that his or her basic approach to planning is conservative. Consequently, the party with the more dominant success chemistry will avoid compromising his position merely because his planning partner has tendencies toward fear of failure that could be detrimental to both. Conversely, if one party finds through self-analysis that he is unrealistic in goal setting, this awareness may make it easier to accept a more workable, scaled-down approach to setting objectives recommended by the other party in the planning process.

The artist without a manager will be forced to plan alone. Nevertheless, the same principles and concepts will apply. In order to guard against the dangers of unrealistic optimism or overly cautious planning, the artist going it alone would be well advised to find someone with business savvy and industry exposure to act as a sounding board. The worst possible consequence is to take the time to plan only to base the future on flawed or unworkable premises or conclusions.

ESTABLISHING GOALS

Another key element of the career plan is setting goals. Goals, which are the objectives of the artist's career, may range from getting a record deal or successfully performing the nightclub circuit to charting a top-10 record or earning $1,000,000 in a year. Goals vary depending not only on the particular circumstances, needs, and desires of the artist, but also on their talents, abilities, and resources as well.

A goal should stimulate and motivate the artist toward a particular achievement. The career planner should avoid setting his sights too high, thus making the goal extremely difficult or impossible to achieve. Nor should he set the goal so low that it's quickly accomplished, consequently losing its motivational value. A happy medium must be reached. Too many goals may further complicate the process. The career planner will have to study the feasibility of each desired goal and rank them according to priorities. By applying the principles of open discussion and honest self-evaluation, the proper goals can be selected.

The speed of goal accomplishment is another important element of the career plan. As we alluded to earlier, the planner must take into consideration unexpected events that could delay the scheduled accomplishment of certain objectives. A timetable for goal attainment must be constructed to match each particular goal realistically. It can't be too soon, thereby not allowing sufficient time for its accomplishment. Nor can it be too distant, thereby losing motivational impact. To design a realistic timetable, goals should be staggered over long, short, and intermediate periods. A certain objective can be set for achievement in six months, thereby giving the artist something to work for with immediate results. Another goal can be set to be reached in one year, and still another set for three to five years. All the goals, of course, should be designed to lead to some ultimate objective, but the short-term and intermediate objectives give the entire plan a logical stair-step effect. Although the timetable is different for each level of achievement, the overall design is geared to the ultimate goal.

SELF IMAGE AND GOAL SETTING

Another interesting factor influencing goal selection and accomplishment is the psychological makeup of the planner. While we have previously discussed the role of the planner and how personality, character traits, and management style can affect the planning process, we are concerned here with how the less obvious dimension of self image can manifest itself in goal setting. Some individuals have a subconscious fear of failure. Consequently, this fear may reveal itself in terms of easily attainable goals over a very short period. There are others who have a hidden fear of success. This fear is camouflaged by setting goals that are almost impossible to attain. These individuals do not have to worry about success, since their goal will never be accomplished. They have a built-in excuse: "I knew I couldn't reach that goal—it's just too high," or, "I would have succeeded, except . . ."

Another important point is the psychological assistance goals give in achieving success. The fact that a goal exists provides a good reason to start. Writing down the goals is also valuable. Periodic reading or repetition of the goal will imprint that objective in the subconscious. Thus conscious actions which are mandated by the career plan are supported by these subconscious thoughts. This can be very helpful when things don't seem to be going well and self-doubt sets in. At this point, a positive subconscious can help put an artist back on the route toward his goal.

DECIDING ON A GOAL STRATEGY

Once a realistic goal has been selected, the next step is developing an approach for reaching that goal. We'll refer to these approaches as "goal strategies." The goal strategy is the planner's idea of the shortest, most effective route to a particular point, the goal. The artist's manager should realize that the goal strategies will almost always differ from artist to artist, depending on his particular talent, needs, and circumstances. His past experience, personal motivation, expertise, knowledge of the overall structure of the music industry, and his sense of timing all play an important part in strategy selection. For instance, many artists wish to break into the national concert market. Several strategies could be employed to accomplish this goal. The artist could work on recording with the aim of having a hit record that would lead to concert bookings as an opening act and later as a headliner. As an alternative, the artist could record and release records through a small regional label with hopes of developing a market in that area as a concert attraction, consequently attracting attention from a major label or national agents. Yet another approach would be to invest more time in developing a high-energy stage show that would attract the attention of agents or established concert artists who might book the artist as an opening act.

All of these strategies could ultimately achieve the desired result. The pivotal question for management is, "Which strategy will be the most desirable for this particular artist?"

Strategies are the pathways to goal attainment. They may be designed to follow just one route, or change directions on numerous occasions throughout the artist's career. Nonetheless, they should all lead in the same direction—toward the artist's goal.

DEVELOPING CAREER TACTICS

The final step to career planning is developing tactics to implement the predetermined strategies. Career strategies set the direction toward particular goals, while career tactics are the actual moves of the strategy. They're the day-to-day activities of an artist's life. These seemingly unimportant details may account for a month's or even a year's work toward the accomplishment of certain goals. The control of these activities is a critical aspect of goal achievement. Many people enjoy the talking, planning, and dreaming phase of planning. But the tactical phase isn't concerned with tomorrow; its focus is today. The manager and artist should ask what's being done *right now* toward accomplishing the predetermined career goals. It's at this point in the career plan where many lose control of their future. If a successful future is the goal, start with being a success today. To have high aspirations and to succeed takes hard work. To work efficiently and consistently takes discipline. Daily tactics inject discipline in the career plan. That can mean rehearsal, writing, recording, interviews, visits to radio promotion people. Any tangible movement toward the objective is a career tactic.

An important factor here is the planner's ability to efficiently utilize time. Because of the rapid fluctuations in popular trends and styles in the entertainment business, time is of the utmost importance to the artist and manager. The artist who has achieved success must maximize it before a new style emerges that may divert his following to a new rising star. Too many artists think that once they have a hit record, the work is over and the fun begins. Nothing could be further from reality. Any established artist and their manager will tell you that getting there is tough, but staying there is a lot tougher. This is especially true for a young artist, not aware of the costs associated with the business. Studio rental fees, publicists, attorney's fees, accountant's bills, union stage hands, sidemen for recording, concert halls, and on and on are part of the backhanded reward for hard-won success. Working efficiently means knowing how to control such costs. This is, to a great extent, accomplished by controlling time.

UPDATING THE PLAN

As a final point, once the career goals, strategies, and tactics have been determined, the plan should be reviewed periodically. A review enables the planner to gauge results and to determine if a tactical or strategical change is necessary. Once goals are attained, new ones must be formulated. Career momentum has only two directions, up and down. Failure to keep a career on an upward path means it's going down.

Often you hear someone comment, "How did that record make the charts?" or "How could that artist be successful?" If you look behind the record or artist to the people planning the career, the success of the record or artist may become more apparent. Determined, positive-minded people with a well-thought-out, realistic career plan can greatly affect the prospects for success. They know where they're going and how they're going to get there. This is the essence of the career-planning concept.

[PART THREE]

MAKING THE PLAN WORK

10

Making Your
Own Breaks

Talent, organization, and planning are all essential elements of a successful career in show business. However, unless an artist's talent receives the proper exposure or unless the career plan is implemented, the artist is no better off than before he initiated his management program.

Making the plan work is the key to success for any artist. It can also be the most demanding part of a manager's job. It requires daily attention to detail and constant follow-up. It means creating opportunities, making things happen, and turning dreams into reality. This is where a manager can be an invaluable asset to the artist.

For the new artist, the implementation or breaking-in phase probably represents the most difficult and frustrating stage of his career. The commitment of the artist and his manager is tested severely. It requires a tremendous amount of persistence, drive, and skill to cope with the inevitable obstacles that stand between an unknown artist and the ultimate goal of stardom. Many talented performers and their managers are not equipped financially or emotionally for the "dues paying" that is associated with this phase of the artist's career. As a result, many artists who receive initial rejections from agents, producers, and record companies become discouraged and quit.

If there is anything that is an absolute certainty in the music business, it's rejection. Artists and their managers shouldn't prepare for rejection *if* it comes, but rather *when* it comes. Success comes to those capable of rising above certain adversity. Those who can't will never make it. That is a guarantee.

Even artists who do enjoy a measure of recognition and financial reward soon learn that success is relative. There's always the potential that hard-earned success will disappear as quickly as it materializes. Every artist is only as successful as the most recent accomplishment. The competition for the limited number of slots on record company artist rosters and the *Billboard* charts is fierce and ongoing. Unless the artist and his management stay constantly aware of this, they'll soon find themselves in the role of "has beens." This suggests that implementation and execution of the career plan is a never-ending process.

This chapter and the ones that follow are designed to acquaint the manager and artist with the specific problems they'll undoubtedly face in implementing their plans. They also suggest approaches and tech niques for understanding and dealing effectively with these problems. While every manager develops his own techniques and approaches for achieving the career goals of the artist, we feel that information and advice contained in this section will provide a strong foundation for helping him adopt a coordinated program for making the plan work.

INGREDIENTS FOR SUCCESS

Successfully implementing the artist's career plan involves the interaction of a number of factors. A clear understanding of these elements provides the starting point for making things happen.

Talent and Appeal

Unless the artist possesses at least some degree of talent and appeal, the most experienced manager, working with the best plan conceivable, won't succeed in making that artist successful. The ultimate decision-maker is the general public, but it is record companies, booking agents, video channels, and all the other "distributors" that make the crucial decisions of whether the public will ever get the chance to embrace or reject an artist. Since talent and commercial viability are so subjective, it is up to the manager to decide if there is enough potential to merit the effort it takes to sell the industry on the artist so it might, in turn, let the public decide what it will ultimately accept or reject.

The Manager

While the manager can't insure success, he does have a great deal to say about how the artist presents his talent to the industry and the public, along with the type and degree of exposure he receives. Record charts, television ratings, and motion picture box office receipts bear witness to the fact that people of only average ability have achieved stardom through astute, effective management.

This leads to the question, What are the elements of astute, effective management? We have alluded to some of them before from the perspective of the artist looking for a manager, but it would be appropriate at this juncture to take a closer look from the manager's viewpoint.

The first prerequisite is a thorough understanding of the various aspects of the entertainment industry. Intelligence and judgement are no substitute for a working knowledge of the particular field of entertainment in which his artist is involved. This knowledge takes many forms. Every manager should know the mechanics of the particular area in which he's involved, whether it be recording, publishing, performing, merchandising, and so on. This means knowing the inner workings of each, knowing what the prevailing industry practices are, and having the ability to speak the language of that particular aspect of the business.

It's also essential that the manager know the decision makers within each branch of the industry, or at least know who they are. The entertainment business is a "people business." Personal contacts can mean everything when it comes to getting a deal for an unknown artist. Many recording executives, agents, producers, and publishers depend on word-of-mouth reports or personal recommendations to reduce the risk and help them screen new or unproven artists, writers, and actors. This is a necessity because of the sheer numbers who are drawn to show business by the promise of fame and wealth. This reality of the industry is often criticized by new artists and many managers, but the truth is that as more artists try to break down the barriers to a show business career, industry pros will step up their retreat behind what they view as a necessary self-defense mechanism. Consequently, for a manager to pierce this protective shield and present his artist to an entertainment decision maker, it becomes even more crucial for the manager to know someone. Like it or not, access is a reality of the business. Without it, the most knowledgeable manager representing the most innovative artist is irrelevant when it comes to getting things done.

While it's clear that knowledge of the industry and personal contacts are necessary tools of any effective manager, this in itself does not ensure success. The truly successful manager possesses the intangible quality of "having a feel for the business." This is a combination of perception, understanding, judgement, and timing which can't be acquired from books or at cocktail parties. It means knowing how to calm a temperamental artist or communicate a certain mood to a studio musician. Having a feel for the business also means understanding the subtle professional and personal interrelationships that exist in the various components that make up the business.

An illustration of this intangible ability is an accurate prediction by a manager of how a certain television appearance or video production will affect an artist's concert drawing power and record sales. Another illustration is the ability of a manager to sense the underexposure or overexposure of an artist by reviewing his itinerary three months ahead of time, and then to adjust it accordingly. All topflight managers share this talent for making the right move at the right time.

"How do I acquire these essential management skills?" is a question asked by every aspiring manager or self-managed artist breaking into the field. Books such as this one provide a starting point. Weekly trade magazines such as *Billboard* are published to keep managers and artists informed of current happenings and trends in the business. A more complete listing of resource materials is provided in the appendix.

These two sources are highly recommended. However, books and trade publications can't establish personal contacts or provide the intangible qualities of insight, judgement, and timing. Actual experience in some aspect of entertainment is the only means available to the aspiring manager to gain the necessary insight and feel for the business. Practical experience also affords him the opportunity to meet others in the industry. Because the music business is relatively small in terms of number, decision-making tends to be concentrated primarily in a few entertainment centers, such as New York, Los Angeles, and Nashville. It's possible to meet a wide cross-section of entertainment industry figures by working and living in an entertainment center. Because the music business is a small industry and people advance themselves by accumulating practical experience and personal relationships, chances are good that a friend who's struggling today might be one of tomorrow's top decision makers. This all adds up to an inescapable conclusion: there is simply no substitute for being in the middle of what is happening, where it is happening.

Preparation

Preparation by the artist and manager is another necessary ingredient for success. Planning is one form of preparation already discussed. Always being ready to carry out that plan is another aspect of preparation. Show business is unpredictable. Opportunity often knocks when least expected. Both artist and manager must always be in a position to capitalize on a "break" when it appears, because it might not present itself again. So many of today's stars attribute their success to being able to take advantage of an opportunity. These brief and often chance events are the best reasons for constant preparation, planning, and rehearsal. If the artist and manager are "ready," it will just be a matter of doing what both have prepared themselves for when the right opportunity presents itself.

Flexibility

The artist and manager should always be willing to change the game plan to fit the circumstances. Trends in entertainment can change overnight. Being able to anticipate and change with them is essential to achieving and maintaining success. Elvis Presley, through the efforts of astute management, sustained and expanded his career through three decades. By being able to remain flexible, Elvis made the transition from rock 'n' roll recording idol to movie star to Las Vegas headliner.

Flexibility is not only important for the established artist but applies equally to the artist in the breaking-in stage. The unknown artist must constantly adapt to existing commercial opportunities. What might have been in vogue a year ago means nothing if the public won't accept it today.

Realism

Being realistic is an attitude that must be maintained at every career level. Entertainment lends itself to big promises that have a way of never materializing, and of firm commitments that often dissolve into "maybes." Part of the manager's job is to sort through these promises, offers, and alternatives and make a realistic assessment of the value of each. He must help the artist maintain a realistic perspective while also sustaining his own enthusiasm and commitment. This requires an ability to recognize a true commercial opportunity and take steps to turn it to the artist's advantage. It also means rejecting offers that may look good on the surface, but turn out to have little real merit. It's often difficult to effectively perform this function, especially in light of the many glamour offers that "can't miss." However, unless the manager can retain his perspective and make accurate judgements, the chances of his artist making it to the top and staying there are slim.

As mentioned earlier, persistence and determination, in addition to everything else, are in many ways the most important qualities of all. The ability to accept disappointment and setbacks without giving up marks the difference between stars and ordinary people with talent. This type of single-purpose drive is necessary not only to unknowns, but to established artists as well. One of the best examples is recording-artist Kenny Rogers, who enjoyed a hit record in the late 1950s as a single artist. After that early success, he faded from the charts. He later came back with a new group, the First Edition, which enjoyed a string of hit records throughout the late '60s and early '70s. After what seemed to be a period in which success was guaranteed, another dry spell hit. The group broke up and Kenny moved to Nashville and began recording country-oriented material. After a few years of absence from the charts, he enjoyed another comeback, recording the biggest hits of his career. During the decade of the 1980s, Kenny and his manager, Ken Kragen, consolidated this hard-won success through a variety of outlets from records, concerts, and videos to charitable activities and a lucrative corporate spokesmanship with the Dole Corporation.

The underlying reason for Kenny's success is that he never gave up. He was determined to find a new approach that would put him back on the charts, not just once, but twice. This type of roller-coaster effect is typical of a show-business career. The artist and manager should accept this from the outset. If the talent is there and the commitment is strong enough, something will usually happen sooner or later. The time in between is for paying dues. This is something both artist and manager should be prepared to do if they really want to make it.

Luck

All of the qualities described in this chapter can, at least to some extent, be controlled by the artist and his manager; however, there's one element that can't. That element is luck. Luck is as much a part of entertainment as talent. Simply stated, luck is being in the right place at the right time. There are many artists who have been in the right place at the right time, but were not properly prepared to make the most of the opportunity. This is the essence of making your own breaks. Although a good manager can't make a lucky break materialize, he can help create the circumstances of commercial opportunity through his contacts and his understanding of the industry. He can, through preparation, flexibility, and realism, help ensure that the artist will be ready to take advantage of that opportunity he has helped to create. This is what successful artist management is all about—helping the artist to make his own breaks, rather than leaving success to chance. This is the difference between an artist sitting back waiting for a break that may never come and an artist with a well-planned and executed management program designed to make sure that the break will come. Sooner or later.

The Artist's Development Team

Previous chapters have dealt with the importance of organization, planning, and action by the artist and manager to help create commercial opportunity. At this point, we'd like to introduce the concept of the artist's development team and its role in the career success of the artist.

The term "artist's development team" refers to the various entities or people within the entertainment industry who have a direct monetary interest or stake in the artist's career and with whom the manager and artist must deal on an ongoing basis. For instance, let's assume the artist's income is derived primarily from the sale of records, songwriting royalties, personal appearances, and commercial endorsements. Those entities or persons who stand to directly benefit from the artist's success would include his record company, music publisher, booking agent, publicist, and advertising agency. These entities comprise the artist's development team. Each of these entities is vitally concerned that the artist succeed because their fortunes are tied, at least in part, to that artist. Each member of the team has certain resources and assets they are willing to expend in order to further various aspects of the artist's career. Any experienced manager knows that without the help of these various entities, career development toward the artist's predetermined goals would be almost impossible. By the same token, maximizing the contributions of each member of the team in a coordinated, efficient manner consistent with the artist's career plan can ensure that those goals are attained. When it's done right, everyone benefits.

THE PRINCIPLE BEHIND
THE ARTIST'S DEVELOPMENT TEAM

The concept of the artist's development team relies on a fundamental principle of the entertainment industry: No one can ever hope to achieve success alone. The most resourceful manager, working with the best plan conceivable and the most talented artist imaginable, must also have the support and help of others within the industry in order to make it.

With this basic principle in mind, the manager should strive to maximize the career development of his artist by working with the various members of the team for the mutual success of all involved. Through a program of coordinated interplay with the artist and the respective team members, the manager should be able to accelerate the career plan. The manager's role is to act as both a coordinator and motivator to tie the team together and get the most each member has to offer.

The concept of an artist's development team, by its very nature, suggests a positive approach. To apply it successfully, the manager must necessarily establish harmonious, cooperative working relationships with those individuals who make up the team. This requires the manager to be an open-minded, cooperative person who is willing to listen to recommendations and suggestions. This is not to suggest that the manager be just a follower, always deferring to others. He must know where his artist is going and set the pace for the team. It also does not ignore the manager's responsibility to assert and protect the artist's rights. However, a successful application of the team approach should allow the manager to maximize the benefits for his client without having to compromise his rights or artistic integrity.

We're realistic enough to acknowledge that disputes between team members and management are sure to arise during the career of any artist. But the role of management is to shield the artist from such disputes as much as possible, while making an effort to resolve these conflicts through compromise or alternative approaches. Under the artist's development team approach, the manager should try to minimize points of disagreement when they arise so not to impede the progress of career development any more than necessary.

Certain disagreements are inevitable, especially in a creatively driven industry where personal taste and preference play such an important role. Most unnecessary disputes arise as a result of ego. A manager should remember that he's working to build his artist's career, not to gratify his own self-image. The manager's sense of self-discipline and restraint will be very important in helping to avoid many petty, time-consuming disagreements. By the same measure, the manager's ability to communicate and counsel his client can help avoid artist-related ego hang-ups. One helpful device for avoiding these types of problems is for the manager and artist to acknowledge and weigh the counterproductive effects of such disputes before a potential problem surfaces. By consciously making this assessment, both manager and artist will often realize that the dispute is simply not as important as they originally thought. Many artists and managers waste valuable time and energy on trivial, unimportant problems. Eventually, through experience, the rational pragmatist will learn how to avoid them.

While a realistic, resourceful manager can help avoid creating his own problems, he must be attuned to potential snags that are generated by others on the artist's development team. The best approach to problem-solving is for the manager to try to negotiate a solution without compromising the artist. This often means that the manager must swallow his pride to achieve the desired result. Another tack he may take is to approach a problem from a different perspective or provide the other party with alternatives. In any event, he must remain cool and keep the lines of communication open. By doing this, a manager will find himself winning far more than he loses.

FORMING THE TEAM

The first step is to identify the team members or potential team members. For example, if the artist is presently affiliated with a record company and a music publisher but not a booking agent, the former two companies would be team members, while any of a number of booking agents would be potential team members. Provided the need existed and the artist was ready, the manager's next move would be to secure affiliation with an agent or agents to fill the vacancy on the team. Other members would be added based on the overall career plan and needs of the artist.

Other possible team members might be a record producer and a publicist. Members of the team will often be added or dropped, depending on their involvement with the artist at any given point in his career.

ESTABLISHING PERSONAL
RELATIONSHIPS WITH TEAM MEMBERS

Once the various entities comprising the team are identified or essential members subsequently added, the manager should move to form personal ties with every individual that will have a role in the development of the artist's career. We stress the importance of "every" person who has a contribution to make, not just the president of the record company or the responsible agent in charge of booking the artist. Every person within an organization is potentially important to the artist's career from secretaries to department heads on up to the top executives. For example, at a booking agency, this means taking the time to meet and get to know not only the agent primarily responsible for booking the artist, but his assistant as well as other agents and supporting personnel in other departments, especially publicity.

Besides just getting acquainted, the manager should tell these people about his artist, what he is doing artistically and where he is trying to go with his career. This will help the team members to better understand the artist. A better understanding can be the beginning of genuine excitement and belief in the artist and his music.

Though it takes time, the successful manager makes the extra effort to establish personal relationships with as many people as possible. It makes a difference when it comes time to getting things done or having quick access to information. Everyone involved with the artist, regardless of his or her specific duties, has a contribution to make to the artist's career. It's human nature for these people to give a little extra or be more responsive or cooperative when they are dealing with a manager they know and like on a personal level. People appreciate being appreciated. They like knowing that the manager thinks their input is worthwhile. The difference will become apparent in a hundred little ways, each one of them important to advancing an artist's career.

Besides the manager's efforts in building personal bridges, it's often a good idea to introduce the artist to these same people. This personal contact helps to make their efforts more meaningful while also allowing them a personal link to the artist.

COORDINATING THE TEAM'S ACTIVITIES

A managerial prerequisite to effectively dealing with the artist's development team is a detailed understanding and appreciation of the structure and function of each component. In short, this means that the manager should not only understand what record companies do and how they do it, but he must also understand the workings, personnel, and politics at the particular record company with which he is dealing. The same is true with every other member of the development team.

Beyond this, he must also understand how each member relates to the other. One of the most frequent criticisms of managers by record company executives, producers, agents, and publishers is that they often don't understand the various aspects of the business. As a result, they're unprepared to work effectively with the various members of the artist's development team. Even if a manager understands the business, but not the particular company or individual with whom he is dealing, his results are likely to be disappointing. People get fired, budgets are cut, companies are constantly being reorganized. More than one artist has been caught in a crossfire of company politics. It's the manager's job to spot trouble on the horizon and take the appropriate steps to either convert it to an advantage or protect the artist as circumstances dictate. When it comes to dealing with the artist's development team, the manager must emulate the artist and be ready to respond effectively when opportunity knocks.

After the members of the team have been identified, personal relationships are in various stages of development, and the manager is sufficiently prepared to deal effectively with the team, the actual process of artist development begins.

The manager should strive to maximize the resources available to the artist from the various components of the team. To do this, the manager must help each team member achieve his own specific objectives while ensuring that those goals are beneficial to the artist's overall career plan. This requires a high degree of coordination and communication with each team member to make sure that everybody is pulling toward the same objective. For instance, the manager will want to see that an extensive personal appearance tour is timed to maximize the promotion of the artist's latest record release. This requires coordination between the marketing, advertising, publicity, and promotion departments of the record company along with the artist's booking agency and the publicist. When the manager effectively serves as the liaison between these team members, he can help each to realize their specific goals. The personal appearance will reinforce the company's promotional efforts, thereby resulting in increased record sales for the company. Because of the new record release, there's increased interest in the artist, thus making him more appealing to promoters. This, in turn, makes the agent's job easier in booking the tour. The efforts of the artist's publicist complements the work of everyone.

To be an effective coordinator, the manager must maintain constant communication with the appropriate development team members. He should keep them informed of the artist's activities and plans while also monitoring the plans and desires of the various team members. The manager should remember that he's the focal point for all information concerning the artist and all communication between the team members and the artist. The manager should make himself readily accessible to the various team members.

In addition to controlling the information and communication functions, the manager should try to anticipate the specific goals of the various team members. For example, by anticipating the direction that the record company wants to go with an artist, the manager can plan accordingly. If he agrees with the direction, he can arrange the artist's schedule to coincide with those plans so as to gain maximum benefit. If he feels the company's plans don't fit into what he and the artist have determined to be the proper direction, he can propose alternatives or present his view of what should be the next move in a logical, persuasive manner before time pressures lead to a confrontation or a serious disagreement.

The manager should also make an effort to understand and appreciate the limitations and specific problems of the particular team members as they relate to any given project. By knowing what's possible and what's unrealistic, he can phrase his requests in a way that will help him get what he wants.

The resourceful manager will take the initiative to help the team members achieve their goals by submitting proposals and ideas. He should, whenever possible, act as a catalyst without appearing to tell someone else how to do their job or to demand that his ideas always be utilized. Rather, he should approach various individuals with suggestions and alternatives and ask for their views or opinions. Working effectively with the artist's development team should be a cooperative process aimed at trying to give an individual team member the benefit of a different viewpoint or alternative from which to choose.

The artist's development team concept is one the manager must utilize according to his best judgement. Some individuals might feel a manager's initiative is a criticism of their abilities or a threat to their egos. Some people prefer that managers not be so actively involved in their particular area of responsibility. The manager should be sensitive to and respect the wishes of these individuals and treat them accordingly. However, there will be inevitable conflicts requiring the manager to protect the rights and position of the artist. When that happens, the manager must do what he thinks is necessary, taking into consideration the long-term best interests of the client to whom he owes his first loyalty.

SUCCESS IS A SHARED CONCEPT

Almost every manager we've talked to has cited the concept of the artist development team as one of the key factors in breaking an artist and keeping him or her on top. The business of creating and sustaining a career in today's entertainment business is just too complex and sophisticated for any one person or firm to adequately handle. Ask the manager of any major artist and they will tell you that success depends on the interrelationship of a lot of talented, hard-working people. The driving force that motivates, informs, and guides this process is the artist's manager. The bottom line is that the manager should strive to deal as effectively and efficiently as possible with each individual concerned with the artist's career. Every manager will have his own particular techniques for getting the job done. These techniques will necessarily vary with each particular person with whom the manager deals. Common sense, flexibility, and follow-up are the key words to remember. Regardless of the approach used, the manager should remember that the more he contributes to helping the various development team members achieve their own success, the more he is contributing to the success of his artist.

12

The Record Deal

A successful record company affiliation is the key to any career in the music industry. Besides being a potentially lucrative source of income, the record is the most effective career development tool the artist possesses. It allows him to reach millions of potential fans with his music via radio airplay. This widespread national and international exposure translates into record sales, as well as a demand for concert and television appearances, offers for endorsements and commercial work, and songwriting income. Every element of the artist's career revolves around his relationship with the record company.

Getting signed to a major label has never been easy, but given today's spiraling production, marketing and promotion costs, the always tight radio playlists and the increased numbers of talented and sophisticated artists competing for the relatively few places on a label's roster, the task is more difficult than ever. Record company A&R departments are swamped with new artists and their managers or attorneys who are all trying to "get a deal." The division head of a major label's Nashville operation told us that his office alone receives over a thousand submissions a year. Out of this number, he'll sign four or five new acts.

The good news, if there is any, is that over the last decade the music business has experienced a broadening in musical tastes. This has translated into specialized markets and greater opportunity for those with the talent and vision to respond to what consumers want to buy. The Rap phenomenon is an example of one of the music industry's new self-contained subcultures which has created a growth market complete with its own video programming, fan magazines, and charts in *Billboard*. Artists like Tone Loc and DJ Jazzy Jeff and the Fresh Prince have become overnight sales and airplay chart giants. The obvious question raised by any fad is: Will it last? While it's impossible to know with any certainty, the odds are that it will survive in some form. A look at the current charts suggest a greater variety of commercial genres than ever before, all of which seem to be coexisting nicely. For instance, the disco explosion of the '70s is still going strong under the '80s alias of dance music. New R&B artists Bobby Brown and Anita Baker share the *Billboard* Black Album Chart with legends like Bobby Bland and Aretha Franklin, which is an indication that there is room on the charts for the old and the new. Country music playlists accomodate the lean, traditional styles of Randy Travis, George Jones, and Reba McIntire next to the innovations of Lyle Lovett, K.D. Lang, and K.T. Oslin. The Rolling Stones are pushing 50 and are bigger than ever. All of this seemingly spells opportunity. However, it's probably worth pointing out that while the number of specialty charts have increased, there are also more artists than ever before fighting for those chart positions and the radio airplay that can help them get there. And as far as the *Billboard* Hot 100 goes, which is still the barometer for measuring an all-purpose hit single, there are still just a hundred slots available to accomodate a big world of innovation and ambition.

This chapter is designed to help familiarize the new artist and his manager with the recording aspect of the artist's career. This information, hopefully, will help them to achieve a successful record company affiliation.

MAKING A QUALITY RECORDING

The first objective in the recording phase of the artist's career is to produce a commercial recording of professional quality. There are two approaches the artist can take. The first is to try to record a finished master recording that can be sold or leased to a record company. The other is to produce a high-quality demo (demonstration recording) that will create interest in the artist by a record label. There are pros and cons to both approaches.

The Finished Master Recording

A finished master recording is desirable from several standpoints. If the record company likes what they hear, the tape can be pressed and released in a short period of time. Some companies prefer to listen only to finished masters because they know what they're buying and won't be required to spend additional time and money on re-recording. This allows the company to concentrate on the marketing and promotional aspects of the record business.

As a practical matter, almost every major label will consider your recording a demo regardless of what it sounds like or how much you spent on it. Because the business today tends to be driven by name producers with a track record the company hopes can be parlayed into a hit, the major companies will most likely want to match the artist with a hot producer and re-record the tracks. The recent exceptions have been in the Rap area where the labels had to catch up to music that was coming from the streets. Of course, like everything else in the music business, this is a trend that is subject to change. Assuming it does or even might, it is useful to look at some of the other factors involved in making a master quality recording.

A negative aspect of the finished master approach is the expense involved. Despite the astounding developments in recording technology during the '80s such as sampling, DAT, etc., recording and mixing two finished sides can cost the artist several thousand dollars or more in studio time and musician payments. A finished master-quality album can cost as little as $10,000 to as much as the artist wants to spend. The average rock or pop album released by a major label can run $150,000 to $250,000. Budgets for established acts capable of selling double or triple platinum have been known to exceed 1 million dollars and a few have flirted with the 2 million dollar mark.

Because of lower production values, country albums are significantly less, but still on average cost between $75,000 to $100,000 and more. That's a lot of money for any artist to front on the come.

Another problem with this approach is that many new artists lack the recording experience necessary to turn out first-class commercial recordings in the early stages of their careers. A finished master makes it difficult to make changes a record company may want. As a result, the company may reject the recording entirely.

The Multi-Track Demo

An alternate approach is for the artist to record a quality multi-track demo that will give the record company a chance to listen to the artist's material and singing style. The company may make suggestions to improve the recording or suggest other material the artist could record. This approach allows the label to get involved in every detail of the artist's recordings at the outset of the artist's career.

The problem with this approach is that some companies prefer not to commit the time needed to develop an artist from a recording standpoint. Rather, they prefer the artist be capable of recording a finished product before they'll offer a contract. Unless a demo is of professional quality and has a high degree of commercial potential, the record company may choose not to get involved with the artist. Signing an artist is a business decision. As a result, the companies are looking for the "sure thing" when they can get it. Since the demo isn't a finished product, the risk factor is increased for the company. Whatever you show the record company had better be good. That includes not only the vocals and instrumental performances, but also the arrangements and the song. Most of all the song. Artists seldom get a second listening by a record company. The competition is too stiff. The advice here is to make sure you are taking your best possible shot with anything presented to a record company. If you can improve any aspect of the presentation, take the time to do it. You may never get another chance.

FINDING A PRODUCER

Regardless of the approach used, in order to turn out successful recordings, the artist must coordinate a number of factors. The first is to find a producer. If a major label is interested in a new artist, they will certainly be involved in the choice of producer and at the very least will want veto power over the choice.

It's the job of the record producer to mold the elements of artist, song, arrangement, studio, engineer, and musicians into a finished product. Many experienced artists are producers themselves. Many others don't feel capable of performing this important function. Whether the artist attempts to fill the dual role of producer or retain the services of another, it's essential that someone be in charge of the recording.

Choosing a producer is much like choosing a manager. They all have their own way of doing their job, but their methods aren't nearly as important as their results. The qualities an artist and manager should look for in a producer are experience, track record, and an ability to understand the musical direction of the artist and to work with him on a creative level. Often, the producer may be the artist himself, although the new artist is probably better advised to find someone with experience. In some cases, the manager may be qualified to serve this dual function. In other instances, the artist may retain the services of an experienced, independent record producer. Whatever the choice, artist, manager, and producer must be able to work closely with each other to help develop the artist's recording career in a manner that is consistent with the artist's ability and career plan.

Contractually, there are two basic approaches to the artist-producer relationship.

The Exclusive Personal Services Agreement

One approach is for the artist to sign an exclusive personal services agreement with an independent producer who becomes responsible for payment of a negotiated royalty to the artist. The producer in turn, seeks a recording affiliation by offering himself and the artist to the company as a package. Under such an arrangement, the producer signs an agreement with the record company, who pays all advances and royalties directly to the producer, who in turn accounts to the artist.

A major advantage to this approach is that a well-known independent producer, through his contacts, may be able to make a deal that the artist or manager may not otherwise be capable of obtaining. In addition, the name value and experience of a hot producer can make a big difference in breaking a new artist once a deal is made.

The major disadvantage is that the artist is exclusively tied to the musical tastes, production style, and fortunes of the producer. If the producer encounters a cold streak, the artist doesn't have the option of looking elsewhere for recording guidance. If a disagreement arises between the label and the producer, the artist's career could suffer as a result.

The Producer-for-Hire Approach

The other alternative is for the artist to be signed directly to the record company. In this situation, the artist would employ a producer on a project-by-project basis for either a flat fee or a percentage of the artist's royalties or a combination of both.

This approach is certainly preferable from the standpoint of giving the artist and manager more control over the recording aspect of the artist's career. The fortunes of the artist are not tied to one producer. However, the producer-for-hire approach is not always available to the new artist because of the expense involved and the inability of the artist to get a deal without the help of an independent producer.

Should the artist enter into an exclusive production agreement, he and his manager should try to limit the terms of the contract to provide for termination of the agreement in the event the relationship is no longer beneficial to the artist. This is a negotiable point and will depend on the bargaining positions of the parties.

After becoming familiar with the artist's ability, style, and goals, the producer will help the artist select the material to be recorded. The right song can play a crucial part in the success or failure of the artist's recordings. The producer will first look at any songs the artist might have written. If the artist doesn't write, or if his material is not appropriate, he'll survey music publishers and other writers for material that would suit his style.

After songs with sufficient commercial appeal have been selected, the artist and producer will work on an arrangement of the song that complements the artist's style and enhances its commercial appeal. If needed, the producer will employ the services of a professional arranger, usually on a flat-fee basis.

FINDING A STUDIO AND PERSONNEL

The next decision to be made is the selection of a recording studio, engineer, musicians, and background vocalists. Today, fully equipped, professional-quality recording studios can be found throughout the country, not just in recording centers such as New York, Los Angeles, and Nashville. Million-selling records have been recorded in such small towns as Macon, Georgia and Muscle Shoals, Alabama, as well as in big cities like Chicago, Miami, and Detroit. Due to technology advances, it is now possible for artists to build state-of-the-art facilities in their homes at a fraction of the cost of even a few years before. Because of this diversity of facilities, geographic location of a recording studio is not really as important a consideration as it once was.

Most studios furnish a recording engineer as part of the studio rental cost. This person's job is to attend to the technical end of recording, working under the supervision of the producer. Often, an established artist or producer may want to bring in his or her own engineer. In other instances, the producer may double as the engineer.

Experienced studio musicians can make a difference in the artist's recordings from both a quality and cost standpoint. A professional with studio experience works faster and with better results than a musician not accustomed to studio work. The same can be said of background vocalists.

Unlike the location of the studio, geography can play a significant role in the quality of musicians and vocalists. Experienced session men are found in recording centers because of the opportunity for steady work. Nashville and Los Angeles are both known for the quality of their studio musicians and vocalists. Other large centers such as New York, Detroit, Philadelphia, and Memphis, among other cities, are home to quality session men. Many studios have their own staff musicians who can provide solid basic rhythm tracks. Another approach is to employ the artist's band members on the session. Because of the uniformity of equipment, it's not uncommon for an artist to record his basic tracks in one city and later add horns, strings, and backup vocals in a studio located in a recording center.

Studio rental is usually handled on an hourly basis, depending on the number of tracks used and other specialized equipment available. Most master sessions employ 16- or 24-track professional recording equipment. The basic hourly rate will vary depending on equipment, location, and volume of recording activity. The rate for a top flight, multitrack studio can be as much as $200 per hour and up. The artist, manager, and producer should shop around for the best rate available. Studios often will block-book time at cheaper rates or offer a reduction for non-prime-time periods.

Musicians who play on master sessions are paid in accordance with applicable American Federation of Musicians (AF of M) scale rates. Vocalists' payments are governed by the American Federation of Television and Radio Artists (AFTRA). These respective organizations should be contacted by the manager as to applicable rates and procedures.

REHEARSALS

An artist recording for the first time shouldn't tackle a full-scale master session until he's gained recording experience. Most studios offer less-expensive demo rates on 8- or 16-track equipment. Band members or other less experienced musicians can be employed for this purpose. Union rules provide for a reduction in scale payments on demo sessions. The demo session is an excellent means to gain experience while trying out different material and production techniques.

Once an artist feels that he has sufficient recording experience, commercial material, and satisfactory arrangements, he should try to rehearse this material with his musicians, if possible, or prepare written charts that they can study. Because of cost considerations, the studio is no place to rehearse.

Multi-track equipment employed in professional studios allows each separate instrument and voice part to be recorded separately, making it possible to refine and perfect a recording until it captures the exact sound desired by the artist and his producer. After all parts of a song are recorded, the producer will mix the volume levels, tones, and effects on the various tracks into the final master product. Like anything else, experience and familiarity with the recording process contribute to better, more commercial recordings. The new artist should gain as much experience as possible before he undertakes a full master session.

SECURING A RECORDING CONTRACT

Assuming producer, artist, and manager are satisifed they have recorded a commercially viable master or a high-quality demo, the next step is to shop the tapes with record companies in order to secure a recording contract. This aspect of the manager's job is one of the most difficult, especially if he's dealing with a new or relatively unknown artist. It's important for the manager or other persons charged with the responsibility of shopping tapes to know how to approach a record company and appreciate what they're looking for in a new artist. This knowledge, used wisely, will improve the artist's chances for success. To do this, the manager should try to put himself in the shoes of the record company.

What Does the Record Company Want?

Record companies are in business to do one thing: sell records. When a label signs a new artist, they're making a business decision that involves the commitment of substantial expenditures, not only in the form of royalty advances to cover recording costs, but also the costs of manufacturing, promotion, and tour support. One label executive estimates that every time he signs a new act, his company will spend a minimum of $250,000. He goes on to point out that this figure is usually low, and doesn't include any extra promotional efforts or the man-hours of his staff. Because of this expense, the company wants to be sure that they're dealing with an artist capable of recouping this amount and earning a profit for the company. Many factors go into deciding whether to sign an artist.

First and foremost, the record companies are looking for artists with talent and ability, capable of making records that will appeal to the mass record buying public. Being good or just having talent isn't enough. Record company A&R men hear hundreds of good tapes by talented artists every year. They're looking for more. They want a unique voice or a distinct sound; something that isn't already on the market. The worst thing a manager can say to a record company is, "I've got an artist who sounds just like. . . ." The companies aren't interested.

When evaluating a record, the company is listening primarily for the lead voice. In all but exceptional cases, musicianship can be recreated by experienced session men; the voice, however, cannot.

Even if the voice is unique, the record must be commercial. Commerciality is a fluid concept that depends on many variables. The producer, artist, and manager must be aware of the marketplace when making an assessment of what is acceptable and what is not. This will depend on the circumstances of each individual artist and the trends that exist at a given point in time in the entertainment industry.

The record company is also interested in the artist's material. Does he write his own songs? If not, what is the source of his material? The record company generally considers the ability of an artist to write his own songs as an asset, since it insures a constant source of material for future recordings. While we're not suggesting that an artist must write his own material, in some cases this could be a factor in the company's decision to sign an artist/writer when a non-writing artist of equal ability is available.

A critical aspect of the artist's career from the record company's point of view is the live personal appearance. Many labels won't sign an artist who's not a working act. Concert and club appearances remain one of the most effective means of promotion a record company possesses. If the artist isn't able to perform his recorded material in a live performance situation, this promotional tool is lost. This illustrates the importance of obtaining live personal appearance experience before approaching a record company.

Aside from the creative components of an artist's career, record companies want assurance that they'll be dealing with professionals with a realistic and cooperative attitude. If this element isn't present, many companies will choose not to sign an artist who may have met all the other criteria.

A critical area of inquiry is the artist's management. A good record company, just like a good manager, thinks in terms of careers, not just one-shot hit records. This is especially true because few first albums recoup the total investment the company has made. Often, it may take two, three, or even more album releases to break an act. If an artist has ineffective management or no management at all, the company will often choose not to take a chance on him. In some cases, the record company will try to help the artist establish a management relationship. The major labels consider strong management to be a must for any artist.

As with management, the record company will want to inquire about the status of the artist's booking agency affiliation. This goes hand-in-hand with insuring that the artist has a tight, well-rehearsed concert and club act.

Other members of the artist's development team are also of interest to the label. They include his record producer, music publisher, publicist and others.

The artist's attitude and experience will weigh heavily on the company's ultimate decision. We have repeatedly stated the talent alone isn't enough. The record company must be able to work with the artist on a very personal level. Unless the artist is realistic and willing to help build his own career, neither record company, management, nor anyone else will be able to make him a success. A company would rather pass up a promising artist than sign him and the potential headaches he may cause later.

The foregoing considerations have dealt with factors within the artist's control. However, there are other elements in the decision-making process that have nothing to do with the merits of the artist and his management.

A record company may be overcommitted to artists already on the label. In some cases, the company's budget may have been expended on signing new acts during the then-current fiscal year. There may be an overabundance of artists already signed who are similar in style and appeal to a particular new artist trying to get a deal. In some instances, a company may have recently gone through an internal shakeup resulting in a halt on acquisitions of new artists.

A manager can improve his artist's chances for a deal by studying the artist rosters of various labels to determine the needs of the various companies. For instance, a label may be overloaded with female rock singers, but may need a male country artist.

The manager should read the trade magazines for news about company shakeups, shifts in emphasis, and expansion moves. Often, knowing when to approach a label can mean the difference between a rejection and a record contract.

How Should the Company be Approached?

We've reviewed the general points a record company uses in its decision-making process. With these in mind, let's turn to how a company should be approached.

As stated in an earlier chapter, record companies aren't interested in dealing with amateurs or thrill seekers. They're in business to make money, not to educate people about the entertainment business. Record executives want to deal with professionals. To do this, they often rely on recommendations from others in the business they know and respect. The best way to get an appointment is by either knowing someone personally at the label or someone else in the business who can recommend the artist or help set up an appointment. Often an entertainment attorney or someone else associated with the artist, such as the producer, will be more effective than the manager because of a personal contact.

If a manager has no personal contacts, he should get the name of someone in the A&R Department and try to make an appointment. It is the A&R man's job to listen to tapes submitted to the record company. When communicating with the A&R man, the manager should be as professional as possible. This means being organized, brief, and to the point. Some A&R men will set up an appointment, while others will ask the manager to mail them a copy of the tape. Of course, an appointment is more desirable. However, if the A&R man wants to listen to the tape in the privacy of his office, which most do, the manager should at least try to deliver the tape personally and establish some sort of rapport with him. The manager must be persistent, without making a pest of himself.

According to all the record-company executives we surveyed, unsolicited mailing of tapes to record companies, almost without exception, is a waste of time. It's also generally a good idea for the artist to let either his manager or some other party make contact with the record company rather than do it himself.

When submitting an artist to a record company, the manager should generally make a tape copy of the three or four most commercial recordings the artist has done. It's also a good idea to submit a lyric sheet, especially if the songs on the tape comprise original material written by the artist. In some cases, the manager may want to submit an entire album, depending on the preference of the company. An A&R man doesn't have time to sift through a number of recordings. If he's interested in what has been submitted, he'll ask to hear more.

The manager should also submit a press kit that includes photographs of the artist, a professionally written biography, a list of past appearances, an itinerary of upcoming performances, and any other relevant information that will help the company better evaluate the artist.

During the interview, the manager should give the A&R man basic information about the artist in a straightforward manner. Record companies don't want hype. Nor do they want excuses made about the tape, such as, "You have to take into consideration that the mix isn't very good," or "The artist had a cold when this tape was recorded." If the tape is a demo, the manager should give him that information. If it's a master, the manager can tell him so, if he feels it would be helpful. If there's immediate interest in the tape, the manager might offer to take the A&R man to a live performance. The key to a successful interview is to be firm and remain in control, without becoming obnoxious.

Even if the A&R man shows interest, he'll almost always want to play the tape for others at the label. The manager should give the A&R man his card and tell him that he'll follow up the interview after he's had a chance to hear the tapes. At the worst, the manager will get an on-the-spot rejection. In this case, he must stay cool. There's no sense in arguing; the A&R man's mind is made up. Instead, the manager should ask how to improve his artist's recordings. He should try to establish a rapport that might help get him in the door the next time. Then, regardless of the outcome of the interview, the manager should write a letter thanking the A&R man for his time and consideration of his artist.

In the event the tape is rejected, it's important that the manager and artist not become discouraged and give up. Rejection by record companies is just part of the business they must get used to. There are many stories of record companies rejecting artists and material that later went on to become hits. Even the Beatles were turned down by a number of companies before they were eventually signed. This fact should serve as inspiration to any artist and manager who have ever received a turn down. Just make the best of it, and move on.

NEGOTIATING THE RECORDING CONTRACT

In the event the record company does become interested in the artist and wants to add him to their roster, artist and manager must turn their attention to negotiation of the recording contract.

The first step is to retain an experienced attorney specializing in music law. He'll be able to advise the artist and manager of the complexities involved and points to be covered. Even if the manager has knowledge and experience in this area, it's still best in most cases to let the attorney do the negotiating. This course of action shields the artist and manager from the bargaining process, which can often be tedious and sometimes damaging to the artist/manager/record company relationship.

Whichever approach is selected, both artist and manager should keep in mind that a record company affiliation is a business relationship, regardless of how enthusiastic or friendly the A&R Department has been. The record-company negotiator, who is usually someone from the label's Business Affairs Department, will be trying to get the best terms possible for his company. From his point of view, signing a new artist is a dollars and cents proposition. The label takes advantage of its relative bargaining strength wherever possible. Naturally, the company will be in a better position when attempting to sign a new artist than it will be in negotiating a renewal of an established artist's contract or signing someone with a past track record.

With this basic premise in mind, we'll briefly discuss some of the points that should be considered by a manager in a record-contract negotiation. This is by no means meant to be a comprehensive or exhaustive discussion, but only a general outline of relevant considerations. This is far too complex a subject to deal with on an in-depth basis in the context of this book. It is also not meant as a do-it-yourself shortcut to avoiding legal fees. The manager should seek the advice and counsel of his attorney in any record negotiation. Remember, that once the contract is signed, the artist and manager will likely have to live with its terms for a long time. This should give the artist and his representative more incentive to make sure that it's the best possible deal that can be negotiated under the circumstances.

PROVISIONS OF THE CONTRACT

Generally, the recording contract is an exclusive personal services agreement whereby the artist furnishes master recordings embodying his unique vocal and/or musical performances to the record company. In turn, it's the label's obligation to manufacture, promote, and market these records to the public, and pay the artist a royalty on the records sold. While this sounds simple enough in the abstract, the process is quite complicated and involved.

Royalties

One of the most important provisions of the contract, from the artist's point of view, is the artist's royalty. Royalties are usually based on either a percentage of the suggested retail price or the manufacturer's wholesale price. For major labels who calculate royalties on the suggested retail price, such as Warner Brothers, the royalty range for a new act generally runs around 11 to 12 percent. Established acts can command 15 to 16 percent with some superstars able to get as much as

20 percent. These figures are usually doubled if royalties are computed on the wholesale price, which is roughly half the retail price. Often, where a contract contains option periods, as most do, an escalating royalty rate is provided. It's also possible to negotiate rate increases or bonuses based upon sales performance. As this book went to press, the suggested retail price of records with their general corresponding percentage of retail sales by configuration was as follows:

Compact Disks—$13.98—$15.98 (25—30%)

Tape Cassettes—$9.98 (65%)

Vinyl Albums—$9.98 (5%)

11 to 12 percent sounds pretty good, doesn't it? However, before you start totaling up your bank roll off a platinum LP, let's talk a little bit about various deductions and rate reductions for specific types of sales.

Industry custom provides that royalties be computed on 85 percent to 90 percent of records sold. This 10 percent to 15 percent deduction was originally devised to cover breakage. Although breakage is not the problem it once was due to improved manufacturing techniques, the custom remains, though in some cases it can be either reduced or eliminated by negotiation depending on bargaining power.

There's also a customary deduction for jacketing or packaging costs. This figure usually runs from 10 to 15 percent for records and from 15 to 25 percent for tapes and CDs. The packaging costs should be limited as much as possible and specified in the contract. It's also standard to deduct all excise taxes and duties applicable to the records. Besides these customary reductions in the base figure on which royalties are calculated, there are similar reductions for foreign sales ranging from 50 percent to 85 percent of the royalty rate payable on domestic sales.

Additionally, the artist and manager should be aware that it's standard in the record industry to pay royalties only on records sold, and not on those returned by the distributors. In recent years there have been attempts by major labels to modify the longstanding industry custom of allowing distributors a 100 percent return privilege on any unsold product. However, there are still returns, which can further erode an artist's earnings. Consequently, companies will often escrow a percentage of the artist's royalties as a reserve to cover these returns. The artist's attorney should try to limit the impact of returns as much as possible and provide for prompt liquidation of the reserve after a stated number of accounting periods.

Besides deductions from amounts payable, there are also various reductions in the applicable royalty percentage payable in certain specialized sales areas. For example, a lesser royalty rate base of 50 percent of the normal retail sales percentage is applied to record-club sales, budget records, special mid-price marketing programs, educational sales, records sold to military bases, and seemingly, whatever else the record company can conjure up and get the artist to accept. Generally, no royalty is paid on disc jockey or promotional copies or bonus goods given away to distributors or to record clubs to generate orders or new memberships. The artist's attorney will strive to minimize these reductions whenever possible, as well as limit the discretion of the company in areas of budget records and free goods.

Last, but by no means least, the artist and manager should be aware that in most cases, all recording costs paid by the company are deemed to be advances against future royalties that will be recouped before any payment is made to the artist. The same is true of video production expenses which might have been advanced by the record company. Efforts should be made to specifically define these costs and if possible, avoid cross-collateralization of royalty recoupment of one record against royalties earned by other records. The record company will generally resist this approach, especially with a new artist. Oh, and one more thing. The producer's override royalty of 3 percent up to 5 percent in the case of a top name also comes out of the artist's royalty. Not exactly a get-rich-quick proposition, is it?

For those artists and managers who feel the record company is taking unfair advantage of the artist through various deductions and rate reductions, it should be pointed out that few first albums by new artists fully recoup the company's investment. The record business is a high-risk proposition which requires a substantial financial and personal commitment on the part of the record company to break an artist. The label is trying to protect itself as much as possible. Without many of these devices, a record company could simply not afford to sign as many new artists as they do. It should also be noted that an artist can dramatically improve his bargaining position through sales performance, thus becoming more valuable to the label. This will help him gain more concessions and higher royalties in the future or even an early contract renegotiation in extraordinary cases.

Contract Term

Another area of importance to the artist is the length or term of the contract. Old procedure was to make the term one year with a number of additional one-year options usually exercisable at the election of the record company. Depending on the particular state in which the contract was entered, there were often restrictions on the maximum number of option periods. For example, California limits any contract involving personal services to seven years. More stringent restrictions are involved when the artist is a minor. Many of these problems are avoided by the new system which measures an artist's obligations in terms of the number of albums he or she must deliver over the term of the agreement. Usually, the standard clause calls for delivery of one album with consecutive options for six to seven more, exercisable at the election of the company.

From the artist's standpoint, the attorney should seek to limit the number of option periods as much as possible, unless there are substantial guarantees involved. If the artist is successful, a shorter term will allow him to renegotiate sooner. If the artist's albums are unsuccessful or should he or she become unhappy, a shorter term allows the artist the freedom to seek an alternate record affiliation. Obviously, the record company will resist this approach, arguing it needs product guarantees to insure it recoups its investment, especially if early releases prove unsuccessful.

Recording and Release Requirements

Recording and release requirements are another vital area of artist concern. Generally, the company will advance the costs of the recordings and will usually have the option to require that more sides be recorded. Normally, the company is under no obligation to release any of the artist's recordings. The artist's negotiations should seek some type of release commitment from the company. Usually the requirement to release a specified number of records during any one year of the contract is a precondition to the exercise of the next option period by the company.

Promotional Support

Another important element in contract negotiations, especially for the new artist, is promotional support. The artist will seek financial commitment from the record company in the form of trade ads, media time buys, and other forms of advertising.

Tour Support

Another form of involvement is tour support. The artist will request that the label help finance his personal appearances to enable him to promote his records. Tour support is usually in the form of direct cash subsidy or label responsibility for any expense deficit incurred by the artist in connection with a particular tour. The strength and ability of the manager and booking agent and the types and importance of dates the artist will play will weigh heavily on the company's decision in this area. The company doesn't want to commit money to help promote a tour that will be mismanaged or ineffective.

Artistic Control

Artistic control of the material to be recorded is a point often considered vital to an artist. This right is often granted to established artists with a sales track record. It's not granted as often to a new artist because of inexperience and lack of sales history. As a practical matter, the A&R Department and artist/manager/producer will work together in the selection of material, with the company reserving veto power in the event of a dispute.

Royalty Accounting

Royalty accounting procedures are extremely important to the artist. Most companies account semiannually. The artist should always seek the right to audit the company's books of account at reasonable intervals. A procedure should be set up to enable the artist to terminate the agreement in the event of nonpayment of royalties or other material breaches by the company. Companies will often oppose this type of clause or seek to word it very narrowly.

Controlled Compositions

Another standard practice by record companies is to seek a reduction in payments it makes to writer/artists representing mechanical royalties for copyrighted selections controlled by the artist and released on any album produced under the agreement. The usual practice is to pay 75 percent of the prevailing statutory rate. This in effect represents a sharing of mechanical royalties by the writer/artist and the record label, with the argument being that the record label is the vehicle that allows a copyright to be launched in the first place; thus a share of that income should go to the company to help defray the costs involved. Needless to say, music publishers and writers object to this. Recently, there have been calls to pass legislation outlawing this practice. However, because of the strength of the record label, use of the Controlled Composition clause persists.

GET A GOOD LAWYER

These are just some of the major elements of the recording contract from the artist's standpoint. There are many more fine points that are far beyond the reach of this book. The best and only advice here is to get a good entertainment lawyer involved at the outset of the negotiation process. It's not just a good idea, it's essential.

REMEMBER—IT'S BUSINESS

As mentioned earlier, the record contract is strictly a business relationship. The company will, whenever possible, try to negotiate terms favorable to itself. The artist and manager should do the same. Often, the record company will be accommodating on certain points and inflexible on others. The key point to remember is that the label's negotiator won't offer concessions; the artist's representative will have to ask.

▌|3▐

Music Publishing

One of the most complex, least understood, yet most important aspects of the entertainment industry is music publishing. An in-depth treatment of this intricate subject, however, is beyond the scope of this book. Our purpose here is to deal with music publishing only as it relates to career decisions that will surely confront the artist and manager when dealing with the essential building block of the music business—the song.

Confusion over the subject is not confined just to the beginner. Many experienced artist managers confess to knowing very little when it comes to the subject of music publishing. This isn't surprising. Publishing requires, among other things, a working knowledge of domestic and foreign copyright laws, experience in negotiating and administering detailed contracts, an understanding of how performing rights societies and mechanical collection agencies are structured, and in-depth experience in royalty accounting, not to mention the ability to recognize and help develop a good song. No wonder so many people are in the dark.

Before discussing the interplay of management and publishing, it's first necessary to grasp a clear understanding of the basic function of the music publisher and gain an overview of this key segment of the music business.

THE MUSIC PUBLISHER

The music publisher's world revolves around the song. Any publisher will invariably tell you that the song is the foundation of the music industry. Without it, there would be no artists, no managers, no record companies, and no booking agents. Undoubtedly, there's a great deal of truth in this statement.

Conceding the importance of the song, the more specific question is, "What exactly does a publisher do with a song?" Briefly stated, the function of a music publisher is to locate and commercially develop songs (often referred to as "copyrights") in much the same way that a manager locates artists and develops their careers. In both cases, publisher and manager are working to transform artistic potential into commercial success.

The music publisher searches for songwriters with ability and songs with potential. Once the publisher finds a song with commercial potential, he acquires the publishing rights in return for a promise to pay the writer a royalty based on gross income earned from the commercial exploitation of the composition. The publisher then takes steps to protect the song by obtaining a copyright registration on the words and music. An active publisher will work with the writer to perfect the song or possibly help develop and improve his writing style. Tape demos and lead sheets will be made. Once the song is in final form, the music publisher will try to match it with a recording artist whose style fits the song, trying to persuade the artist to record it or incorporate it in his television or live performances.

The reason a publisher will expend the time and money to find and develop potential hits is simple. Every time an artist sells a record embodying the song, the music publisher and songwriter make money. Every time the song is performed on television or radio, the publisher and writer make money. Every time a copy of sheet music or a printed folio containing the song is sold, the publisher and writer make money. Every time the song is used in a motion picture soundtrack, a commercial, or in a concert performance, the publisher and writer make money. When income is realized, it's the responsibility of the publisher to collect the money and account to the writer for his royalties while retaining the balance. The split is roughly 50-50, with the songwriter's royalties designated as the writer's share and the amount retained being referred to as the publisher's share.

The foregoing is an oversimplified account of the publisher's role. The process involves endless hours of listening to tapes, changing lyrics, reassuring songwriters, and all of the other things that go into finding and perfecting a hit song, or better yet, a standard. The creative side of publishing is paralleled by a seeming avalanche of contracts, licenses, memos, letters, forms, and phone calls.

Success for the music publisher is measured by how many times a particular song is recorded, how many times it's played on radio and TV, and how many other commercial uses are made of the song. The more activity, the more money is earned for the songwriter and his publisher.

From a management standpoint, the music publisher should first of all be viewed as a source of material for his artist. Many recording artists don't write their own material and therefore must depend totally on songs written by others. Other artists who do write are not consistently able to turn out quality songs suited to their own recording styles. These artists find it necessary to supplement their own songs with material of others. Even the great singer/songwriters such as Willie Nelson or Paul Simon will on occasion record songs written by others if they feel the material will help give their career a boost up the charts. Every artist needs good material to sustain a career. As a result, most artists will be open to the possibility of recording someone else's song provided it fits their style and sound.

A manager, artist, or producer seeking material should realize that a music publisher is only too happy to submit songs for consideration by the artist. While this is especially true of an established artist with a recording contract, it also applies to a new artist trying to secure his first deal. For this reason, the manager or artist should not shy away from the major publishing houses when seeking material. Nor should the manager overlook the smaller companies also trying to establish themselves. Often, a lesser-known company will expend more effort than a larger firm to find the right song for a new artist, hoping to build a relationship with him and his manager.

When approaching a music publisher for songs, the manager, producer, or artist should speak with the professional manager or someone in the Professional Department. This part of a publisher's operation is very similar to the A&R Department of a record company. It's the Professional Department's job to find and develop new songs and match them with artists. The professional manager is also involved in adapting previously recorded songs to the styles of currently popular artists. When approaching a professional manager, the artist or manager should specify the type of material that the artist records or performs, such as country, adult contemporary, heavy metal, and the like. The professional manager should also be given a tape of two or three songs indicative of the artist's singing style and voice quality. This helps the Professional Department identify songs that might be appropriate. If the artist has a certain tempo, instrumentation, or sound in mind, let the publisher know this also.

It's also helpful for the manager, producer, or artist to specify whether he's looking for previously unrecorded material or proven copyrights which could be given a new arrangement. The distinction can be important from a legal standpoint. The revised United States Copyright Act, which went into effect January 1, 1978, gives the copyright owner (usually the publisher) the right to determine the first artist to commercially record a particular song. But after the song has been recorded and distributed to the public for the first time, anyone has the right to re-record it without permission from the copyright owner, provided they pay the owner a royalty set by the Copyright Royalty Tribunal, an administrative body set up by the Copyright Act. This practice is commonly referred to as the "Compulsory License." Because of this legal requirement, the artist can't record a previously unrecorded work without the copyright owner's permission. The manager, producer, or record company should therefore make sure that permission to record the work is granted by the copyright owner before any money is spent in the studio.

Another consideration in recording new or unproven material controlled by a music publisher is to insure that the song hasn't been recorded earlier by another artist who might release the record ahead or at the same time as the artist's release, thereby creating a competitive relationship between records. While a publisher can't always guarantee a first recording, especially in the case of previously recorded material, he can let the manager know of other artists to whom the song has been submitted. If the artist is of sufficient stature or is seriously interested in recording a new copyright, the manager or producer might request the publisher grant an "exclusive" on the song. This means that the publisher won't grant a license to anyone else for a stated period of time to enable the artist and record company sufficient time to record and release the song.

Still another aspect of recording previously unrecorded material is the possibility of a participation by the artist in the publishing income from the song as an inducement to record it. This is a practice that is understandably unpopular with music publishers. However, an established recording artist with a large record-buying following can, in some instances, persuade a publisher to give up either part ownership of the copyright (publisher's share only) or a percentage of the income earned from the sale of the particular recorded version due to the powerful lure of a guaranteed level of sales and performances on radio and television. Many publishers have policies against such practices, arguing that the integrity of their copyrights should remain intact. Other publishers maintain that there's never any guarantee a particular recording will be a hit, thus there's no justification for giving up part-ownership or a portion of the potential income. The final decision often comes down to bargaining strength. How much would you be willing to give up to have Madonna or Anita Baker or perhaps the Judds release one of your copyrights as their next single?

Besides providing an artist with quality material, many publishers contribute to the promotion of a record embodying their copyrights or can even help open the doors at record labels for exclusive writer/artists. At this point, the music publisher becomes a member of the artist's development team. Often, a manager can persuade the publisher to either purchase or co-op a trade ad or employ independent radio promotion men to push a recorded version of one of their songs. Some of the larger publishing companies have their own promotion staffs to complement the efforts of the record company.

An active publisher is also an excellent source of information regarding radio airplay and sales activity of a particular record. A manager is well-advised to develop contacts with the top music publishers to insure a steady flow of material for his artist. An experienced publisher will always be thinking of songs for the artist and won't waste a manager's time by submitting weak or inappropriate material.

In the event the artist does record a song controlled by an active music publisher, especially in the case of an "A side" single release, the manager should keep the company informed of all pertinent developments in the artist's career. This will help insure a maximum contribution by the publisher to the success of the artist's record.

MUSIC PUBLISHING AS INCOME

Let's now examine music publishing as a source of income for the artist/writer. The ability of the artist to not only perform but also write his own songs adds an important dimension to his career. First of all, a singer/songwriter is guaranteed a steady source of material geared to his vocal and musical style. This generally makes the artist more attractive to record companies, booking agents, and managers than an artist who must depend on the writing of others. Secondly, the artist/writer has a much greater income potential than the non-writer. For example, the Beatles were an extremely successful group, with all four artists sharing equally in record royalties and personal appearances. However, John Lennon and Paul McCartney, who wrote the majority of the group's original songs, far surpassed the other members in earning power as a result of their songwriting royalties. More than 20 years after the legendary group played their last concert, those same songs are still generating huge annual amounts. This illustrates the often repeated observation that hit records and rock stars come and go, but the real money in the music business lies in owning copyrights.

Before considering the artist's publishing alternatives, let's briefly review the nature and sources of income that can be derived from the exploitation of copyrighted musical compositions. Generally, a writer will, by contract, convey all rights of ownership in the musical composition to the publisher. This grant includes the right to secure copyright protection in the name of the publisher. In return, the publisher agrees to use its best efforts to commercially develop and exploit the song and to pay the writer a percentage of the proceeds. We refer to this royalty as the writer's share and the balance as the publisher's share. Income is realized from five main sources: mechanical royalties derived from the sale of records and tapes embodying the song; radio and television performances; movie synchronization fees; sale of printed music; and miscellaneous uses. Most standard songwriter contracts call for mechanical, performance, synchronization, and miscellaneous income to be divided 50 percent to the writer and the remaining 50 percent to the publisher. A lesser percentage or set amount is paid to the writer as a royalty on the sale of printed music. This reduced payment takes into consideration the publisher's expense in printing, distributing, and selling sheet music and folios.

Royalties from the Sale of Records and Tapes

The Copyright Act of 1976 sets a statutory rate of compensation that must be paid to copyright owners by anyone who manufactures and distributes phonorecords embodying the owner's composition in lieu of a negotiated rate. The current statutory rate is 5.25 cents or .95 cents per minute or fraction thereof, whichever is larger for each record manufactured and distributed. This rate for "mechanical royalties" is subject to periodic adjustment by the Copyright Royalty Tribunal, which is an administrative body created by the Copyright Statute. Assuming an artist/writer writes ten compositions embodied on an album that sells 100,000 units at the statutory mechanical royalty rate, the total amount of mechanical royalties payable to the copyright owner would be $52,500, assuming there are no deductions for collection fees. Of this sum, $26,250 would represent the writer's share and the remaining $26,250 would be retained by the publisher. Although payment is computed in pennies, they can mount up in a hurry if a hit record is involved.

Performing Rights

A second lucrative source of income consists of performing rights. The performing rights of publishers and writers in the United States are controlled by three performing-rights societies, ASCAP, BMI, and SESAC, with ASCAP and BMI controlling the bulk of all compositions written in this country. SESAC is a much smaller, privately owned society specializing in certain areas of music including gospel and country. The societies license radio and television broadcasters as well as concert halls, nightclubs, and other users of music. Each respective society has a complicated payment system whereby it distributes the proceeds from these licenses to its publisher and writer members based on the number and type of performances of the respective copyrighted musical compositions they represent.

Movie Synchronization Fees

Movie synchronization fees account for another source of musical copyright income. Songs are usually licensed for use by the publisher on a negotiated fee basis. Producers of major motion pictures are willing to pay substantial amounts for a license to use the "right" song in their productions. The recent innovation of the music video also requires a synch license whenever the copyrighted composition is synchronized with visual images.

Sale of Printed Music

Printed music consists of individual sheet music and song folios containing multiple compositions. This has proven to be an expanding source of revenue especially with the popularity of the "personality folio," which features songs in printed form that have been made popular by the recordings of a particular artist.

Miscellaneous Uses

Miscellaneous uses of material include the use of songs on greeting cards and song quotes used in books and articles.

It's clear from this overview of potential income sources how much a successful artist/writer stands to gain from a hit song. The question facing the manager is how to realize maximum benefits while still allowing time for other career pursuits such as recording, touring, commercials, television, and personal appearances.

FINDING A PUBLISHER

The most obvious course of action is to find an experienced music publisher to handle an artist's songs. This is especially advisable in the case of a new, unproven writer without a recording contract who seeks an outlet for his material. An active, experienced music publisher who believes in a writer can offer a variety of services otherwise unavailable to a writer/artist. One of the most attractive features of this type of arrangement is that a reputable publisher's fee is based entirely on a percentage of earnings from the writer's songs. Consequently, the publisher has increased incentive to exploit the writer's songs. By choosing this option, the artist/writer and manager take advantage of the publisher's expertise in copyright law, publishing, administration, song development, promotion, and exploitation. There is also a cost savings for obtaining copyright protection, preparation of lead sheets, production of demos, and costs associated with submitting the songs to other recording artists. The major drawback is that the writer gives up approximately 50 percent of potential earnings in the form of the publisher's share.

The artist/writer has two alternate ways of working with a publisher to exploit his songs, depending on the strength of his writing and the desires of the parties. He can either publish on a song-by-song basis, or he can elect to sign an exclusive writer agreement whereby all songs written during the term of the agreement will be submitted to the publisher. If the latter approach is chosen, the writer should usually expect to receive a sum of money as a signing bonus or cash advance recoupable against future writer royalties.

Certainly, any type of unrecoupable payment should be sought. Too many young, impressionable artist/writers have been seduced by the cash advance, thinking it is free money with no strings attached. Any time such a payment is made subject to recoupment, manager and artist should recognize it for what it is—an interest-free loan. Since the publisher has the duty to collect and account for monies received, it will make sure the debt is paid back by deducting any outstanding advances out of the writer's share. For this reason, an artist/writer might be better advised to refuse advances where possible, or trade offers of front money for a shorter contract term that would allow for renegotiation with the publisher on better terms if success is realized.

When selecting a music publisher, it's important that the artist and manager choose a legitimate, active publisher who will work to secure recordings of the writer's songs rather than merely act as a "copyright collector." This type of publisher finds songs, signs songwriter contracts, and then deposits them in a filing cabinet hoping something will happen either through the efforts of the writer or perhaps by luck. The writer should feel comfortable with his publisher and be able to relate to the company's personnel on a personal level. This is important if the publisher really intends to help the writer develop his songwriting skills and techniques. Even though artist/writers may be convinced of a publisher's sincerity, it's also important that the publisher has the time to devote to exploiting the writer's songs. There's nothing worse for a writer than to be lost in the shuffle, especially when he's writing commercial material.

Regardless of whether the artist/writer chooses to work with a publisher on a per-song or exclusive basis, he should seek the help of an attorney experienced in music publishing to negotiate and draft his contract. While many contractual terms are more or less standard, many others are not. Important items to be considered include the scope of rights granted, duration of the contract, territory, royalty rates, deductions from writer's royalties, time and method of royalty payments, right to audit publisher's books, and royalty advances or guarantees. Foreign aspects of the publisher's contract will be dealt with in a later chapter.

The main trap a writer wants to avoid is granting publishing rights to a publisher who's either unwilling or unable to exploit his songs. Depending on the bargaining strength of the parties and the importance of the writer and song, the artist/writer's negotiator may request a clause in the contract whereby all rights to a particular song will revert to the writer after a stated period of time if the publisher hasn't been successful in securing a commercial recording of the song. Many publishers object to this type of clause, maintaining it may take an investment of considerable money and time to commercially exploit a writer's songs. Such a recapture clause would undermine the total commitment necessary to achieve this success. This argument is particularly valid if the publisher has advanced unrecouped monies to the writer. But certain companies won't object, provided that they're given a reasonable time to secure a recording and the writer agrees to repay any unrecouped advances against royalties.

Before leaving the subject of finding a publisher, we should point out several realities of the music business which could have a significant impact on the artist/writers. Most every record company will have an affiliated music publishing firm to take advantage of its capacity to generate publishing income through the commercial release of its records. It is standard procedure for labels to package the offer of a record deal with a co-terminus publishing contract. Because of the antitrust laws, the label can't compel the artist to sign with its publishing affiliate, but from a practical standpoint, they will have considerable leverage. The legal and practical advice from an experienced attorney on how to handle this likelihood can be of great value, especially where the artist and management have reservations about such an arrangement.

A point worth alerting new artists and managers to is the trend toward concentration in the music publishing field. A pattern of consolidation and acquisitions over the last decade has created two international publishing mega-giants: Warner/Chappell and SBK/EMI Music. The combination of these two mammoth companies along with other major label affiliates could well change the face of music publishing in the coming years. The implications are not at all clear, but it would be in the interest of artist/writers to monitor potential changes in the structure and practices of music publishing. Your music lawyer will be able to advise you of these developments and offer sound advice on how to respond.

THE ARTIST AS PUBLISHER

An alternative available to the artist/writer who doesn't want to work with an established publisher is to act as his own publisher or let his manager or another employee administer his catalog. This is common in the case of an established recording artist who writes all or substantially all of his own material. This type of undertaking requires sufficient financial resources to hire persons with publishing experience or a manager with sufficient time and experience to handle this additional responsibility.

The advantage of this arrangement is obvious. The artist retains not only the writer's share but the publisher's share of the income as well. But the disadvantages are many. First, the artist/writer must bear all the expenses that would otherwise be borne by the publisher. Because of the lack of an organized staff, the artist/publisher may not be as effective as a regular publisher in obtaining cover recordings of his material by other artists. Finally, unless the artist or someone on his staff has experience in the field of publishing administration, the artist could jeopardize his entire catalog.

There are other drawbacks. Normally, publishing administration doesn't come within the normal scope of management duties. Many managers simply aren't qualified to undertake this very complex and multi-faceted job. Even if a manager is qualified, he may not have sufficient time to devote to the management of the artist's career as well as administration of his publishing affairs. But if the manager does decide to undertake these duties, a separate agreement covering the scope of his publishing duties and compensation is advisable. In this event, the manager and artist may want to modify the management agreement to exempt publishing income realized by the artist's publishing firm from the income base on which the manager's fee or percentage is computed, provided, of course, that the manager is receiving separate compensation for his publishing activities.

The structure and operation of the artist's publishing company is beyond the scope of this book. However, the artist and manager are advised to consult an attorney thoroughly knowledgeable in the area of music publishing. He can provide counsel on the advisability of such a move and can help organize and structure the artist's publishing operations. The respective performing rights organizations and mechanical collection agencies should also be consulted regarding their rules and procedures.

OTHER ALTERNATIVES

For many artist/writers, especially those with record company affiliations and established followings, there may be alternatives that a manager might consider that fall between writing for an established publisher and acting as a self-contained publisher. The first of these arrangements is a joint ownership agreement with an established publisher. Often, a name recording artist/writer with a guaranteed outlet for his recorded product has sufficient leverage to enter into an agreement whereby a music publishing company owned by him and a full-time, active publisher can jointly own the copyrights to his songs. This allows the artist to take advantage of the active publisher's administrative, exploitative, and promotional capabilities while still collecting his writer's share and a portion of the publisher's share of income. Although the artist gives up part of his copyright ownership, he's still able to increase his income and maximize the long-term development of his copyrights.

Another approach is an agency representation agreement with an active publisher. This is similar to joint ownership, except full copyright ownership remains vested in the artist/writer's company. The established publisher is paid a percentage of the total publisher's share of income, but only from monies earned or accruing during the term of the agency agreement. Obviously, the inducement to a major publisher to enter into this type of arrangement is not nearly as attractive as a full or joint copyright ownership arrangement.

A third alternative is an administration or collection agreement with a major publisher or a publishing administration service company. Here the artist's publishing company retains an administrative specialist to render specific services such as copyright registration, performing right clearance, and administration and/or royalty collection and accounting in return for a negotiated fee or percentage of publishing income.

One last alternative that must be considered is the possibility of the artist publishing his material through a company owned or controlled by the artist's manager or jointly owned by artist and manager. This raises possible conflict-of-interest problems with the manager. Will a manager in this situation be tempted to make a publishing decision that might be good for him personally but detrimental to his client's career? What happens to ownership of copyrights in the event of a breakup between the artist and manager? Finally, should the manager's fee be calculated on a percentage of the writer's share of income derived from material published by the manager's company? These are all potential problem areas. This isn't to say that such an arrangement isn't advisable. There's nothing wrong with it as long as there's full disclosure by the manager and artist of their positions, understood and agreed to by all respective parties. The best advice here is for the artist and manager to consult their attorneys as to the structure of any such arrangement.

RESPONSIBILITIES OF THE
ARTIST/WRITER AND MANAGER

Regardless of the publishing alternatives selected, both artist and manager should be aware that there are certain responsibilities related to songwriting and music publishing that are the sole responsibility of the writer and his representative. The most notable of these is selection and affiliation with a performing rights society. Performance royalties are paid directly by the societies to publisher and writer members on a separate basis. A writer can only be affiliated with one society and must make that decision himself based on which society is best for him. As mentioned before, ASCAP and BMI are the leading societies in terms of license fees collected and royalties paid. SESAC has a smaller, more specialized membership. Performing rights societies are highly competitive and each offers certain advantages over the others. Their Membership Departments will be glad to talk to writers and managers concerning the relative merits of their respective organizations. The artist/writer and manager should be cautioned that failure to affiliate may result in loss of writer performance credits even though a song is copyrighted and published.

Once the writer has affiliated with the performing rights society, the writer member and his manager must deal with the society directly in the area of writer-related affairs. Although the publisher may offer guidance in this area, it's not his responsibility. The manager is well-advised to contact a representative of his client's society as to the duties and responsibilities of the writer. There is no one "right" answer as to which music publishing alternative or performing rights society an artist and manager should select. The decision should hinge on what's right for the artist/writer at a given stage of his career. Publishing and songwriting royalties are important long-term sources of income that can continue to accrue long after record royalties and personal appearance income have diminished or come to an end. As a result, decisions in this area should not be made hastily, especially in the early, breaking-in stage of a career where the temptation is often the greatest to compromise potentially valuable copyrights for some ego-warming praise and immediate cash. As in every other career area, it's much better to make publishing decisions with an eye to the future when being a star is longer possible or even desirable. Awareness and knowledge of music publishing by a manager and artist, accompanied by careful planning and intelligent decision-making, can result in long-term financial security. Just ask Paul McCartney.

14

Music Videos, Television, Radio, and Motion Pictures

The 1980s saw the beginning of a technological and creative revolution that would change the face of the music business forever. Music videos fostered an entire new genre that had not existed before. Many music professionals credit this new art form with turning a badly depressed music business around in the early '80s.

Now, a few short years later, MTV, VH-1, The Nashville Network, and a number of other developing cable formats have taken the basic three- to five-minute video and merged it with more traditional television programming aimed directly at music consumers. In the process, they have created an entertainment staple that will not soon disappear.

The hardware/software combination of the VCR and music video is only one manifestation of how technology and imagination have changed the music industry. At the same time as the video revolution was being felt, network and syndicated radio programming began enjoying similar unprecedented success rather than the demise that many media experts predicted only a few years ago. For the first time since its heyday in the 1930s and '40s, radio experienced a comeback in variety, concert, and interview programming centered around music acts. Led by an assortment of syndicaters and entrepreneurs, a wide range of new music-based programming for radio came into being, beyond the standard top-40 format.

As the decade of the '90s begins, Pay Per View (PPV) television programming promises to be the latest music software innovation. Artists as diverse as The Rolling Stones, Wayne Newton, Bon Jovi,

Elton John, and Hank Williams, Jr. have either played or are planning PPV concerts with possible one-night grosses in the tens of millions of dollars. High-resolution television could fuel an accelerated move to PPV and other new audiovisual programming innovations. While specific formats and configurations are nearly impossible to predict, it is a safe bet that entertainment in general and music in particular will never be the same.

The management implications of all this are overwhelming. Failing to appreciate and understand the changes and opportunities brought about by new technology can spell the difference between a successful career as an artist or manager and being left behind to pick up the pieces of what might have been.

MUSIC VIDEOS

Thanks to the invention of the videocassette recorder, the growth of cable television, and the pioneering efforts of MTV, the music video is now an entertainment staple. Record company A&R departments have been forced to factor video potential into their decisions of whether to sign an artist. Fans now expect to *see* their favorite artists as well as listen to them on record or experience them in an infrequent live concert. A whole new category of awards now recognizes video excellence and popularity. The music video is here to stay.

From a management standpoint, exactly what role do videos play in an artist's success? The answers vary considerably and will probably be somewhat surprising. The majority of managers and record executives we surveyed harbored serious doubts about the ability of a music video to break a new artist or record or even to directly generate record sales. However, most agreed that a well-produced music video can have a significant, indirect impact on solidifying and increasing sales. They were even stronger in their belief that the music video is an indispensable tool for creating name and identity recognition of an artist with fans, which ultimately translates into long-term record and concert ticket sales.

If a divergence of viewpoint regarding videos exists between a manager and his artist's record label, a potential conflict could arise if the manager wants a music video while the artist's label feels that money earmarked for video production would be better spent on some other manner of promotion. This conflict is fueled by the fact that it is almost always the record company that advances the money to produce a video. Because most videos do not have sufficient commercial appeal to recoup the rather substantial sums it takes to produce them, record labels are forced to deal with videos as expensive promotional tools. As a result, videos are often budgeted only after a record breaks, if at all.

There are of course, notable exceptions—artists who are viable in the home video market. One of the most successful is Michael Jackson, who is able to compete with motion pictures, comedians, and popular exercise videos for sales and rentals. Because videos represent another source of income in excess of costs for an artist with the unique talents of a Michael Jackson, he chooses to finance the productions himself and keep the profits. Such an arrangement is clearly the exception. At least for now, it is the record company that makes the decision to produce a video for promotional purposes and is also usually the entity that provides the funding. Consequently, they will also expect a substantial voice in the creative content of the video along with control of its exploitation.

MUSIC VIDEO COSTS

Music videos aren't cheap. Even the most bare-bones production will cost $50,000. The average price range for a rock video produced in Los Angeles or New York is $100,000 to $250,000 depending on the stature of the act. Country and rap videos are generally less expensive, with the average cost running from $75,000 to $100,000. And, of course, it's possible to spend just about as much as you can write a check for. There have been some videos that have run a seven-figure tab. That's a lot to recoup, but sometimes it is done, often more for ego than for record sales.

That leads to the next question: How does the record company get its money back? This varies according to the label, but the standard approach is to deduct a portion of the cost from the artist's record royalties. This figure is usually 50 to 75 percent and sometimes higher. The balance comes from revenue generated by commercial sales, rentals, and licenses. Because of their investment, the record company also demands extensive right of ownership and control over the video production. Any new artist should expect the record company to demand exclusive audiovisual rights along with the right to own and license the copyright in and to any music video produced pursuant to the terms of the overall contract. Generally, record companies will offer artists a video royalty equal to 50 percent of net revenues after recoupment of all production costs, distribution fees, and other expenses. Finally, the label will regard a video as a controlled composition and will demand a free synchronization license as well as waivers of other applicable copyright fees on the video production.

Managers should be cautioned against an overly broad grant of exclusive rights to the record company which might impair the artist's ability to pursue motion picture and television opportunities, i.e., a grant of exclusive audiovisual rights. Artists and their managers should also attempt to use any leverage they might have to modify or limit the record company's standard recoupment policies and liberal definition of terms such as "recoupable distribution fees and other expenses." An experienced music lawyer is indispensable when it comes to negotiating the fine points of audiovisual rights with record labels and publishers. Certain artists, such as Michael Jackson, have the money and bargaining power to finance and control their own productions. As of this writing, that is the rare exception. As a substantial commercial market develops, if it does, that could change, but for now, the record company is in the driver's seat when it comes to music videos.

TELEVISION

It's virtually impossible to be engaged in the entertainment industry and not be affected by the impact of commercial television. Network and cable TV have significantly changed the character of entertainment around the world. Prior to television, an artist could reach a mass audience primarily through live network radio, which had only a fraction of the programming alternatives available through television or personal appearances. Television has changed all of this.

Today, an appearance by an artist on the right television show can be seen by tens of millions. Given the profusion of channels and formats which include music video programs, in-concert series, cable and network specials, talk and interview shows, late night and variety programming, and even game shows, made-for-TV-movies, dramatic series, and sitcoms, an artist's name can be turned into a household word literally in a matter of weeks. There's almost limitless potential for instant career acceleration. However, the prospects for career development offered by television must be balanced against the ever-present dangers inherent in the medium. The same mass exposure that can make an artist an instant success can just as quickly overexpose him into an overnight has-been. The manager should be careful to choose only those types of appearances that will enhance the artist's career plan. Doing a game show might be fun, but it can quickly trivialize an artist unless it is handled correctly, if at all. By the same measure, an appearance on a Saturday morning kid's show might strike just the right chord by winning over a new following of kids and their parents. The same is true of charity events.

The amount and type of television exposure is always a judgement call subject to second guessing. Decisions should be made with care. One way to ensure they are is to see that the career plan contains specific television goals and guidelines. There's nothing more potentially damaging to a career than indiscriminate, randomly selected television appearances. The manager who takes a make-it-up-as-you-go policy or nonpolicy is flirting with disaster.

Some Basic Television Planning Considerations

To clarify an effective television policy, let's look at some basic considerations that should go into TV appearance decision making.

Television producers, programmers, and sponsors are always looking for artists or celebrities with "name value" to enhance their programs. When evaluating name value or drawing power, they're generally looking for someone with wide national appeal rather than with a regional or a localized following. As a general rule, an artist's value is directly proportional to his current activities, unless the artist has achieved living-legend or celebrity status. A hit record, recent award, or national concert tour will undoubtedly make the artist more attractive and give the producer and manager a hook on which to justify an appearance. Visual appeal and personality are also factors considered by television professionals. Overall name and identification value is yet another consideration.

The most common types of appearances for the musical variety artist, aside from music video programming, are network or cable specials, talk shows, in-concert series, and musical variety or concept shows. The major multifaceted booking agencies maintain very strong contacts with the producers and talent coordinators of these programs. A strong agency contact is often instrumental in getting an artist the "right" slot on the "right" show. Many of the major record companies also maintain contacts in this area because of the impact such appearances can have on promoting record sales. Many top-level managers also make it their business to maintain strong television contacts.

The talk show and musical variety or concept guest appearance should be viewed primarily as a promotional tool. Talk shows rarely pay guests above AFTRA scale, which is less than $1,000 for a network program. From a career development standpoint, this should be the least of an artist's worries. Such an appearance can often be the one break the artist needs to boost him into the national limelight.

Financial remuneration for a musical variety or musical concept appearance can be more substantial, depending on the artist's name value and the budget of the particular show. However, just as with talk shows, money should not be the only factor considered. A slot on the right show can be of untold value to an artist in terms of promotion and exposure. A case in point is the first United States national television appearances of the Beatles on the Ed Sullivan Show in the early 1960s. This was the major push that helped launch the group in the United States. This exposure helped them to achieve superstar status in relatively short order.

The TV "special" is probably the most attractive alternative available to the established artist from a financial, promotional, and artistic standpoint. This is especially true if he's able to exercise a measure of creative control over the program and guest selection process, which many do. Here, the procedure is somewhat different than in the previous examples. Often the artist/manager and/or an independent television producer will formulate a concept for a special and then sell it either to a television network or directly to a sponsor. Naturally, the more name value and following the artist possesses, the easier it will be to sell the show. In addition to hosting a special, established artists are often asked to appear on such programs as guests, many times at the invitation of the artist/host. Some major artists limit their television appearances to this type of format to avoid the problems of overexposure and negative image projection.

Making the Right Television Decisions

As mentioned earlier, careful attention should be given to any television offer based on some of the following factors. First, the manager and artist should consider the type of show. Is its format consistent with the artist's image, career plan, and goals? For instance, a serious singer/songwriter would stand to gain little by a guest appearance on a TV quiz show or situation comedy. However, such a format might be consistent with a comedian's image and career objectives. The second factor to consider is the show's ratings. This will determine the exposure value of the particular program for the artist and may indicate the quality of the program and how it's perceived by the public. Then there is another consideration: Who are the other guest stars? The artist wants to be presented in the best possible light. The stature of other performers, billing, time slots, and so forth will have a bearing on whether the artist will want to appear on the show. Potential for overexposure is also a major consideration. Once the artist is too accessible on television, the concertgoer and record buyer won't be nearly as interested in paying to hear or see the artist when they can get the same thing free on television. There's also the danger that too many appearances will cause the audience to tire of the performer. Their adulation can quickly turn to indifference. This has ended the career of more than one artist. Making the right decision here isn't easy. It requires a great deal of judgement and perception on the part of the manager and the willingness to say "no" to lucrative offers for the sake of preserving the artist's career.

While most of this discussion has been couched in terms of the established artist, the same guidelines are generally applicable to the new artist. The major difference is that the artist without established name value will find it much more difficult to get television exposure, especially the right exposure. The new artist should be encouraged to develop strong management, booking agency, and record-company connections to help break the national TV exposure barrier. Alternative formats, such as regionally syndicated shows and specialized cable television, may serve as a means of gaining experience and exposure. For example, an excellent option available to new country artists is The Nashville Network, which is dedicated to programming country music in multiple formats. Programmers maintain close contact with Music Row labels, managers, and agents and are constantly on the lookout for up-and-coming artists. Due to the popularity of country music, and because TNN is available on a high percentage of the country's 800 cable television systems, a new artist can be exposed to tens of millions of potential new record buyers and concertgoers.

Based on the success of MTV, TNN, and other music-oriented cable networks as well as the promise of other new and exciting formats and hardware such as Pay Per View and high resolution television, the video/television segment of the music business represents unlimited opportunity for resourceful and forward-looking artists and managers.

RADIO

Another important aspect of an artist's career, especially a recording artist, is radio. In the early 1950s, television succeeded in replacing radio as the primary vehicle for reaching the mass audience with the live performance. Almost simultaneous with this change came the increased importance of the phonograph record. As the radio networks dropped their variety-oriented entertainment and stations became more independent, there was a need for new programming ideas and concepts. Likewise, the record companies needed new promotional avenues to help boost sales. The result was a shift to programming of records on radio stations. This concept has grown since that time to the point today where AM and FM radio airplay is probably the most important promotional vehicle available to the record companies. Record airplay is also the lifeblood of radio programming.

It's essential that recording artists and managers realize and understand the crucial importance of radio airplay to their careers. Without it, the mass record-buying public will generally remain unaware of both the artist and his or her records. The strategic role radio plays is demonstrated by the significant sums of money record companies budget in order to promote radio airplay of their product. An awareness of the Promotion Department's job and the radio station's needs and objectives by the artist and manager will contribute greatly to the overall success of the artist and his records.

The primary rule every artist and record company should keep in mind regarding airplay is that radio stations are in business to make a profit. They can only make a profit if they can attract advertisers. Since advertisers are attracted by a station's ratings, the station's record playlist is formulated to obtain the best possible ratings. In other words, programming is not designed to help a record company or an artist sell records, though many artists and managers are unwilling to accept this reality.

Because ratings are all important, a top-40 AM or FM station will program only those records it thinks will draw listeners. Playlists are usually restricted to between 20 and 30 records. The programmed releases are usually already hits or have been recorded by hit artists with past track records. Very few new artists are added to these tight playlists. Those that are must have a record with super commercial appeal that's not too long, not too short, and fits into the station's format. It's a reality of the business.

While some progressive FM, black, and Adult Contemporary stations may be a little less restrictive in their programming, the same general rules apply.

The artist and manager are urged to become familiar with primary and secondary radio stations in various markets around the country that have formats consistent with their recordings. Getting to know program directors and air personalities can often be helpful. Besides the radio people, the manager should also get to know the record company's promotion staff. Unless the promotion man believes in an artist's record, there's little chance he can convince a program director or programming service to program it.

Learning "radio" is a major educational project in itself, but well worth the effort. The importance of this aspect of entertainment to a recording artist and his manager cannot be overemphasized. Knowledge and appreciation of radio and radio promotion is an essential rung in the career ladder.

Besides traditional radio programming, the last decade has seen a dramatic increase in radio syndication activity reminiscent of the pre-television era when the medium dominated the nation's entertainment scene. The artist and manager should factor in the increasing opportunities for nationally syndicated radio programming focusing on talk and music formats. This is simply one more promotional tool available to an artist seeking to break or sustain a career.

MOTION PICTURES

The final subject area dealt with in this chapter is motion pictures. This is a complex component of the entertainment industry, with its own peculiar rules and complexities. As with television, the motion picture industry offers the opportunity for long-term career maintenance to those artists who have the talent and ability to act. Just because a person is a successful recording artist doesn't necessarily mean that he'll be a hit on the big screen. There have been successful recording artists and songwriters who have possessed acting ability and screen appeal, allowing them to add an extra dimension to their careers. Barbara Streisand, Bette Midler, and Cher come immediately to mind. Other singers who have crossed over from music to movies are better left unmentioned. Acting, while having some similarities with recording and performing, requires a different talent and discipline. Those versatile enough to master both can reap tremendous rewards, not the least of which is assurance of career longevity. For these reasons, a manager is well advised to think in terms of possible involvement of his client in motion pictures as a career alternative or supplement.

The ins and outs of breaking into and succeeding in motion pictures could easily fill a separate volume. Here are just a couple of words of advice for managers looking for a way into Hollywood. While most major motion picture studios are also active in the production of television programming, movie people and TV people tend to live in separate worlds. Consequently, they rarely talk to each other. As a rule, movie and TV people never talk to record people and vice versa. However, they all talk to agents and lawyers. For that reason, your best bet for gaining an entry is through your attorney or the responsible agent at a major, full-service booking agency.

The second point deals with the dangers of bad roles and overexposure. The rules applicable to television appearances are generally the same for movies. Our advice is to be careful. A movie is fine if an artist can act, but it is potential catastrophe if he or she can't. Late night cable movie re-runs will make sure your client's deficiencies are forever remembered. Even if you get a top money offer, the best decision is to pass on the big screen if the part doesn't fit into the career plan or if the stretch from singer to actor is just too far. If a movie is part of the career plan, manager and artist are best advised to get a good lawyer and a well-connected agent. Whatever you do, don't plan on giving up the singing career until after the second Oscar.

15

Personal Appearances

One of the most potentially lucrative aspects of the music business is the personal appearance. A hot artist with a hit record and an explosive stage show can command as much as a $100,000 and up for a single appearance while grossing millions over the span of a successful concert tour. In addition to the live gate, the personal appearance remains one of the best vehicles for boosting record sales and capturing valuable media attention. The ability to "turn on" an audience can be a valuable negotiating asset when dealing with record companies, booking agents, and promoters. From a long-term career standpoint, an artist's live performance has the potential to outlive and out-earn his recording career. Many artists who have been moderately successful as recording artists have maintained lucrative careers for years strictly on the basis of strong live appearances.

But before you assume that the personal appearance is a certain path to riches, stop and consider the changes in the decade of the '80s that have made it harder than ever before for an artist to make a living on the road. The dramatic rise in tour costs has made the personal appearance a much trickier proposition than ever before. High-tech special effects, increased transportation costs, lighting, sound, and ever-expanding entourages of support personnel to bring a live show together have combined to drive up the costs of going on the road. This is especially true of hard rock and heavy metal acts as well as established superstars whose fans demand a lot in exchange for paying $15 to $25 for an evening of live entertainment. The manager of several headlining concert attractions estimated that an artist who could net 25 percent of a six-figure gross would be doing well.

Besides cost, artists are confronted with a national trend of top club venues going out of business. This is primarily due to a change in attitudes about alcohol in this country. The 1980s saw almost all state legislatures raise the legal drinking age to 21 and pass stern measures against driving and drinking. As a result, a number of high-profile clubs that proliferated in the late '70s and early '80s are gone. Fairs and outdoor festivals have, in many instances, replaced the nightclub. Unfortunately for many new acts, these venues demand established artists to satisfy larger numbers of concertgoers who are drawn by known commodities they have heard on the radio or have seen on music videos. Consequently, while the potential rewards connected with the live performance are probably greater than ten years ago, so are the challenges. This underscores the need for strong management to make the personal appearance a viable part of an artist's career.

Regardless of the spiraling costs and other problems inherent in live performances, the personal appearance remains the lifeblood of an artist's career. The excitement generated by a tight, well-produced concert date remains a unique and necessary experience for both the artist and fan. The record-breaking attendance figures at concert halls, stadiums, and festivals across the country make it very clear that there is no acceptable substitute for live music. The challenge is to provide the best show as efficiently and as inexpensively as possible without sacrificing quality. That task falls on the shoulders of management.

There are many different levels of live performance available to the artist. Depending on the client's career goals, track record as a recording artist, and his style of performance, the manager can select the most favorable type of personal appearance. Basically, the alternatives available to the manager fall into three categories: clubs, private parties, and concerts. These broad categories can be divided into many levels, or what we refer to as "stages."

CLUBS

While nationally there are fewer clubs than even a few years ago, this stage still comprises a substantial segment of the demand for live music. Clubs can be divided into lounges, rock and show clubs, showcase clubs or listening rooms, and large hotels and national chains.

Lounge

For the sake of our discussion, let's define a "lounge" as a restaurant or bar usually employing four artists or less. The format of this type of engagement normally requires soft music to facilitate the sale of cocktails or enhance the atmosphere in a restaurant. The broad heading of lounge entertainers would include everything from a solo pianist at an exclusive dinner club all the way to a four-man country or rock group performing at a Saturday night "watering hole." There will obviously be exceptions; some lounges may employ a group larger than four artists. Normally, however, a lounge will attempt to keep the number of artists employed to a minimum. Another characteristic of a lounge engagement is that the audiences are small. Generally this "stage" is not conducive to the performance of original material.

The lounge market employs thousands of artists, providing jobs for many individuals involved in the entertainment business on a part-time basis, or artists in the early stages of their career. Moreover, many artists who have become weary of the concert circuit or of larger clubs prefer the low-key environment and relaxed atmosphere of lounge engagements.

Rock and Show Rooms

The next club stage consists of rock and show rooms. Traditionally, these types of clubs have more of a music or dance-oriented atmosphere than do lounges. Because of the emphasis on music and dancing, these types of clubs are livelier than lounges, and are more conducive to the performance of original material. Rock and show rooms usually employ groups of artists ranging from four to ten members. More emphasis is placed on using popular entertainers from the local or regional area. For this reason these clubs have budgets that are larger than those of lounges. Despite the decline of clubs, almost every city of moderate size still has at least one rock or show room. Surprisingly, many smaller cities have show rooms with high budgets.

We've purposely omitted discos and dance clubs from this survey because of their emphasis on recorded music as opposed to live entertainment. The discos and dance clubs that do utilize live music would otherwise be included in this category.

Showcase or Listening Room

The showcase or listening room is another very important category of club, especially from the standpoint of the artist's career development. In many major cities, especially entertainment centers, there are key clubs that have a policy of only booking recording artists. The format and atmosphere is listening-oriented and is well suited to the presentation of original material. These clubs are usually well covered by trade press from publications such as *Billboard, Cash Box, Variety,* and *The Hollywood Reporter.* They are also frequented by the general press, industry figures, and record buyers. The potential for exposure and the concert-like atmosphere make this stage an extremely important one for breaking in a new recording artist.

Because of the importance of showcase clubs, booking an artist into them can often be difficult. The competition is stiff and the money is usually minimal. One example of the bargaining power that owners of important showcase clubs possess is what is known as a "pay to play" policy. Some of the important hard rock clubs in Los Angeles have instituted a policy whereby a band must guarantee the sale of a minimum number of tickets before they will be permitted to perform. Because many of these groups regard exposure in these clubs as an essential step to a record label affiliation, they do what is necessary to turn out their fans at these venues.

Certainly, not all showcase clubs have a pay-to-play policy, but they do want only the top up-and-coming talent to attract and hold their clientele. As a result, clubs look to those with connections in the industry to help supply the talent. This is why a manager seeking to position an act on one of these stages should seek the help of influential booking agents and record companies to help secure these dates. If an act is already signed to a label, the record company will often help subsidize the artist's appearances in showcase rooms through tour support, radio and print advertising buys, or by buying a block of tickets for radio program directors, the trade press, and anyone else the label feels can help them sell records. This support is often necessary since the showcase club usually doesn't have to pay top dollar because of the intense competition among artists.

The Artist-Sponsored Showcase

A common technique for an unsigned artist trying to create some excitement is to sponsor his own showcase much in the way a record company would for a newly signed artist. The first step is to perfect original material and a tight show in rehearsal and later in lounges or showrooms. Once the act is ready, the manager uses his connections to turn out record executives, agents, publishers, and anyone else who could help boost the artist to the next career level. Because industry pros are a tough audience, it's also advisable to pack the club with as many enthusiastic fans as can fit through the door. While such a showcase performance is obviously staged, it is perfectly acceptable to all concerned. It not only gives potential career partners a chance to see a new artist in action, but it also provides an opportunity for a manager to showcase his organizational ability and resourcefulness. Because artists seldom rate a second chance for such concentrated exposure, everything must be right before the manager gives the go signal for such a showcase.

Large Hotels and National Club Chains

The last stage available to the artist in the club market is large hotels and national club chains. This category includes hotels in large cities such as the Hilton or Hyatt chains, or the major hotels in Las Vegas, Atlantic City, Miami and other resorts. Because the budgets are usually substantial in this segment of the club market, these rooms are capable of attracting top-caliber talent. There are no restrictions on the number of artists employed. From single performers to extravagant productions, the hotels and chains have the resources to buy the best. At this level, the artist's fees are high and so is the standard of excellence.

These types of rooms serve several functions. Performers who may not have been tremendously successful as record sellers, but who are nonetheless super entertainers, find this level appealing and financially rewarding. Acts such as Wayne Newton and Sammy Davis, Jr. are the leading examples of those who sustain superstar careers while rarely releasing records. This is also an attractive career alternative for artists who have built names through record sales, but who are no longer considered chart toppers. Tom Jones is an excellent example of a performer with the ability to do a first-rate live show who has made the transition from million-selling recording artist and television star to a highly sought-after and paid showroom headliner. Another attractive aspect of this segment of the club market is their international scope. Artists with the ability to connect on an international level can expand their career options in direct proportion to the number of markets they can appeal to around the world.

PRIVATE PARTIES

A second major category of live appearance is private parties. This level includes high school proms and dances, college fraternity parties, corporate parties, military base functions, and other private engagements utilizing live entertainment. This level of personal appearance offers the young artist numerous opportunities to develop and perfect his talent. Many national artists have come directly from this circuit. Colleges offer young artists the chance to build an extensive following long before a record affiliation is established. This following can be translated into future record sales. The format of most of these types of engagements is largely dance-oriented. The audiences are generally receptive and lively, providing the young artist a chance to polish his stage show and musical ability while also providing reasonably good compensation to help finance the move up the career ladder.

CONCERTS

The last broad heading of live appearance is the concert market. This segment can be broken down into three parts: college concerts, festivals, and promotions.

College Concerts

Most every college, regardless of its size, presents concerts of some kind for its students during the school year. The college concert circuit is a good way to popularize or introduce new recording artists as well as maintain and expand the following of established acts. College audiences also represent an important source for record sales. One of the most attractive features of the college audience is the acceptance of a wide range of performers and styles of music. Because of the enrollment base of most colleges and universities, these institutions are able to allocate high budgets for concert entertainment. This aspect makes the market both attractive and competitive to artists who have become established through hit records. College venues can range from 1,000-seat auditoriums to 20,000-seat coliseums.

Festivals and Fairs

The decline of clubs has been accompanied by the popularity of the outdoor festival and the increased use of talent by state fairs. Today, almost every major- and secondary-market city in the country has its own event, which is usually held in the spring and summer months. State Fairs usually follow in late summer and fall. Other specialty events focusing on specific types of music, such as The New Orleans Jazz and Heritage Festival or the Concord Jazz Festival, as well as numerous blues, country, and bluegrass festivals held throughout the United States and Canada, also provide numerous slots for entertainers that didn't exist even 10 years ago. The major, full-service booking agencies have separate departments that concentrate on these lucrative venues.

Promotions

The final category of concerts is promotions. Some of these involve independent promoters and promotion companies who book artists for an isolated concert promotion all the way to multi-city tour packages. Where the college concert and festival buyer isn't motivated to book an act based solely on profit potential, the promoter is. Normally, the veteran promoter has established a relationship with various booking agents and managers of national artists. Once a promoter has proven himself financially sound and reliable, agents and managers entrust him with the promotion of more dates and subsequently entire tours.

The promoter is the purchaser of entertainment. He'll sign the artist performance contract as employer, thus guaranteeing the artist's fee, arrange the location for the concert, promote the event, and coordinate the actual performance the night of the show. He must also make sure that the artist and all who participate in producing the show are paid, plus be responsible for applicable taxes associated with the production of the concert. He takes all the risk for a potential profit.

With the rising prices of artists, arenas, radio, printing, and amusement taxes, the promoter must select the artist he promotes cautiously. For this reason, the professional promoter will attempt to book complete tours in order to insulate himself from a fatal loss on a one-night promotion.

Veteran promoters are primarily interested in headliner acts and tour packages. The novice promoter usually gets the lesser-known acts. However, this is how a promoter begins to develop his reputation. If he can help an agent, manager, or record company develop the market potential of a new artist by promoting a tour, and the artist subsequently becomes successful, he'll have gained their respect. As a result, he's likely to get additional dates for the artist he helped to develop.

Many college students who serve as entertainment buyers for their schools establish friendships with booking agents and managers. These college students often prove themselves trustworthy and capable promoters. Consequently, the agents will sell them dates during the summer for their own entrepreneurial promotions.

It must be emphasized that both booking agents and managers of national artists exercise the utmost caution when dealing with unknown promoters. The financial repercussions to agent, manager, and artist are simply too great to entrust a tour or a string of dates to a beginner. If a particular promotion isn't successful and the promoter doesn't have the financial capacity to cover the loss, who'll pay the artist? Take this isolated situation and multiply the loss times eight, ten, or fifteen cities on a tour! The artist could conceivably play a multi-city tour, and after paying hotel, transportation, equipment rentals, actually *lose* money. Even if the artist is protected by contract, the cost and time to litigate may make the collection process economically unfeasible. For these reasons, booking agents normally require substantial deposits from promoters. The economic consequences to the artist are simply too serious not to exercise extreme care in this area.

In some instances, a well-known artist will retain his own promoter to set the entire tour. This is possible when the artist is so popular and is in such demand that normal promotional efforts to ensure a profitable show aren't needed. Despite this popularity, a local contact, in most cases, will still be utilized to coordinate necessary details. An artist desiring to set his own tour usually will have his own promoter or coordinator contact a local promoter and will pay him a flat fee for assisting in making the arrangements in certain cities. Under this approach, the local promoter doesn't risk his money, but just performs a task for a fee.

Promotions vary in size, but the more expensive attraction forces the promoter into a larger arena to make the show economically feasible. Generally, the professional promoter is concerned with concerts that have the capability of filling 10,000 seats and up. The optimum promotion obviously depends on the artist, size of the city, arena, and overall cost considerations.

Recording artists and their record companies utilize the concert appearance to promote record sales. A successful performance in a stadium seating 50,000 people or an arena seating 20,000 can translate into significant record sales. For this reason, the major record companies feel that well-promoted, successful concert appearances by their artists are a must in their overall marketing program. The experienced manager, artist, and promoter recognize this and work closely with the record company when promoting a concert tour.

THE CONTRACT

The contracts used in booking artists for live appearances overlap in their terms and conditions, depending on the type of engagement involved. The name of employer, engagement location and address, date and time of engagement, rehearsal hours, and wage terms are all standard information contained in any artist performance contract. Also found in most contracts are clauses regarding the inability of the artist to perform due to sickness, accident, strikes, civil turmoil, epidemics, mechanical malfunctions, acts of God, or conditions totally beyond the control of the artist.

The American Federation of Musicians has a standard contract form used by all licensed affiliated booking agents. The beginning manager is well advised to familiarize himself with its terms.

The artist performing in the club market will frequently encounter clauses providing for room accommodations and discounts for food and beverages. These extra gratuities are sometimes essential in order to make some engagements economically feasible for the artist. The manager should insure that all the terms are contained in the performance contract to avoid any dispute during the engagement and to facilitate financial planning of the artist's tour. In the club market, it's also often necessary to set forth the exact hours of rehearsal time during the day in clubs that have constant customer traffic.

The basic performance contract for concerts, promotions, and private parties is very similar to the club contract, although, unusual features do occur. Many artists performing in these markets have certain additional requirements necessary for the successful presentation of their show. These extra requirements are contained in an attachment to the performance contract called a "rider." Some riders are quite extensive and contain costly provisions for the employer. For instance, many artists require the employer to furnish a specific type of sound system that can cost several thousand dollars. In addition, musical equipment, room accommodations, and special transportation, as well as food and beverages, often appear as requirements in riders. The artist and manager must be cautious when preparing a rider so it does not take on the appearance of a scavenger hunt list. On the other hand, the employer should review the rider requirements carefully so as to be totally aware of all cost considerations relative to the purchase of a specific artist. An experienced booking agent will normally advise the purchaser of the requirements contained on the artist rider before a date is booked.

The artist performance contract for promotions will require that the price of tickets and number of available seats be included. Furthermore, the number of gratis seats is normally restricted. This occurs especially when the artist is to receive a guaranteed amount against a percentage of the total proceeds of ticket sales. Other clauses or terms are usually included that pertain to the percentage split of proceeds over a certain amount between artist and promoter.

THE BOOKING AGENCY

The most direct way for an artist to secure club, private party, or concert engagements is through a booking agency. In many instances, concert, festival, and top-line club dates are impossible to secure *without* an agent. Regardless of the type of date, the booking agency serves as a meeting place for artists and purchasers of entertainment. Some agencies represent certain artists exclusively, thus requiring other agents to purchase from them if they have an engagement for that artist.

Booking agencies come in all sizes. There are a few that are international, multidimensional firms, such as William Morris or ICM. These superagencies maintain offices in major cities throughout the world and have numerous departments representing entertainers, athletes, television personalities, authors, actors, and other types of celebrities.

The next strata of booking agencies are the ones working primarily in the area of musical entertainment. These types of companies will often specialize in one or more types of entertainment such as country music, black contemporary, or jazz. They may also specialize in certain markets such as club attractions, dance music for private parties, and so forth. Besides the firms that operate on a national basis, there are hundreds of regional booking agencies throughout the United States.

The manager should select a booking agent or agents capable of securing the type of engagements best suited to the development of the artist's career. The first step is for manager and artist to determine on what "stage" the artist should appear. Once this determination has been made, there are literally hundreds of agents representing the entire entertainment spectrum. Finding the best agent for an artist may turn into a trial-and-error process. The manager must be alert and cautiously watch over the artist-agent relationship.

Agent fees generally range from 10 to 20 percent. Normally an agent's fee for booking a club engagement is 10 percent while the fee for a private party or concert ranges from 10 to 20 percent. The fees for booking are somewhat negotiable, depending on the strength of the artist and the service the artist requires. The American Federation of Musicians has an exclusive Agent Artist Agreement, which attempts to govern this relationship between its members and affiliated agents. While the agreement covers broad areas of an exclusive agent-artist relationship, there are usually certain specialized terms associated with each situation.

As with every other member of the artist's development team, the manager and artist should choose the person or firm not simply by track record with other clients, but also based on the dedication and belief that agent has in the artist. Getting lost in the shuffle at a booking agency can be disastrous, especially if the personal appearance figures prominently in an artist's career plan.

Once the right agency situation is in place, the artist and manager should make an effort to cultivate their relationship with their agents, encouraging comments and criticisms and working closely with them to shape a realistic and effective career plan. While it might be fashionable to gripe about agents the way most people do about lawyers, experienced managers know they can be one of your surest links to long-term success in the music business.

║║║ 16 ║║║

Merchandising, Commercials, and Corporate Sponsorships

Ten years ago, income from merchandising, commercials, and corporate sponsorship was, for the most part, icing on the cake for artists in the entertainment industry. Record/songwriting royalties and personal appearance income comprised the bulk of most artists' earnings. Not any more. A maturing baby boom generation coupled with an ever more affluent younger generation has supported an explosion of consumer products in every industrialized nation of the world. This phenomenon has created a worldwide mass marketing revolution, driven in large part by the two essentials of the music industry: songs and celebrities. The result has been the formation of a powerful new alliance between corporate manufacturers and marketers and the music business.

In the past, certain celebrities have been able to command fees or royalties totaling more than a million dollars from merchandising, commercials, and endorsements. That trend has accelerated in terms of both the number of celebrities selling products and the types of imaginative arrangements that resourceful artists and managers have been able to set up. The continued refinement of mass-marketing techniques, combined with the increasing importance and influence of entertainment figures, will no doubt continue to enhance potential earnings in these areas in the 1990s. An astute manager aware of the possibilities in these fields can help raise his artist's income level and make effective use of these vehicles for promotion and image projection.

MERCHANDISING

Merchandising is one area of ancillary income and name projection that continues to be critically important to an artist's bottom line. "Merchandising" generally refers to the marketing of products to the public on the strength of the artist's name or likeness. These products can include T-shirts, souvenir photograph books, posters, dolls, toys, and games. The range of products possible is limited only by one's imagination.

The key to effective merchandising is to give the public a product they want and to present it so as to enhance the artist's popularity rather than to diminish it. This is not always an easy task. Good taste and thoughtful planning should serve as primary guidelines for any merchandising campaign.

The new artist negotiating his first record contract should be especially conscious of the potential value of his name and likeness. Many record companies will try to secure exclusive merchandising rights from the artist in return for a royalty based on the net sums they receive. The amount is usually 50 percent. The manager should try to retain these rights, at least in areas not bearing on promotion of his records. For instance, it might be advantageous for the artist to give nonexclusive merchandising rights to the label in specific areas that could be used to promote record sales, such as T-shirts and posters. However, toys, dolls, and games would generally be outside the scope of legitimate record-promotion tools. If rights are granted, the artist and manager should retain all rights of approval mentioned earlier.

As with record companies, the artist should not give merchandising rights to specialists in the field until the artist's career merits such an arrangement. There's always the danger that a premature grant of rights can result in less favorable contract terms for the artist because of lack of bargaining strength. However, when the artist's career has reached such a level, the artist and manager should carefully consider the consequences before committing themselves to a campaign.

COMMERCIALS

Commercials comprise another important source of income and provide the artist with a vehicle for exposure. Entertainment personalities of star caliber can command fees in the six figures for a national advertising campaign. They can also be expected to be seen by millions through television, radio, and magazine exposure. However, as with everything else, there's the potential for damage to an artist's career if the manager's dealings with the "commercial" market are not handled properly.

The word "commercial" may encompass any means by which an artist is used to promote, advertise, and sell a product. It may take the form of an on-camera television spot or a voice-over on a radio jingle. In other instances, the commercial may be a printed advertisement in a national magazine or may even involve using the artist's picture on outdoor billboards or in connection with in-store product displays. In the case of a comprehensive national campaign, all of these different formats may be used.

Just as a commercial can take many forms, so it can be aimed at specific markets. It can be targeted at national, regional, or local markets. All of these variables will have a bearing on the desirability of the particular commercial and the money the artist can hope to make in return for his services.

Most major national advertisers retain advertising agencies who have the responsibility for developing and producing their advertising campaigns. When developing a campaign that will call for the use of an entertainment personality, the agency will usually contact the major, multi-faceted booking or talent agencies and other agents with access to important national acts. As a general rule, these agencies are based either in New York or on the West Coast. Since the advertising agencies' area of expertise is not entertainment, they depend on the agent's knowledge and experience in the field. In some instances, an agency will have an in-house music department that might have contacts directly with artists, managers, producers, and record companies. In this case, the advertising agency might choose to deal directly with the artist or his personal representative. The best way for a manager to get his artist commercial work, if he has no advertising contacts of his own, is to develop a relationship with an agent who regularly works in the commercial field. It may often be possible, depending on bargaining position, for the manager to work with one agent for personal appearances and another for commercial work.

Basically, there are two approaches to advertising. One is "product sell." This consists of using the artist to make a direct appeal to the consumer to buy the sponsor's product. The other approach is known as "image advertising." This is a more indirect concept. Here, there is no effort to make a direct sale. The advertising agency appeals to the buyer by suggesting their product is a desirable commodity that should be a part of the consumer's lifestyle. Many national advertisers use this form of advertising in their national campaigns to supplement a local "product sell" approach. Image advertising is generally well suited for entertainers because of their mass appeal to large numbers of people. The key here is to tie the product to the artist, thereby taking advantage of the artist's popularity.

When a campaign calls for use of an entertainer, the agency will usually come up with a type of person who would fit what they're doing. For example, let's suppose the agency wanted to do an image-advertising television commercial for a soft drink manufacturer. The largest target group of buyers of this product consists of pre-teens, teenagers, and young adults. The commercial is designed to center around a high energy pop/rock male artist with a high approval rating with the target age group. The agency will draw up a list of five or six singers who fit this description and the general budget range they have to work with. The advertising agency will then contact agents to inquire about an artist's interest and availability. Generally speaking, advertising agencies don't work with much lead time. Often, an artist's unavailability will end his chance of doing the commercial because air dates, once they're set, are usually inflexible. Once the agency finds an artist who fits their requirements, a contract is negotiated and a production schedule is set.

The Pros and Cons of Doing a Commercial

There are a number of factors bearing on whether to accept or reject a commercial. Naturally, the money involved must be sufficient to warrant involvement by the artist. There's also the consideration of how a commercial will affect the artist's image and career development. What product is being advertised? It must be consistent with the artist's image. For instance, an artist with a reputation for an unorthodox lifestyle would probably not want to do a bank commercial. A beer commercial wouldn't be appropriate for an artist sporting an all-American, wholesome image. The terms of the contract to be negotiated with the advertising agency will also bear on whether the artist should accept the commercial. For instance, an artist should avoid a long-term commitment unless the financial return is sufficient. The artist may not want to grant unlimited rights to use his likeness in things such as in-store displays, posters, and billboards, arguing this would cheapen his career.

Another point to consider is the effect a commercial will have on the artist's future worth in the commercial market. Every time an artist does a commercial, his value diminishes. This is especially true if the campaign is national in scope. Eventually, the artist will no longer be fresh and unique. Therefore, a manager hoping for a more lucrative contract may want to defer accepting any commercial offer until later in the artist's career. Or he may want to think about a regional commercial to gain experience and some financial return without running as great a risk of lessening his artist's value.

A manager should be especially wary of the danger of overexposure. Too many television guest shots, coupled with an extensive national advertising campaign, could result in oversaturation. Consequently, demand for the artist's concert performances and records might fall off, severely damaging his career. No commercial is worth taking if it will have an extreme negative effect on a developing career. On the other side of the ledger, a well-produced national television commercial for a good product can give an artist's career a significant boost.

In short, the proper degree of exposure is a question of judgement. The manager must make a calculated projection of a commercial's effect based on all relevant information at his disposal.

ENDORSEMENTS

A related area of ancillary income is from endorsements. This area has many of the attributes of merchandising and commercials. It involves the artist's name and likeness being directly connected with a specially manufactured product line. Professional athletes serve as a frequent example of endorsements, such as Michael Jordan and Bo Jackson, both of whom are paid millions of dollars to endorse a wide range of sports and athletic products. Endorsements are also available to entertainers for a variety of products. The same basic considerations discussed in merchandising and commercials also apply to endorsements.

THE CORPORATE SPONSORSHIP

Probably the most significant development over the last decade in the area of commercials and endorsements has been the increased involvement of corporations in the careers of music artists.

Along with the growing appeal of recording artists to corporations eager to tap into expanding markets, the 1980s brought skyrocketing costs to almost every aspect of an artist's life. Artists who once toured the country in station wagons and panel vans suddenly found it necessary to use jets and tractor trailers. Crowds demanded state-of-the-art sound, lights, staging, and special effects. Fewer clubs and more out-door festivals and promotions ushered in a new era of personal ap-pearances. It all added up to more people and more money. Acts who once depended on personal appearance income were going in the hole just to promote their records. All this set the stage for new alliances with the corporate world.

Today, imaginative managers and corporate marketers are entering into a new era of corporate sponsorships which include packaged tours; multi-year corporate spokesmanship arrangements; television, radio, and print ad combinations; and a host of other complex joint ventures. One of the most successful arrangements involved Michael Jackson and Pepsi Cola. This relationship went well beyond the traditional one-shot product commercial, allowing Pepsi to tap into Jackson's huge follow-ing. It reputedly cost the soft drink manufacturer millions of dollars to attract hundreds of millions in sales. Obviously, Jackson and Pepsi thought the arrangement was mutually beneficial. In the wake of this deal, the area of corporate involvement entered a new dimension.

All of these new options have created a host of new decisions for artists and their managers. Should an artist take advantage of lucrative commercial offers, or would it be more advisable to hold out for a more lucrative spokesmanship package at a later stage of the artist's career? This is always a gamble because a manager can never be sure that an artist will be able to sustain a career over a long period of time, or even if more attractive offers will ever materialize. There is also the matter of an artist appearing to sell out their art for corporate money or sponsor-ship. And then, how much money is enough? What other benefits can be derived? What are the potential risks? How will fans react?

The right strategy clearly depends on the artist and the opportunities that present themselves. This is an area that will surely test a manager's acumen and judgement. Whatever the decisions, they should be made against an awareness of the competing factors that are involved.

UNDERSTANDING THE LEGAL BASIS

The legal basis of merchandising, commercial, and endorsement con-tracts as well as corporate sponsorship arrangements rests on a commit-ment by the artist to provide his or her unique personal services along with the grant of a license to utilize the artist's identity in connection with the sale or promotion of a product or company. The personal services aspect is similar to commitments in which artists promise to use their unique talents to make records or concert appearances. As with any other contractual arrangement, scope and term of the commitment along with creative input into the final product are critically important factors.

Licensing one's name, likeness, or another aspect of personal identity such as a distinctive voice is a separate right belonging to the artist that is protected by the developing legal doctrine known as the Right of Publicity. When negotiating with product-related companies, merchandisers, and corporate sponsors, the artist's manager should make every effort to place a value on these attributes that make the client unique and thus incapable of being replicated by a substitute personality. Obviously, the more versatile and distinctive the artist is, the more value can be attached to them for ancillary income purposes. Obviously, Michael Jackson's management did an effective job when it came to convincing Pepsico executives that *Thriller* and Pepsi-Cola had enough in common to merit opening up the corporate change purse.

NEGOTIATING THE CONTRACT

Some of the more important factors to be considered in the negotiation process are the length of the contract and date from which the term will be measured. For example, assume a television commercial is to run for one year. Should the year begin running from the date the contract is signed, or from the date of the first production of the commercial, or from the first date of airing? This is a negotiable point. Other key terms include territory: national, regional, or local airing. Another issue to settle is scope of rights, such as television rights only, television and radio, print, outdoor advertising, and point of purchase (which includes in-store displays and posters). In addition, advances, guarantees or flat fee, and creative control of production are other points that must be negotiated.

Normally, an artist is paid on the basis of either an advance against residuals or a guarantee of residual remuneration based on a negotiated percentage of applicable AFTRA (American Federation of Television and Radio Artists) or SAG (Screen Actors Guild) scale. Depending on bargaining position, an artist's manager may negotiate a contract that pays the artist at the rate of scale, double scale, or higher. This rate is then multiplied by the number of radio and/or television airings the commercial receives according to AFTRA and/or SAG rate schedules, and is paid to the artist in much the same way a songwriter is paid by performing right societies. The manager should become familiar with AFTRA and SAG rates and procedures. Representatives of these organizations will be glad to talk to managers about their organizations.

In the area of commercials, timing can mean everything. The manager should make sure a commercial will have either a positive career effect or will provide the artist with substantial income. But an artist should never damage his image or sacrifice his career development for the sake of the money he can earn from doing a commercial. However, the right commercial at the right stage of an artist's career can be beneficial career-wise as well as financially.

THE BETTE MIDLER "NO COMMERCIALS" POLICY

To illustrate some of the various legal and practical considerations that go into placing a value on a given artist's unique characteristics, consider the real-life example of singer/actress Bette Midler. Over the span of her career, Bette Midler has proven to be one of the most versatile entertainers working. She parlayed early success as a cabaret singer in the 1970s into a string of top-selling records and film soundtracks. She also became a headlining concert act and a successful motion picture actress and film producer. Her greatest assets were an outrageous personality, distinctive voice, and versatility, which made her an unforgettable stage personality. Bette Midler and her management were also shrewd enough to recognize that the substantial sums she could earn from commercials could potentially offset her demand and popularity in other ventures. Consequently, she adopted a policy of not doing commercials. Ford Motor Company later tried to persuade her to do a voice-over of one of her well-known songs for a commercial they planned to shoot. When she refused, they enlisted a singer from her backup group and instructed her to imitate the famous singer's voice as closely as possible. The soundtrack was played over a commercial without Midler's permission, giving the target audience the impression that the famous singer was endorsing the product. She brought a lawsuit against Ford and won, even though her name or face were never connected with the commercial.

An analysis of this case demonstrates several valuable lessons for managers confronting possible commercials and endorsements. First is the question of whether to do commercials at all, and if so, what kind. At least part of Midler's decision rested on an assessment of how such work would impact on her demand in other areas. After weighing the options, she chose to pass up the potential income in favor of other considerations. In Midler's case, she passed on all commercials. Some artists in this situation might well pass up a car commercial, but have no trouble doing a soft drink promo. Robert Palmer, George Michael, and Michael Jackson are prominent entertainers who have done just that in the late 1980s, apparently suffering none of the down-side repercussions Midler feared. From a long-term standpoint, because Midler has yet to do a commercial thus far while still in the prime of her career, her asking price at a later date, if she chooses to reverse or modify her policy, will more than likely go up. In fact, her never having done a commercial combined with her recognizable, one-of-a-kind personality were most likely the very things that attracted Ford's interest in the first place. This real-life example also demonstrates that artists who choose not to license others to use their name or likeness for commercial purposes have legal recourse. It should be noted here, however, that while the Right of Publicity is a generally accepted legal doctrine, it is not uniformly interpreted by the states. This is why an attorney should be consulted before any decision is made in this lucrative area.

COMMERCIALS AND CORPORATE TIES: NO EASY ANSWERS

The fields of merchandising, commercials, endorsements, and corporate sponsorships provide the artist with additional avenues to financial fulfillment and career development. But they can also present some very tricky decisions for the artist and his manager. The rule in this area is to think twice before making a commitment. Once a basic direction is determined that complements the overall career plan, make sure your attorney is involved. Making the right decision about ancillary exposure of the artist can be a crucial plus or minus in realizing career goals. Artists and managers who merely view this as an isolated opportunity to make a little extra, quick cash could be making a serious miscalculation over the span of a career.

17

International Considerations

During the decade of the '80s, the entertainment industry witnessed the unprecedented growth of international markets. Like other sectors of the economy, the global marketplace has become a reality that cannot be ignored.

The United States remains the world leader in entertainment. Demand has never been stronger for American films, television, and music. This has had a significant beneficial impact on the earnings of United States-based record companies, music publishers, and artists. Foreign markets now account for a substantial share of gross income earned by these various entertainment entities. This share is sure to increase as more nations of the world achieve a higher standard of living, acquire more leisure time, and continue to improve and be served by the communications network. Given the potentially lucrative overseas markets, it is no surprise that more artists and managers than ever before are thinking in international terms. The popularity and interest in American artists has never been greater. This favorable situation presents the artist and manager with the opportunity to broaden their appeal and increase their incomes.

The acceptance around the world of artists' records or songs can make a big difference in a record company or music publisher's annual balance sheet. Artists such as Elton John and Julio Iglesias are top draws throughout the world. These artists enjoy the same type of global popularity that many artists receive only in their own country. The result is increased record and live performance revenue in direct proportion to increased international appeal.

FOREIGN RECORD SALES

A very important aspect of the world entertainment market is record sales. Generally, when an artist signs with a major American record company, the label will demand world rights to the artist's recordings. In the case of a few major artists, certain territories may be exempted.

Foreign record sales are usually achieved in one of two ways. The first is through major American record companies, such as CBS and RCA, which have affiliated companies in the major developed nations of the world. These companies license master rights to their foreign branch affiliates. The second approach involves American companies without branch affiliates who enter into licensing agreements with foreign record labels. These agreements can either take the form of a blanket, worldwide foreign agreement with a major overseas company that has its own branch affiliates, such as London-based EMI, or they can be on a country-by-country basis through independent companies.

As a general rule, an artist is paid a royalty calculated at 50 percent of the rate normally paid for American sales. This rate may be negotiated up to as much as 75 percent of the domestic rate, depending on the artist's bargaining position and whether or not the American record company is dealing with its affiliated branches or unaffiliated independent licensees. This reduced rate is justified by the record company because it receives substantially less on foreign sales than on domestic.

Most recording contracts make no guarantees as to release of the artist's records in foreign markets. Depending on bargaining position, the artist should try to negotiate a guaranteed release of his records in key countries of the world, especially if the record company insists on securing world rights. But he must be prepared for the record company's reply to this type of proposal. They may say that they don't always have control over what will be released in a given country, especially if independent licensees are employed. Another frequent argument is that the foreign record company won't want to release a record in their territory unless it's either a hit in the United States or unless the artist has a previous track record in the particular foreign country.

The status of foreign record deals may be somewhat different where the artist is signed to an independent producer who, in turn, deals with the U.S. record company. An established producer may succeed in exempting certain foreign territories from his contract with the American label. In this event, the producer would be free to make his own licensing agreements on a country-by-country basis in return for an aggregate producer/artist royalty.

The manager interested in expanding his artist's career into international markets should investigate the overseas capabilities of various foreign record labels as one consideration in choosing an American company. Some domestic companies are more conscious of international sales than others. Larger companies with foreign affiliates may be in a better position to release and promote records in foreign territories. However, it is possible a smaller company with strong independent licensees may be able to devote more time to help the artist promote record sales in foreign territories.

Consideration should also be given to the type of material the artist records. Manager, artist, and producer should seek songs with international appeal whenever possible. However, they should be careful not to think internationally at the expense of the American market. This would be self-defeating, especially since many major countries look to success of a record in the United States as an indication of whether it will be released in a foreign market. The goal here is to strike a balance between domestic and foreign appeal.

FOREIGN MUSIC PUBLISHING

The essence of foreign music publishing involves agreements between American publishers and their affiliated or independent overseas licensees. These contractual relationships are referred to as "subpublishing agreements." An American publisher will enter into these agreements much in the same manner as an American record company enters into foreign record licensing agreements. Typically, an American publisher will grant rights on either a song-by-song or catalog basis to foreign music publishers for a negotiated term. The subpublisher will seek to exploit and promote the compositions and collect and account for income received. As compensation, the foreign publisher will retain a percentage of earnings derived from the commercial use of the material. Depending on the commercial potential of a particular composition or catalog, the foreign subpublisher may pay the copyright owner an advance against royalties to obtain rights to the material.

Generally, no provision is made in the songwriter contract for payment of a reduced royalty on foreign income to the writer. However, as a practical matter, a writer's income will be diminished because his royalty is based on a percentage of income actually received by the publisher. Since the foreign subpublisher deducts a percentage of the gross income he collects, there'll be less money to divide between the publisher and writer. For instance, let's assume $100 in mechanical royalties is earned in France. Assuming the French publisher by contract is entitled to 50 percent of all mechanicals earned in the territory, he'll retain $50 and remit the remaining $50 to the American publisher. The American publisher will, in turn, normally be obligated to pay the writer 50 percent of all mechanical income actually collected by him. Consequently, $25 is payable to the writer and $25 is retained by the publisher.

It should be noted here that most subpublishing agreements grant the foreign licensee the right to collect all mechanical, synchronization, and miscellaneous income. With regard to performances, the subpublisher either collects the total publisher's share or just the foreign publisher's share of performances directly from the foreign performing rights society. Generally, the foreign society will collect the writer's share of performing income as a result of reciprocal agreements with ASCAP and BMI. The writer's share is paid directly to the respective American performing rights society after deduction of a small collection fee. The American society will pay the applicable amount directly to the writer.

A major consideration of the writer/artist when signing with an American publisher is a determination of whether royalties paid to the company by foreign subpublishers and ultimately to him are computed at the source and are not diminished on account of any sublicense granted by the subpublisher. For instance, let's assume the American publisher enters into a subpublishing agreement with a French publisher for the territories of France and Switzerland. The subpublisher negotiates a clause whereby it agrees to pay the original publisher 50 percent of the income actually received by it in France. The French publisher doesn't have an office in Switzerland and thus finds it necessary to enter into a subpublishing agreement of its own with a Swiss publisher on a 50 percent royalty basis. The money earned by the Swiss publisher is $100. The division of income in this situation would be as follows: $50 is retained by the Swiss publisher, with the balance being remitted to the French publisher. The French publisher in turn retains 50 percent or $25 and remits the balance to the original American publisher. Out of this $25, $12.50 is remitted to the writer, and the balance is retained by the American publisher. Sometimes, these types of sublicenses are unavoidable, especially in order to insure representation in smaller countries or when the original publisher is in a disadvantageous bargaining position. However, whenever possible, the writer should determine the American publisher's foreign subpublishing structure and learn whether payments are computed at the source from the important foreign territories.

Usually, the American publisher will have absolute discretion as to the terms it negotiates with regard to foreign licensing or subpublishing agreements. This right will, of course, be subject to any limitations in the agreement with the writer. The writer can protect himself from improvident foreign agreements in one of two ways. The first is through a restriction in the original writer's contract, which may be difficult to obtain. The second method is to choose a domestic publisher with an active and successful subpublishing situation.

Translations, Adaptations, and Arrangements

Another aspect of foreign publishing that can affect the artist/writer is the right of the subpublisher to make translations, adaptations, and arrangements of his compositions, including the right to have new lyrics written. Without this right, it would be extremely difficult to exploit the writer's songs in certain territories.

Royalties payable to a local lyric writer will vary depending on local industry practice and the strength of the lyricist. It's customary for the subpublisher to pay the lyric writer royalties based on the mechanical and synchronization uses and sales of printed editions out of its share of the income. The local lyric writer's share of performing rights income will come from the American lyric writer's share. In some cases, foreign arrangers may be entitled to receive a small portion of the American composer's performance share.

As with records, the artist/writer should be aware of the appeal his songs will have in foreign territories. It's the responsibility of the foreign subpublisher to seek recordings of songs by artists in the territories it controls. In order to do this, the subpublisher must have material that will be acceptable to these artists. Because of language differences in non-English-speaking countries, melody becomes a key consideration in adaptability. The writer interested in international acceptance of his material is well advised to acquaint himself with the musical tastes of some of the key foreign markets, such as the United Kingdom, France, Germany, and Japan.

Often a writer may write with a certain artist in mind. As we have seen earlier in the chapter, a successful recording by an artist with an international following can not only account for considerable income from the foreign territories but can also help develop the composition into an international standard that will be recorded literally hundreds of times over the life of the copyright.

PERSONAL APPEARANCES

A third major area of international concern is the personal appearance. As in the United States, concert, nightclub, radio, and television appearances provide a lucrative source of income, while also serving as an effective record promotion tool. The rules regarding coordination of personal appearances and record company promotion in the U.S. apply equally to the foreign market. The large booking agencies such as William Morris and ICM have foreign offices to handle the booking of a foreign tour. Smaller companies often maintain reciprocal working agreements with separate foreign agencies. If the artist is not affiliated with an agency that has international connections, the manager can contact reputable foreign agents or consultants who specialize in arranging overseas tours.

A popular American artist can command substantial fees in certain foreign markets while also boosting record sales and music publishing income. Once dates have been set, the same general principles of personal appearances and the road apply to foreign tours. The manager and road manager should place special emphasis on each country's laws and regulations relative to passports, visas, work permits, and any other potential travel restrictions.

If the artist is to travel to non-English-speaking countries, thought should be given to hiring interpreters or guides to help ensure that the tour goes smoothly. It's helpful for the manager and artist to have at least some familiarity with the geography and customs of the countries they'll be visiting. This will not only contribute to a more successful tour but will add to the enjoyment of the experience by the artist and his traveling contingent. The local agent or contact can provide the artist with help in this area.

Apart from expanding the artist's markets, the foreign tour is an excellent device for avoiding domestic overexposure. An absence of several months from an artist's home country can help create a renewed demand for the artist once he resumes domestic touring.

SMART MANAGEMENT THINKS GLOBALLY

As the world economy improves and technological developments continue, it seems to be a safe bet that the demand for quality entertainment on a global scale will continue to increase. The astute artist and manager should strive to help fill this demand through internationally oriented career planning.

[PART FOUR]

CAREER
MAINTENANCE
AND CONTROL

18

The Manager's Juggling Act

What does a manager do? Or better yet, what doesn't he do? Generally speaking, a manager does anything necessary to further the career of his artist-client. He's a coordinator, advisor, negotiator, psychologist, planner, promoter, and a friend to the artist. We believe the term "juggler" aptly describes a manager's many diverse functions and responsibilities. Just as one problem is solved, new ones requiring immediate attention usually appear. Management is an ongoing process with no real stopping point short of termination of the artist-manager relationship. The manager must be aware of all aspects of the artist's career. He's the focal point of literally hundreds of decisions that must be made daily. The manager's ability to make the right decision at the right time will greatly enhance the success of the artist's career. Conversely, his failure to act in a timely manner as daily problems unfold can severely damage the artist's career.

The best way to accurately describe a manager's duties and responsibilities is to construct a typical day in the life of the artist's manager.

The day begins, as in any other business office, with the opening of the morning mail. The manager finds several artists' performance contracts included in the stack of correspondence. He carefully reviews each contract, giving special attention to the date, time, and place of engagement, and the compensation clauses. If deposit checks are enclosed with any of the contracts, the proper accounting entries must be made and the checks deposited in the artist's bank account. If an accountant maintains the financial books, then the checks will be processed according to the predetermined accounting procedure. If the manager finds anything in the contracts that doesn't meet his approval, he'll contact the booking agent regarding the appropriate modifications. However, on this particular morning all the contracts received are in order, so he promptly signs each one and instructs his secretary to return the remaining copies to the booking agent.

Also included in the mail are offers for live performances received by the booking agent. Each offer must be examined in view of its economic and exposure value. The manager will normally contact the artist if any offer has unusual features. The manager notices one of the engagement offers is for an amount twice the artist's normal asking price. However, the engagement is to be held outdoors. The artist and manager had previously formulated several live-performance guidelines, one being no outdoor engagements. Since the money offered is extremely high, and several other name attractions have already agreed to perform at this engagement, the artist might want to consider this offer. Knowing the artist's daily schedule, the manager decides to contact him later on in the afternoon.

After the mail has been processed, the manager begins making and returning telephone calls. Representatives from the artist's record label, publishing company, and booking agency have all called requesting various information. These people receive top priority. Upon returning the record company's call, the manager is surprised to learn that the artist's album is selling well in four new markets in the Midwest. Excited by this information, the manager calls the booking agent to share the news. He informs the agent of his desire for the artist to perform in these new markets. The agent replies that he'll check with buyers in the markets and will call back toward the end of the day.

Before making any further telephone calls, the manager is interrupted by an unannounced visitor—the artist. In short order, the manager learns the artist is very upset with one of the members of his backup group. With the fall tour just a few weeks off, the artist is pessimistic about being ready in time unless something can be done about the attitude of this particular musician. The manager attempts to get all the facts so he can define the real problem. Is it the musician's playing or singing ability? Is it his attitude, or is there a personality conflict? What's the real problem? After an in-depth discussion, the manager feels he knows what the trouble is and how to remedy it. He reassures the artist that the problem will be solved and encourages him to make the most of today's rehearsal. An appointment is set with the musician for later that afternoon. Before the artist leaves, the manager asks him about the offer for the outdoor engagement. The artist's answer is, "No."

After the artist leaves, the manager is informed that he has an emergency telephone call from the artist's public relations firm. Trouble! The firm can't have the publicity campaign ready in time to correspond with the artist's tour. The manager and public relations man have a rather heated discussion regarding the firm's inefficient handling of the artist's affairs. The manager has had enough excuses and delays. He terminates the relationship with the publicity firm. Immediately following this unfortunate encounter, the manager instructs his secretary to arrange appointments with representatives of three other P.R. firms for the next day. Time is running out. The artist's publicity campaign must be planned and activated immediately in order to coincide with the efforts of the record company for promoting the upcoming tour.

Next the manager receives a call from the booking agent who informs him he has secured firm offers from a promoter for all of the new markets mentioned by the record company. However, the promoter wants to block-book the dates for several thousand dollars less than the normal price. The manager instructs the booking agent to have the buyer submit his offer in written form. The agent says he'll call back when a telegram is received.

The manager contacts the promotion department at the record company to inquire about the feasibility of the label providing extra tour support in the new markets to help offset the lower live performance fee if he should accept the dates as offered. The record company representative tells the manager he'll check and be back in touch.

Lunch time! Today the manager has a luncheon appointment scheduled with the artist's attorney. During the meeting, the attorney advises that all the employment agreements with the road crew now being used should be modified to include several new clauses. Moreover, the lease agreements for the tour vehicles have been approved and are ready for the artist's signature. In addition, the attorney explains the legal ramifications of an incident involving the artist and an irate auditorium manager at a concert performance earlier in the year. It seems that the artist became enraged at the way the auditorium manager's staff was handling the lighting effects and made some derogatory comments to the audience regarding the intellectual capacity of the crew. As a result, the auditorium manager is suing the artist for slander. Finally, the attorney presents the manager with the proceeds of a recent collection suit, which was successfully concluded, involving an overdue concert fee. All in all, the meeting wasn't too bad. The manager has experienced far worse.

The manager hurries back to the office to meet with the artist's record producer. They're scheduled to review the artist's latest recordings. Both the manager and artist agree that the mixes on the recordings are terrible. Unfortunately, the manager must relay this information to the producer in such a way so as not to upset him. The manager conveys the negative feelings of his client to the producer as tactfully as possible. After a lengthy session, the producer leaves convinced the manager is an idiot when it comes to recording and doesn't understand how the artist could put up with such incompetence. Nonetheless, the recordings will be remixed.

Immediately following the meeting with the producer, the booking agent calls with several new offers. After listening carefully, the manager accepts two of them, since they correspond with the tour's routing. Several of the offers merit consideration if the price can be increased or the dates changed. The remaining offers don't make sense from a routing or financial standpoint and are refused.

As the afternoon draws on, the road manager arrives to begin finalizing motel and travel accommodations for the tour. After discussing the budget limitations for various expense items, he begins making the necessary arrangements. The manager instructs him to contact the program directors at the important radio stations in the cities where engagements have been set in an effort to increase airplay for the artist's latest record. The manager sends the road manager into the adjoining office to start accumulating the necessary information to commence the in-house promotion campaign for the tour.

The manager next speaks with the artist's accountant regarding the bookkeeping procedure for the tour. The same system that has been previously employed will be used. The manager arranges a meeting between the accountant and road manager so they can discuss any questions he might have about the system.

Emergency call! The artist is at rehearsal and is in a rage. The monitors of the sound system aren't working. There'll be no rehearsal until they're fixed. The manager immediately locates a repairman and replacement equipment and has the road manager personally direct him to the rehearsal location.

Fifteen minutes later, the manager meets with the musician with whom the artist is experiencing problems. The manager learns that the musician is having some serious domestic difficulties. After a candid conversation, the manager is sympathetic to the musician's situation. However, he explains the great pressure the artist is under due to the immediacy of the upcoming tour and the amount of rehearsal still to be done. The manager assures the musician he'll explain his situation to the artist and will encourage him to be understanding. Since the musician is quite concerned about several legal aspects of the situation, he advises the musician to see an attorney for counsel.

The manager calls the artist and tells him the results of the meeting with the musician. The artist is most understanding of the situation and is quite relieved to learn that the problem isn't being caused by some personality clash between him and the musician. However, the artist is still concerned over the sound system that still hasn't been repaired. The manager assures him that the road manager will take care of it.

Half an hour later, after solving the minor catastrophe with the sound system, the road manager returns and begins contacting radio-station program directors. The manager joins the road manager in talking to these people about the artist's upcoming appearance in their city. He enjoys playing the role of radio promotion man, especially after two stations promise to add the record to their playlists.

Toward the end of the day, the booking agent informs the manager that firm offers have been received on the proposed engagements in the new market areas. Putting the agent on hold, the manager contacts the record company's Promotion Department to see if a decision has been made on extra tour-support money. The proposal is being considered by the Business Affairs Department. The manager advises the agent to delay the buyer until a decision can be made by the record company. Maybe they'll get an answer tomorrow.

That evening, the manager is scheduled to attend the artist's rehearsal to review a portion of the concert presentation being prepared for the upcoming tour. Watching and listening to the rehearsal stimulates the manager's thoughts about his client's creative direction. He has several comments and ideas to offer about the show. This is the area where manager and artist excel as they feed off each other's ideas. The manager's thoughts provoke additional ideas from the artist. After an hour-long discussion, both artist and manager are excited about several new approaches to the live performance they've agreed to try. They're both starting to feel the excitement of the upcoming tour.

Before leaving the artist's rehearsal, the manager again mentions the offer for the outdoor engagement. He asks the artist to reconsider because of the money involved and the positive exposure value. The manager also adds the fact that several other name recording artists will also be performing at the same concert. The artist agrees to think about it and give the manager an answer within the week. The manager starts to leave when he's cornered by two members of the artist's backup band who inquire about the itinerary for the tour. The manager briefs them of the general tour schedule and promises to give them an exact itinerary as soon as the details have been finalized.

On his way home, the manager can't help but think about the problems involved with finding a new public relations firm and activating a campaign in time for the tour. He also makes a mental note to call the record company tomorrow morning about his tour-support proposal. The conversation with the producer also pops into his mind. The manager smiles to himself, knowing the new tapes are going to be remixed, even though the producer thinks he has a tin ear. All the problems of the day are balanced out by the excitement generated by the rehearsal. The creative give and take with the artist make all the problems worth putting up with.

The manager arrives home late. He checks with his answering service for any calls. There's an urgent message to call the booking agent at home. The message has the making of another emergency. The booking agent tells the manager that he's heard a rumor that the artist has been nominated as Best New Artist of the Year by an influential national magazine. The agent points out that this could dramatically raise the artist's asking price for personal appearances on the upcoming tour.

After hanging up, the manager's mind begins to race, thinking of all the implications and repercussions such a turn of events could have on his client's career. The excitement builds for the second time that evening. The manager must either confirm or deny the rumor that the booking agent has given him. He decides to call a friend on the West Coast who may know something about the report. It's almost midnight, but because of the time difference, it's only 9:00 P.M. in Los Angeles. He picks up the telephone for the thirtieth time since the beginning of the day and begins dialing a phone number scribbled on the back of one of his business cards. "Hello Marc? I've just gotten a report that. . . ."

19

Helping the Record Company Help You

Once the artist and manager have succeeded in establishing an affiliation with a major record company, they've cleared a crucial hurdle. In one way, they've finally achieved the success they worked so hard to attain. Yet in another, the work has only begun. Signing a contract with a viable record label and becoming an established recording artist are two entirely different things. To bridge this gap takes the same type of hard work it did to interest the company in the first place. The only difference is that the record company is now a potent ally rather than a closed door that must be pried open.

In order to maximize the artist's potential at this stage of his career, we feel that active, experienced management is an absolute necessity. Many self-managed acts will find it increasingly difficult to continue to develop their own careers once this level of success is attained. Nowhere is this more true than in the artist's relationship with his record company.

The record business today is highly sophisticated and potentially lucrative. The manager's role in the ultimate success or failure of an artist's record career has become increasingly important. He's the artist's personal representative in all dealings involving the label. He acts as the artist's advocate, press secretary, advisor, planner, negotiator, decision-maker, protector, and spokesman all rolled into one where the record company is concerned. He can be instrumental in helping the label allocate its resources and make the most effective use of its assets to break the artist from a record-sales standpoint. The artist simply doesn't have enough hours in his day to devote to the many and varied management duties and responsibilities involved in dealing with the record company.

The most common complaint against managers voiced by the record company executives we surveyed is that many of them don't fully understand or appreciate the function and inner workings of the record business in general and the record company in particular. On the other hand, they were quick to praise those managers who made it a point to understand what a record company could and could not do for an artist. Effective management is impossible unless the manager is able to relate to the record company on its own terms. This means having the same degree of knowledge and skill as those he'll be working with at the label.

UNDERSTANDING RECORD COMPANY OPERATIONS

The record company has one objective—to sell records. Record companies in the United States don't receive performance royalties from broadcasters as some do in Europe and other foreign territories. They don't share in income from the artist's concerts, television appearances, commercials, endorsements, or songwriting royalties. The only way they can make a profit and stay in business is by selling compact discs, cassette tapes, and records. The manager should always keep this basic premise in mind. Any suggestions and requests he makes should in some way be designed to help the record company succeed in their objective. The fact that the manager's plans and requests will directly benefit the artist's career is of no real concern if it will not help sell records.

The manager should also have a thorough understanding of the organizational structure and procedures of the label. Most major record companies in the United States are based in recording centers such as Los Angeles or New York. Many have branch offices in other cities to deal with specific or specialized functions. For example, many labels maintain self-contained offices in Nashville that specialize in country music. Others maintain branches in key markets around the country to handle regional marketing, promotion, and distribution.

Record companies are no different from other businesses. Most are divided into departments charged with certain phases of the company's activities. Each department has a supervisor who reports to the president or other upper-echelon executive. The president, in turn, reports to the board of directors or the parent company which is concerned with the overall direction and profitability of the company.

Although no two companies are structured exactly alike, most are organized along the same lines with regard to division of responsibility according to subject matter. Each label has a chief executive officer and executive staff. They're charged with the overall operation and management of the label. Individual areas of responsibility are usually divided into the following departmental areas: Business Affairs; Legal; Accounting; A&R; Marketing and Sales; Promotion; Press, Publicity, and Advertising; Artist Relations; and Career Development.

Business Affairs Department

The Business Affairs Department, as its name implies, is charged with the responsibility of controlling the company's business direction. It's often staffed by attorneys and other business-oriented persons. This department is historically a training ground for top label executives. Among other broad business-related duties, this department is responsible for negotiating and administering artists' contracts. Once a decision is made to sign an artist, the manager will be in contact with the Business Affairs Department. This department also has input into decisions involving tour support, promotion budgets, and the like. It's valuable for the manager to get to know the people in the Business Affairs Department. Because of their background and responsibilities, they'll be much more likely to appreciate a manager with a businesslike and professional approach to his job. A favorable impression never hurts.

Legal Department

The Legal Department at most companies is involved in drafting contracts, licenses, and other legal documents negotiated by the Business Affairs Department. They're also called upon to render legal opinions concerning various aspects of the label's operations.

Accounting Department

The Accounting Department rounds out the business and financially oriented components of the company. The artist should have a special interest in this department because it's responsible for computing and mailing him his royalty checks.

A&R Department

The A&R (Artist and Repertoire) Department is concerned with the artistic development of a record company. As discussed earlier, the A&R Department is responsible for bringing new talent to the label. In addition, it's their responsibility to serve as the creative contact point between the artist, producer, manager, and the record company. They're involved in helping the artist select material, studio, and producer. Often, the A&R man acts as the production supervisor as well as artist's liaison within the structure of the record company. Many A&R men also fill a dual role of record producer. The A&R Department will generally have input into any decision having to do with the creative matters affecting the label.

Marketing, Sales, and Distribution Department

The Marketing, Sales, and Distribution Department is the lifeblood of the company. This department is concerned with selling records that have been developed through the efforts of the artist and the A&R Department. It's very important that the marketing specialists be excited about the artist's record. Without this enthusiasm, it's difficult for them to convince distributors, rack jobbers, and one-stops of the saleability of the product. The A&R person often will play a newly submitted tape by an unsigned artist or the preliminary mix of one of the label's current artists for the Marketing personnel to get their opinion of the record's commercial viability.

Once an artist is signed and a record completed, the Marketing and Sales staff will structure a marketing approach with the help of other departments such as A&R; Promotion; Press, Publicity, and Advertising; Artist Relations; and Career Development. Once the record is released, this department makes sure product is available to retailers to fill the demand. It closely monitors sales and reports to other key departments at the label, as well as the manager. It's important for the manager to know the people in this department. An experienced manager can make a significant contribution to formulation of the marketing plan and can help the company make it work.

Promotion Department

Promotion goes hand in hand with Marketing and Sales. Once the record to be released is selected and the marketing approach is set, the

Promotion Department will be involved in exposing that record in whatever manner the marketing plan dictates. This can mean getting AM and FM radio play, setting up promotion parties, in-store displays, and so forth. Most labels have field promotion men assigned to a specific territory. The home office coordinates their efforts on a daily basis and reports their progress in terms of airplay back to the department head, much in the same manner that Marketing tracks sales progress. The department head, in turn, analyzes and distributes this information to others in the company, as well as to the manager. This information is important in helping the label, manager, and artist know which move to make next.

Press, Publicity, and Advertising Department

Another key department to an effective marketing campaign, as well as to the artist's overall long-range career, is the Press, Publicity, and Advertising Department. This component of the record company helps keep the artist's name before the public either through press releases, trade and consumer stories, print ads, time buys, and other exposure through the media. This is a tremendous asset available to an artist. The manager can help assure that this tool is used to its maximum effectiveness by constantly keeping the department informed of every aspect of the artist's career and by cooperating in arranging interviews, press conferences, and other publicity activities.

Artist Relations Department

The Artist Relations Department can be very helpful to the manager in areas of scheduling, routing, and attending to the numerous activities of a busy artist. This department serves as a contact point between the artist and label. The manager should strive to keep Artist Relations informed of the artist's schedule and plans.

Career Development Department

Some of the larger labels have a separate department devoted to the artist's career development. This is a strong indication of the modern record company's commitment to the principle of career longevity as opposed to a hit-and-miss approach characterized by the one-shot hit record. Career Development acts much like an in-house manager, attending to many management-oriented functions discussed in this book. The record company feels this is necessary in many cases in order to protect and develop their investment. This is especially true in the case of young, inexperienced artists and unmanaged artists. An experienced and conscientious manager can often accelerate the growth and development of his artist's career by working closely with this department.

Coordination is obviously a problem in large departmentalized, multi-office record companies. Certain labels, such as CBS, use product managers to help solve this problem. The product manager is assigned to certain specified projects. It's the product manager's job to guide a particular artist's record through every phase of the process we've just discussed. The artist's manager obviously can be of great assistance to the product manager in making the record a financial as well as an artistic success. Other labels may use the Career Development or A&R Department as the coordination and contact point for a specific artist or product.

WORKING WITH THE RECORD COMPANY

With this basic outline of the record company's various functions and division of responsibility, let's now turn to some specific things the manager can do to help the record company help his artist. Once the recording contract has been negotiated with the Business Affairs Department, the manager should waste no time in meeting with the label executives to discuss the company's plans for the artist and his records. Most likely, this will have already been done prior to signing. An artist should never sign with a label until he has at least a basic understanding of the company's intentions. However, even assuming this phase has been completed, it's a good idea to reconfirm the previous discussions at the level of the president, if possible.

Next, the manager should spend whatever time necessary to meet everyone he possibly can who is connected with the label. This means going from department to department establishing one-to-one personal relationships with the various record company personnel. As pointed out in the chapter on the artist's development team, this does not mean department heads only. Everyone at the label, regardless of responsibility, has a contribution to make to the artist's career. For this reason, the manager should take time to meet the individual promotion men, the press and publicity staff members, the secretaries, even the guy in the mail room. When he meets these people, he should tell them about the artist and his music, what he's trying to do, and where he's trying to go. He should make himself accessible, and ask for their thoughts and opinions.

After the manager has had a chance to get to know the record company personnel, he may want to introduce the artist to them. This has the tendency to reinforce the positive atmosphere the manager is trying to create. In order for a record or an artist to achieve success with the public, those at the record company must first be excited and committed to the project or artist. These preliminary meetings are the first round in helping build that enthusiasm.

The business of selling records begins with the A&R Department. The manager should meet regularly with A&R to discuss the artist's material and production release schedule. Even though, by contract, the A&R Department may have final say as to material selection and release decisions, most often they'll take into consideration any recommendations and suggestions made by the manager, provided they're realistic and well thought out. The same is true of almost any other contact with the record company. It's just human nature that a positive, cooperative approach will result in more satisfactory results for the artist/client.

Once a collective decision has been made regarding the product that will be released, the manager should turn his attention to the marketing scheme. He should talk to the Marketing and Sales, Promotion and Press, and Publicity and Advertising Departments about the artist's objectives and strategies. The emphasis here should be on arriving at a coordinated, unified approach, consistent with the artist's image and goals and the record company's assessment of how best to market the artist and his recordings.

Prior to these discussions, the artist and manager should have carefully worked out their approach as to which route to take in maximizing the marketing and promotional efforts. The manager is encouraged to work out general proposals in this area to present to the label. The proposals should be flexible enough to conform to the views and circumstances of the record company. By making these suggestions, the manager is at least assured of having some input into the final decision by the company. Even if his ideas aren't adopted, he has demonstrated his competency and ability to the label. Respect for the manager by the various department heads is extremely important.

When making proposals, it's very important for the manager to keep in mind that no one likes to be told how to do his job, though some people are more sensitive to this than others. The manager should always have an appreciation for the other person's psychological makeup and treat him accordingly. There's always the danger of the manager giving the appearance of taking over rather than merely giving suggestions. The rule of thumb here is: Use tact when dealing with record company personnel.

Once a marketing plan has been conceived, the manager's function becomes one of coordination. He must work with various label personnel and other members of the artist's development team to adequately prepare for the record's release. This will include coordinating with booking agents, promoters, publicity firms, television producers, and anyone else who will affect the record marketing process. If a promotional tour is contemplated, tour support must be finalized.

Once the record is released, the manager becomes the record company's point of contact with the artist. He should keep the various departments informed of the artist's schedule as well as any relevant developments pertaining to him. He should also make himself accessible to deal with any problem or new development that might arise. The manager especially will want to maintain close contact with Marketing and Promotion concerning sales and airplay activity. Heavy sales or airplay in particular markets will affect decisions such as which dates to accept and which interviews should be granted.

If the artist is touring, arrangements must be made for press conferences, interviews, and in-store promotions. This will necessitate coordination with the Artist Relations, Press, Publicity, and Advertising and Promotion Departments. The manager will want to review the crowd reaction to the artist's live performances with the Career Development Department and determine the impact the appearance is having on sales and airplay. During the entire process, the manager and label must always be thinking about the artist's next recording session, next record release, and next tour. It's a never ending process requiring almost daily contact and communication with the various departments of the record company. However, it can be enormously rewarding if done effectively.

THE END RESULT

There's nothing more exciting for a manager than watching a record start to gain wide airplay and begin to break sales-wise, knowing that he's largely responsible for making it happen. This is a reward that can't be measured in terms of dollars and cents. It's the end result of months of planning, communication, and follow-up with the record company. Major record labels have the resources and expertise available to achieve these results. It's up to the manager to make sure that these assets are maximized in favor of the artist/client.

20

The Road

The traveling and touring aspect of an artist's career is commonly referred to in the entertainment business as "the road" or "roadwork." To some entertainers, the road offers many exciting opportunities: the chance to meet new people, see new sights, and visit new cities or foreign countries. However, to others, especially the veteran artist, the road is anything but exciting. These performers view it as a boring, monotonous existence that takes them away from family, home, and a normal way of life. Regardless of the artist's viewpoint, the road is an essential element in the careers of most artists.

WHY TOUR?

Touring has a direct and significant effect on an artist's popularity and audience appeal. The personal appearance is absolutely essential to the new artist trying to become known and develop a following. This is one of the few vehicles he has to display his talent and create a demand for himself and his art. This is especially true of new recording artists trying to establish record sales. The road is equally important to the established artist from a career maintenance standpoint. To ensure continued popularity, he or she must maintain visibility and contact with fans. Although records and videos are effective promotion devices, there's no substitute for the personal appearance. This allows the audience to establish a closer relationship with the artist while permitting someone who has been around to add new fans to his following. With the competition for the entertainment dollar being so intense, no one in the industry today can afford to take anything for granted, especially the public. For those who do, there's the probability that the people who buy the records and concert tickets will shift their loyalties and dollars to other more active and visible artists who haven't lost sight of what it takes to get to the top and stay there.

Beyond developing and maintaining popularity, there's another very important reason why artists find the road a necessary part of their career-money. Concert, one-nighter, and club appearances can account for a large portion of an artist's income. Consequently, many artists can't afford to neglect the road from this standpoint.

As mentioned earlier, a successful personal appearance tour is an excellent record promotion device that can translate into increased sales. Record companies frequently require that an artist be a working act before they'll sign him to a recording contract.

The road offers the artist the chance to win over thousands of potential buyers in a single evening. Besides direct sales, word of mouth created by an artist's visit to a city attracts the curiosity of others. All of this coupled with good records, exciting performances, and a positive public image all translate into a hot artist.

Since the road is so important to the overall success of an artist's career, the manager must do everything possible to make sure that every aspect of an artist's personal appearances is successful. This is why a manager will often travel with the artist, or be present at key engagements. When the manager is unable to travel with the artist, he usually employs a road manager. For all practical purposes, the road manager is an extension of the manager. He coordinates the numerous aspects of a personal appearance or tour, making hundreds of decisions daily. Throughout the remaining portion of this chapter, we'll discuss the various functions of the manager and road manager relative to touring. While the following discussion assumes the artist has chart activity at the time of the tour, these basic principles are still applicable in part to the artist without a record.

PREPARING FOR THE TOUR

The manager's first order of business is setting an objective for each tour. (The word "tour" is used throughout to refer not only to a series of dates but also to isolated engagements.) What is the artist trying to accomplish? Is the objective solely to enhance record sales? Is the goal perhaps to capture a specific market or region? Often the artist is trying to make as much money as possible within a particular time frame. The underlying objective will influence many of the manager's decisions when formulating the tour. Artist and manager must know exactly what they want the tour to achieve. Whatever the particular tour objective, it should be compatible with the artist's career goals.

Before accepting any dates, the manager must ensure that the artist's act is ready for the road. That means working with the artist to develop a stage presentation that is both entertaining to the public and compatible with the artist's image. The show must be tight and professionally produced, which means that an adequate amount of planning and rehearsal time should be scheduled. During this time, decisions regarding material, arrangements, sequence, dramatic effects, lighting, sound, wardrobe, equipment, sidemen, choreography, background singers, and conductors should be made. Based on the objective of the tour and the artist's image, the presentation should be formulated and refined until both artist and manager are satisfied that the show is more than just good; it has to be drop-dead great.

Once the artist and manager agree on the format of the show, the on-stage support personnel, such as musicians and background vocalists, must be located and rehearsed. Simultaneously with rehearsal, the manager must employ offstage support personnel, such as sound technicians, lighting crew, equipment handlers, drivers, and a road manager. All these decisions should be made within the guidelines of the tour's objective and image of the artist.

Early in the planning stage of the tour, the manager should meet with the artist's booking agent to discuss the objectives and structure of the tour and set a price range for the act. An experienced agent can provide valuable information concerning the marketability and price range of the artist based on the target markets, arena capacities, style of show, rider requirements, and current popularity of the artist. If the objectives of the artist are unrealistic, it's best to find out at this stage, before the support people are employed. Based on the asking price of the act, the manager will project the artist's overhead and costs associated with the production of the tour. If the general price limits are lower than previously estimated by the manager, modifications may have to be implemented to reduce the cost of producing the show.

Assuming that the booking agent is confident the price for the artist can be attained without difficulty, the next consideration is the availability of the artist. This will depend on the existing schedule of the artist and the type of engagements the artist seeks to undertake.

Once the manager and booking agent have thoroughly discussed and reviewed the scope of the artist's tour, the manager will need to know how long it will take to set the tour. Here's where an artist's popularity pays dividends. If the artist has a hot record on the charts, coupled with a reputation for first-class personal appearances, the agent should be able to set the tour easily, provided that the price is not out of line. It should be noted that, with a superstar, price is usually a lesser consideration because the talent buyer knows that the concert will most likely be an automatic sellout. Conversely, if the artist doesn't have a current record release and isn't known for his ability as a performer, the agent's job will be much more difficult.

Artists often become upset if the booking agent can't deliver the type of dates for the desired amount of money. Although booking agents do have some influence on the marketing process of the artist, they don't control every aspect. They must work with the product as it exists. Once the artist has expended the resources available to him through artist's development team members, such as his record company, public relations firm, booking agent, and manager, the decision to book the artist is up to the buyer. That decision is based upon his perception of the commercial potential of the artist to sell concert tickets. The agent can give his best effort and still not achieve the desired results for the artist because many of the factors influencing the buyer's decision are beyond the booking agent's control. Of course, in some instances, the agent may be the deciding factor that influences the customer's decision. Therefore, it's important that the manager maintain a close working relationship with the booking agent since his confidence, belief, and excitement about the artist can definitely influence customers' buying habits. However, it would be unrealistic to think that the booking agent can control the talent buyer's decision-making process. The act must be able to stand on its own merits.

The Artist Relations, Marketing, Publicity, and Promotion Departments of the artist's record company should also be advised of the tour arrangements. In order to achieve maximum benefit, the various departments of the record company will require a certain amount of lead time to activate their promotional machinery. For the artist, booking agent, and record company to achieve maximum benefit, they must all move in a carefully coordinated manner. The record company, therefore, should also have input in setting tour objectives and target areas. This is especially true when the record company is providing the artist with tour support money.

As the booking agent receives offers from buyers, they're communicated to the manager, who may accept or reject them at his discretion. If the offer is in a desired market and within the price range previously established with the booking agent, the manager will probably accept it. However, supporting dates, routing, travel factors, and overall tour developments could force a negative decision. If the offer is beyond the designated market area or the price is under the minimum agreed on, it will probably be rejected. In some instances, the financial or promotional value of a supporting date will force the manager to depart from the original tour plan. Submitting each offer to the manager affords him the opportunity to follow the development of the tour.

As each date is booked, the agent will usually send a press kit to the employer containing the artist's latest record, photographs, biography, and other promotional material. Often the artist's publicist, record company, and manager will send additional promotional material so that the employer receives adequate publicity. The booking agent will issue performance contracts to the employer. The booking agent will also forward a signed copy of each contract to the local office of the American Federation of Musicians or other applicable labor organization in the city where the engagement will take place.

While the booking agent and record company prepare for the upcoming dates, the manager will be busy finalizing the tour personnel, acquiring needed equipment, and making transportation arrangements. A road manager must be employed if one is not already on staff. In all the tour preparations yet to be discussed, the road manager will work very closely with the manager.

The next phase of tour preparation involves three important areas: travel, public relations, and protective functions.

Travel Arrangements

After the tour dates have been set, the road manager will usually make the hotel and travel arrangements. These will include ground transportation if the artist or support team plans to travel by air. Otherwise, the road manager should inspect any vehicles that will be used—buses, automobiles, and equipment trucks—to be certain that they're safe and efficient. A travel agent is often used to make hotel and travel arrangements. When this is done, the road manager acts as liaison between the travel agent and artist's tour personnel. The road manager must also make sure that all members of the tour have valid passports when traveling abroad, and that they're affiliated with the necessary labor organizations. While many travel arrangements can be made in advance of the tour, there will always be problems or changes in schedule which will necessitate the road manager making modifications in advance plans.

Public Relations

The public relations function of the road manager is often over-looked due to more pressing duties associated with the tour. Public relations awareness on the part of the road manager can prove to be a real asset to the overall career development of the artist.

A substantial part of the road manager's public relations work can be done before the tour begins. A list should be compiled of the names and addresses of key radio stations, program directors and disc jockeys; television stations and newspapers; music equipment stores; local union representatives; as well as record stores, promotion men, and distributors in the cities where the artist will be performing. The road manager should make an effort to develop a friendly relationship with all these people by contacting them in advance of the engagements. It's also a good idea to invite these people to the artist's engagement and to send them press kits. As a follow-up to this initial contact, the record company should be instructed to send complimentary records and other information about the artist.

Additionally, the record company should be kept current on all tour developments. An itinerary of the artist's tour, including the exact date, place, and time of each engagement, should be sent to key record-company personnel. This information will allow the record company to make sure that the recorded product is in the stores and that promotional efforts are being coordinated. As stated previously, many record companies help the artist financially prior to the engagement.

The road manager should also contact the employer (or promoter) to verify that he's received adequate publicity material. At this time, any questions regarding the artist's rider requirements, location of engagement, or other matters relative to the performance can be discussed. Again, we must stress the importance of the road manager establishing a personal relationship with the employer prior to the arrival of the artist. Once the road manager arrives in a tour date city, he should attempt to personally meet all the people with whom he has previously communicated. If this is impossible, and it often is, he should try to call and invite them to the artist's performance.

Protective Functions

The last general area of a road manager's duties involves precautionary measures to ensure the successful completion of the tour. The first preventative step is for the road manager to know where to reach the manager at all times during the tour. This is absolutely imperative. The road manager should have in his possession a route sheet with engagement information. He should also keep photocopies of the artist performance contracts, including all riders and special attachments, in the event a problem occurs with an employer. The road manager should maintain an important papers file containing names, addresses, telephone and social security numbers, local affiliation, passports, and emergency contacts for all members in the tour. All vehicle ownership and registration documents should also be included in this file. If the artist's personnel are covered under a hospitalization insurance policy, the necessary identification forms should be on file. If each member maintains his own medical insurance coverage, the road manager should have a photocopy of the policy and identification card. A duplicate set of the entire file should be kept at the manager's office in the event the road manager's file is lost or destroyed.

Advance plans should be made with the manager or artist's accountant regarding the bookkeeping procedure to be utilized during the tour. The road manager should fully understand the procedure and have an ample supply of accounting forms. In addition, he should have at least two major credit cards and an adequate amount of cash, although carrying large sums of money on the road should be avoided. If possible, all payments from employers for artist's services should be in the form of cashiers or certified checks. When the road manager does receive cash, inter-bank deposits should be used to transfer the money quickly, thus avoiding accumulation of substantial amounts of cash.

Contacting the local musicians' union representative in advance of the tour can be helpful if it's necessary for the road manager to replace a musician for an engagement due to accident, sickness, or other unforeseen emergency. When personnel problems arise during a tour, the road manager must act decisively. Substantial income could be lost unless the problem is solved quickly. The local union representative is a good starting point, especially if the road manager is on a first name basis with him.

If the artist will be traveling by automobile and the equipment will be transported by truck, it's wise for the road manager to know in advance the names of local dealerships representing the brand of vehicle being used. A telephone call and an autographed picture to a dealer in the city in which the artist is performing not only helps if extraordinary service is needed, but may even create another fan. Another precautionary measure regarding ground transportation is to maintain a good relationship with a major rental car company. Again, a personal relationship, or simply knowing who to contact at three in the morning, can help tremendously when the group needs a vehicle to make it to the next date.

ON THE ROAD

Once the tour has begun, the road manager's responsibilities increase and the amount of time to make decisions decreases. The road manager's primary function during the tour is to oversee the artist's timely arrival at the place of the engagement. Whether traveling by air or land, the problem of coordinating departure, arrival, and alternate modes of transportation in the event of schedule changes is ever-present.

Once the artist and support crew arrive at a performance site, the road manager should focus on the stage set-up. Through advance communication with the employer, the road manager can arrange for the arena to be open for the road crew at the desired time. An efficient road crew is not only advantageous to the artist, but also economically helpful to a promoter when union stage hands are being paid on an hourly rate.

Following the stage set-up, the road manager should supervise the sound check and a brief rehearsal, if desired by the artist. The arena should be closed to the public during this phase of activity. Once the road manager leaves the arena, security people should be present until the equipment is dismantled.

While the stage is being set up, the road manager should inspect the dressing rooms to make sure that they're adequate, and he should determine their proximity to the artist's entrance and exit into the arena. If the artist requires food and beverage in the dressing room, this should be arranged.

The road manager should attempt to structure the artist's daily schedule to allow sufficient time for rest prior to each performance. While this can be an extremely difficult task, he must make every effort to see that the artist is well rested before each performance.

On the night of the show, the road manager is responsible for all last-minute details. He must see that the artist's show begins on time and runs smoothly. The road manager acts as a field general for the lights, stage crew, sound man, and all other support personnel. Depending on the type of engagement, it may be necessary for him to review the ticket manifest and receipts to determine if percentage fees have been earned and properly paid.

The road manager should evaluate all aspects of the artist's show. Was the performance too long? Was audience reaction enthusiastic? Did the lighting effects dramatize the performance? A written report of each performance should be forwarded to the manager immediately after each engagement. These reports serve as a diary of the tour. They also serve as a directory of all the people involved in the production of each show. After the tour is completed, these people should be contacted by telephone or letter thanking them for their help. Once an engagement has been successfully completed, the road manager should turn his attention to the next date, until the tour is concluded.

We've attempted to discuss the many functions of a road manager during an extended tour; however, to cover them all is impossible. Whatever problem may occur, it's the road manager's duty to deal with it, while insulating the artist from as much unnecessary distraction during the tour as possible.

AFTER THE TOUR

The manager must make the final determination of the success of the tour. The reports filed by the road manager serve not only as a good control device, but also as a reference in evaluating the tour's results. The record company can provide the manager with sales figures of the artist's product after the tour. This is a good way to measure the degree of the artist's impact on a particular market after the concert. The booking agent will be directly in contact with the employer or promoter after the event. Here, too, is a reliable source of feedback concerning the artist's performance.

After the tour is completed, the total picture can be analyzed. At best, the manager hopes to find universal acceptance in all markets where the artist performed. He's not interested in scattered success in push-over markets. The artist and manager shouldn't be satisfied with a tour that elicits mixed reactions or audience indifference.

THE KEYS TO MASTERING THE ROAD

The road is probably the most demanding and challenging aspect of the artist's career. In many ways, it's also the most important and satisfying. As with every other area of the artist's career, planning, hard work, and follow-through add up to success.

21

Re-evaluation and Critique

It's extremely difficult for a highly successful artist to remain objective about his career. However, to ensure that success continues, he must always be open to re-evaluation and critique from his manager. While the large royalty checks, lucrative performance contracts, and thunderous applause are all evidence that the artist has made it, someone must retain a realistic perspective. The same goes for a new artist who begins to experience success. In both situations, this responsibility falls to the manager.

It's only human nature for anyone, especially an artist, to find criticism distasteful and ego deflating. Their positive self-image is reinforced by the acclaim heaped upon them by the public and press. "If I'm so wrong, why are my concerts still packed and record sales soaring?" they retort. There is obviously an element of truth in that kind of response. Unfortunately, it's not always the whole truth. An artist who can't accept any constructive criticism of his career has begun to lose perspective, which means the life expectancy of his career will be shortened. On the other hand, the mature professional capable of acknowledging the need for ongoing reassessment can breathe new life into his career whether he is riding high or beginning to fade. It's common sense that the manager, record company, producer, and booking agent all want the artist's career to flourish. When the artist succeeds, they succeed. The advice they offer is motivated by a common economic bond. Though it's not always easy, the astute artist will realize this and listen openly to a constructive analysis of his work.

RE-EVALUATING THE ARTIST AND HIS ACT

The manager should review all facets of his client's artistic and professional persona. Has the artist become complacent? Is the artist overexposed or underexposed? Has he developed bad stage habits? What has audience reaction been to the artist's live performance? All areas of the artist's act need review and scrutiny.

Once the manager has presented his assessment of the positive and negative points of the artist's work, both should discuss ways to improve the weak areas without sacrificing the strong points. While the artist and manager always make the final decision on matters affecting the artist's career, their willingness to consider the opinions of others can often help keep their perspective clear.

At this point, any artist who has retained a "yes man" for a manager is probably going to be in trouble. It's unlikely that a manager who can only maintain his job by constantly agreeing with the artist can offer any constructive comments if they conflict with the artist's viewpoint. So instead of having an advisor, the artist has retained another follower, something he could get for much less than the percentage he pays him.

Business Review

The business structure and operation of the artist should also be re-evaluated periodically, usually on an annual basis. All legal documents should be reviewed, insurance coverages updated if necessary, and accounting records audited. The artist's budget should be carefully studied to determine if any breakdowns or excesses have occurred during the year. Often, the annual summary reflects the accumulation of various expenses that have previously gone unnoticed, but prove to be significant at year's end. Once detected, adjustments for such expenditures can be made in the new budget.

All reports to governmental authorities relative to the artist's business should be prepared, explained to the artist, and filed with the proper authority. Since many of the business aspects of an artist's career may not be fully understood or appreciated by him, the manager would be well advised to request a letter from the accountant, attorney, and insurance agent reviewing their particular area of the artist's business for the year. The manager can then wrap up the review of the artist's business operation at a meeting specifically for that purpose. If the artist has questions or desires additional information, the manager can offer the summary letters to help clarify his business status. In some instances, it may be best if the accountant, attorney, and other advisors are present at the annual business meeting to personally answer any inquiries from the artist. Regardless of procedure, at least one meeting a year should be devoted to an evaluation and review of all aspects of the artist's business.

Creative Review

The creative evaluation cannot be forced into a predetermined time frame as easily as the business review. Since styles and trends in the entertainment industry change so rapidly, this area must be constantly under scrutiny. The guiding principle in this area is maintenance and projection of the artist's image. If a major change in image is desired, however, then the artist and manager should consult all members of the development team before embarking on such a far-reaching move. A total departure from an established image could result in professional suicide for the artist.

PROJECTING AND ENHANCING
THE ARTIST'S IMAGE

Let's assume that the artist and manager are satisfied with the artist's current image. Their primary concern, then, is the proper maintenance of that image. Several factors must be reviewed in assessing the efficiency of team members in projecting and enhancing the artist's image.

The Artist's Material

The first important factor is the selection of artist's material for recording and live performances. Where is the material coming from; the artist or other songwriters? The material must be compatible with the artist's voice, style, and abilities. Most importantly, is the material becoming dated or below par. Just because there has been past success is no guarantee of what will happen in the future. Usually the artist who writes his own material has a common thread running through most of his compositions. The artist must take care not to confuse a recognizable "sound" or formula for success with a creative rut that recycles the same song with new words and titles. At the same time, care should be taken not to embark on such a radical departure in material and recording style so as to alienate long time fans.

The Record Producer

Another key influence affecting artist's image that should be evaluated periodically is the record producer. The artist and manager must review the producer's work product in view of the *artist's* changing and evolving goals, not the producer's. For instance, let's suppose an artist and producer have been working together for several years, finally achieving some degree of success on the last album they recorded. The record company wants the follow-up album to be in the same vein to take advantage of the sales and excitement generated by the last album release. However, the success of the previous album has afforded the producer a new-found degree of financial security. Despite the commercial success of the record, he's not pleased with the overall sound of the artist's material and demands a radical change in direction. What should the artist do? He believes in the producer's ability as a result of the success of the last album. But the artist also agrees with the recording direction suggested by the record company. The manager must resolve the dilemma without compromising the direction and image of the artist. If the producer is diverting the artist from his strategic course, then a new producer may be in order if a solution cannot be found through other means. The manager can't let the producer satisfy his artistic aspirations at the expense of his artist. To guard against this situation, the artist-producer relationship should be examined at certain intervals.

The Record Company

The effectiveness of the record company should also be assessed at various stages. The manager must be aware of personnel and organizational changes occurring within the company that could be detrimental to the artist. The resignation or retirement of key record-company executives, mergers, acquisitions, and shifts in company policies all could have some effect on the artist's relationship with the record company. It is also vital that the artist get his share of the resources and attention from his record label. If it becomes apparent that the artist does not figure in the long-term future of the company, it might be time to look elsewhere.

Be assured that all record labels conduct periodic reviews of their artist rosters with the view of cutting the least productive artists to make way for new blood. The examples of artists and labels parting company after long, successful relationships are many. While this is sometimes sad, its also a reminder that the music business at this level is very much a business.

The Booking Agent

The artist and booking agent relationship also requires periodic evaluation. The first measure of whether the relationship should continue centers around the results the agency has gotten for the artist. How many dates? What kind of money? Have new markets been developed or is the artist just playing the same accounts? All of this should be considered and analyzed.

Assuming the relationship has been mutually beneficial, the role of personalities should also be considered. The artist may become affiliated with a certain agency because of a particular individual. The artist may be affected if that individual leaves the agency or is transferred into another department. This is always a consideration in reviewing the artist's agency relationship.

Changing goals and objectives are certainly another consideration when re-evaluating the artist's agency affiliation. As mentioned in a previous chapter, many booking agencies specialize in specific types of performances or are confined to certain geographic regions. While one agency may be ideal for an artist at an early stage of his career, a shift in direction or a new level of career success may render the agency incapable of helping the artist.

For instance, let's assume that an artist has been performing quite successfully in the club market for a number of years. While interested in recording, the artist has never stressed this aspect of his career, since his club dates provide him with a substantial income. The infrequent recordings submitted to various record companies are impressive. The artist is eventually signed by a major label and, within six months, an album and single are released. The response is overwhelming; both the single and album soar up the charts. The record company, astonished with this new-found success, releases another single and it too climbs the charts.

Eagerly, the record company encourages the artist to set a tour to capitalize on the market acceptance. But the booking agency that has been so successful in securing the artist club engagements isn't capable of arranging the concert dates. As a result, the agency attempts to keep the artist in club markets. Asked for a partial release so the artist can retain another agent for concert dates, the agency reacts negatively.

Such situations are not uncommon in the entertainment business. The manager must scrutinize the booking-agent relationship to make sure that this aspect of the artist's business is deriving maximum economic benefit.

Other Image-Related Components

All other components of the artist's image must be inspected to complete the re-evaluation process. The critique should apply to the sound and lighting crews, music director, sidemen, and all other personnel utilized by the artist. The publicist and road manager should also come under the magnifying glass. Their activities are vital to the proper maintenance and projection of the artist's image.

Artist-Management Relationship

The artist and manager should also evaluate their own relationship as objectively as possible. Has the relationship been successful? Has the manager been good for the artist's career? Are both moving toward the accomplishment of predetermined career goals? After an objective analysis, both parties may agree that a termination of the relationship is best for artist and manager. If either party disagrees about prematurely ending the relationship, then their differences should be compromised or attempts made to settle them. If this can't be done, both parties must consider a release as a possible solution to their problem.

Career Goals and Strategies

The artist's career goals and strategies should also be reviewed periodically in order to utilize them effectively. The artist may wish to change career direction, or maybe set new goals. Whatever the case, a periodic re-evaluation will ensure that career goals, strategies, and tactics will be kept current.

STAYING CURRENT IS
THE BEST WAY TO STAY ON TOP

The manager should attempt to give the artist an overview of his entire operation, a concise review of the business machinery, and an in-depth discussion of all the creative factors influencing the artist's image. Critical comments from the artist's development team members also should be considered and discussed. All phases of the artist's career should be reviewed, from the selection of musical material to the color of his shoes on stage. The manager should recap the year in terms of success and discuss any modification of the career plan. The manager shouldn't hesitate to discuss the artist's failures as well as his successes during the year. The key to making this process work is a shared openness to valid, constructive criticism.

If the manager and artist don't stay current through periodic career assessment and re-evaluation, you can be certain that the music industry and the fans will, at some point, do it for them.

PART FIVE

MASTERING SUCCESS

22

Coping With Fame

Louie Richards' career was a success story. At the age of 13, Louie was playing in local rock and roll bands. By the time he was 17, he was a veteran performer with a new recording contract and a promising future. For the next 12 years, no one was more devoted to achieving success in the music business than Louie. But throughout his career he encountered numerous personnel changes within his group, financial hardship, and untold personal problems.

Although Louie had married young, fortunately he had an extremely understanding wife who encouraged him to pursue his music career. She worked to support them while he chased his dream. Time and time again, her income pulled them through the hard times.

Since his first record release while still a teenager, Louie had recorded literally hundreds of tracks. He had the experience, talent, determination, and dedication to be a success, yet after 12 years, he still hadn't experienced a chart record. All his friends and fellow musicians agreed that Louie had "paid dues" long enough.

Then, at age 29, all the experience paid off in success beyond Louie's wildest dreams. Within a year, his recordings were being hailed as the most progressive sounds of the decade. To the general public, Louie was an overnight success. Only his wife and friends knew the truth.

This sudden success brought all the fame and recognition Louie could have ever wanted. And with fame came money. In less than two years after his career had begun to take off, Louie had earned ten times the money that he had in all of his previous years as an entertainer. Louie could do nothing wrong; everything he did was deemed sensational. Three Grammys and a host of other awards were a testament to his critical acclaim and popular appeal.

After the initial shock of success had passed, people close to Louie noticed a change in his personality and attitude. He was far less friendly and down-to-earth. At times, he acted like a spoiled kid. Louie and his wife also started experiencing real domestic problems for the first time in their marriage. Louie's newfound wealth made it possible for his wife to accompany him on the road during tours. During the years Louie was struggling, he and his wife dreamed of the day they both could be together to enjoy the excitement of travel and meeting new people. However, now that the opportunity existed, it was nothing like they'd expected. The more time they spent together, the more arguments resulted. Louie grew tired of having her around. On the road, he was a star, and she didn't fit into his lifestyle. As far as Louie was concerned, they were in different worlds. Finally, the inevitable occurred. Louie and his wife were divorced.

Louie was so wrapped up in being a star that his divorce didn't really bother him at the time. His immediate concern was his health. The hectic schedule was causing him frequent minor ailments. Louie seemed tired all the time. He just didn't seem to have time to exercise or care for himself. Things were moving too fast. Though he knew his diet was poor and schedule too hectic, Louie was still having the best time of his life.

Besides being in poor physical shape, Louie started drinking. He also began using cocaine and uppers to help him keep up his frantic pace. While the alcohol and drugs had a stimulating effect, his physical well-being and mental outlook deteriorated quickly. Time and time again, his manager begged him to slow down. But Louie was making so much money that he was able to bury his problems with cars, new homes, beautiful women, parties, and more drugs and alcohol. These things seemed to cure his emotional and physical problems, and he repeatedly returned to them for comfort. Louie's prescription for his depression was money. He had plenty of it, and as long as it was coming in he could afford the expensive pain-killers.

Three years after Louie had acquired the Midas touch, it slowly started to fade. His manager was the first to recognize the situation. He'd been with Louie from the very beginning and knew him better than anyone else. They'd always gotten along well and had the utmost respect for each other. Sensing a shift in musical styles, Louie's manager recommended that he cut back his live appearances and devote a substantial amount of time to recording. While this would reduce his client's immediate income, the manager believed it would help him physically as well as professionally. Louie panicked. The thought of slowing down, even the least bit, was totally foreign to him. Along with the fear of losing his fans and expensive pleasures, Louie's irrational outlook added to the dilemma.

His solution was simple: "Book me more dates for more money." When his manager attempted to explain the harm in such action, Louie exploded. "Anyone who is making money off me will do what I say, or else." The decision was final. Louie would call the shots with or without his manager. Unfortunately, he communicated his new career philosophy to his agent and record company in the same threatening tone. They had already seen the signs of trouble and began making plans for the future, which suddenly made him potentially expendable.

Louie's gradual career slow-down began to manifest itself in smaller royalty checks and reduced guarantees for live performances. To make matters worse, Louie didn't really care about what was happening on stage. All he wanted was the money. His motivation no longer came from the applause of the audience or from shouts for encores, but only from dollars. Although his income was still substantial by anyone's standards, it wasn't enough to sustain the lifestyle he'd cultivated. His manager attempted to regulate his personal finances by continually warning him he was spending money that should be invested or set aside for income tax payments. All to no avail. Louie became fed up with his manager's overprotective attitude and continual advice. He simply tuned him out. Finally, the manager, realizing he could do nothing for Louie, reluctantly and sadly resigned.

The scenario continued for less than a year, until Louie's drinking problem and growing drug dependency became so bad that it dominated his entire life. This, in turn, resulted in blown dates, bad reviews, and ultimately failure of his record company to exercise its option for his services. The press started reporting on his erratic lifestyle and career reversals. The negative publicity accelerated a precipitous drop in popularity.

Four years after Louie's dream had come true, it had ended. Now, without his wife's comfort and his manager's advice, he was facing a bleak immediate future.

Farfetched? Hardly. The foregoing hypothetical example is actually a composite of several real-life careers. Contained in this scenario were many "success crisis" signals that may be helpful to artist and manager attempting to avoid this trap.

Unfortunately, the story of Louie Richards is repeated all too frequently in the entertainment industry, sometimes with even fatal consequences. These stories all pose the same question: How do artist and manager cope with fame?

AVOIDING A SUCCESS CRISIS

One of the main factors causing a success crisis is the sudden accumulation of substantial amounts of income in a short period of time.

The development process of most artists takes many years. As with Louie Richards, artists receive relatively little compensation during this "dues-paying" period. It is a time of sacrifice, usually without financial reward. But when success does come, the reverse is true. Almost overnight, artists can find themselves with more money than they can spend. This gives a false impression of the future because the money being earned at this peak won't continue forever. The initial shock of increased earnings must be handled cautiously by artist and manager. Much attention should be devoted to the financial-planning aspect of the artist's career at the first sign of such a situation.

We contend that the earnings for many successful artists tend to follow a pattern. That is, low income during the development phase, followed by a substantial jump once success is achieved, which will rise to its highest point, followed by a gradual decline to a point higher than where the artist began, but lower than the peak point of earnings. The artist's income cycle often will peak and fall several times during his career. The objective of the manager is to achieve the highest income point for the artist and then sustain it as long as possible.

It's certainly understandable why an artist could lose perspective of financial reality. After starving and sacrificing for a long period of time and then, almost in a flash, start receiving checks for $10,000, $50,000, and more from record companies, publishers, and concert buyers—yes, that would tend to distort anyone's view of the future. The manager should make the artist aware of this trap and have a general idea of what he'd do in the event such a situation occurs. Although some may label such a plan as daydreaming, it could well become a reality. If you don't think so, just look around for the real-life Louie Richards stories. They're not hard to come by.

WARNING SIGNALS

Success in large doses can often bring about physical abuses. An artist with enough money to buy anything he wants can be a disaster, especially for the artist who isn't prepared for it. Without a proper handle on life, the money earned by a successful artist could afford him access to alcohol, drugs, sex, and material possessions in excessive quantities. All people face this potential danger, but few have the economic capacity to truly indulge.

The manager must caution the artist to avoid a "materialistic rampage." Needless to say, this can be a very delicate area, but the manager must speak out if his artist's health or financial wellbeing is threatened, even if the artist himself is the adversary. In situations where the artist refuses to take counsel and continues on a destructive course, the manager must exercise extreme caution. Often, another successful artist or close family member or friend might be able to talk some sense into the out-of-control artist. If advice and persuasion fail, the manager should best leave a trail of paper to support his objections to the artist's damaging activity. If and when the inevitable crash does occur, an artist might start looking for a scapegoat. This is especially true of artists whose egos have obscured the facts. Not being able to accept responsibility for their actions, they're forced to find a guilty party to protect their inflated, do-no-wrong self-image.

Some situations may become so unbearable that the artist not only refuses to take the manager's advice, but begins to hold the manager in contempt as being an incompetent. For the experienced manager, this situation has only one solution—termination of his relationship with the artist. While the economic consequences can be painful, the manager must think about his future. If an artist has gotten totally out of control, cancelling engagements, refusing to record, and taking his public for granted, his conduct reflects directly on the manager's reputation. When everything has been done to salvage the artist's career, it's best to let the artist suffer the consequences of his own actions and avoid having *two* careers needlessly destroyed. Certainly, we're not suggesting that managers cut and run at the first sign of trouble. Loyalty and obligation come into play even in the worst of situations. However, if all else fails, the option of termination must be considered.

Another warning signal of a pending success crisis is complacency or laziness. The artist could be handling the emotional and financial aspects of a successful career, but fall into a far different trap. It's the "I've made it" attitude. In the entertainment business, an artist is only as successful as his accomplishments today. Yesterday doesn't count. One of the characteristics of the music business is the constant change of styles and tastes that lead to frequent star turnover. Unless the artist is ready for retirement, he must be prepared to work just as hard once success is achieved as he did earlier.

TOMORROW IS GUARANTEED
TO BE A NEW DAY

All too often an artist will have a hit record and believe there's no end to success. But this is a fallacy. You need only look at the current record charts to confirm this fact. How many new artists are included on the

Hot 100 now who weren't there a year ago? By the same token, the number of veteran artists who have sustained their careers is evidence that an artist can overcome change in styles and fads and retain and enhance his popularity and appeal.

Any artist who obtains a measure of success is well advised to be constantly aware of how to deal with the many dangers we've discussed. Whatever the fate of a particular artist, the entertainment business will continue, with or without him. Over the years, the industry has lost gigantic superstars because of death or self-imposed retirement, yet there's always been someone to fill the void. Contrary to what any number of ego-driven artists have thought over the years, no one is that important or that necessary. Music and life go on.

The financial rewards of a successful career, if handled properly, can provide lifelong compensation for a job well done. The accolades of the public can help the artist achieve the total self-fulfillment that few people ever have the opportunity to experience. Effective management, a realistic approach to fame and fortune, and common sense are the qualities every artist must master. Failure to adequately cope with sudden fame and unexpected fortune carries the seeds of professional and personal destruction.

23

Money Management

What exactly is money? It is generally defined as "anything that serves as a common measure of value, or as a means for the payment of debts or services rendered." "Save your money, spend it sparingly and wisely, work hard, and get to bed early," said Poor Richard.

Money provides much of the lure for seeking a career in the music industry. The accumulation of money affords the opportunity to fulfill needs, both physically and psychologically. But can we really ever have enough money to buy or obtain everything we may want in a lifetime? No! It's all relative to the earnings of an individual. The up-and-coming, starving artist wishes for enough money to pay his car note and guitar payment. The moderately successful artist is plagued with paying for a home, sports car, and a couple of guitars. The star who's earning plenty of money still has problems. By the time Uncle Sam takes his chunk, there's barely enough money left to make the payments on his three homes, four cars, and that sixteenth guitar he must have. No matter how much an artist makes, there will never be enough to satisfy an ever-increasing appetite, whether it be for more material possessions, financial security, or philanthropic and charitable causes.

There's an art to making money. Certainly, part of the purpose of this book is to help artist and manager obtain success, which is often measured, at least in part, by money. But earning it is just part of the problem. The greater challenge is *keeping* the money that a successful career has generated. The effective management of money requires at least as much talent as it took to make it in the first place.

The areas of money management can be divided into five areas: income/expense control; investments; tax planning; retirement; and estate planning.

INCOME/EXPENSE CONTROL

The Budget

A well thought-out budget is the first step to financial planning. It serves as a road map to one's financial future. Assuming expense and income budgets have been carefully prepared, several control devices should be implemented. An accounting system must be set up on a weekly, monthly, or quarterly basis to accurately record the income and expense flow of the artist. Many artists have unique accounting systems to fill this need. These "roadsheets" are the first line of financial record-keeping and are essential to maintaining an accurate financial picture of the artist's expenses.

Profit-and-Loss Statement and Balance Sheet

At the end of each accounting period (monthly, quarterly, semi-annually, or annually) the accountant should prepare a profit-and-loss statement and balance sheet. As stated earlier, the budget is analogous to a traveler viewing a road map before a trip. The profit-and-loss statement is the traveler's log of what has happened during the trip and a description of the exact route taken. The balance sheet is a picture of the artist's economic condition, assets, and liabilities at a given time. It's comparable to a photograph of the trip at a certain point. These three financial tools will provide the artist and manager with the basic information needed to maintain control over operating incomes and expenses. Of course, as the artist becomes more successful and his income increases, the accountant may want to implement additional procedures to keep a closer watch over the artist's financial well-being.

The manager's awareness of income and expenses becomes an extremely valuable tool when modifications have to be made in revenue inflows or outflows. For example, if the artist's popularity starts to fade, causing his engagement price to fall, the manager may want to implement cost-reduction procedures to insulate the artist from personal loss of income. Conversely, if the artist is making too much money, the manager may recommend increasing some expenses to help reduce net profit in order to put the artist in a lower tax bracket.

The same accounting procedures should be followed for the artist's personal earnings. Once the booking agent, manager, support crew, attorneys, publicist, travel costs, and other expenses have been paid, the artist will receive the balance. The amount of money earned by the artist should be controlled just as carefully as business earnings. The artist should maintain a personal budget, profit-and-loss statement, and balance sheet. Again, it makes it much easier to spot unnecessary economic drain and helps the artist be aware of where his money is going. Remember, no matter how much an artist makes, there's never enough for everything. The successful artist will have to establish some priorities. Once this is done, his cash outflow can follow a logical pattern instead of resembling an irrational spending spree.

Credit

Another important aspect of income-expense control is the proper utilization of credit. Used wisely, credit is a most valuable ally; uncontrolled credit, however, can result in harsh consequences.

A hypothetical story will help illustrate this point. A group of young artists had just made the transition from "weekend warriors" to full-time professional entertainers. Faced with considerable travel commitments, the group leader procured credit cards from every major oil company. The cards were used indiscriminately, depending on which dealer was the most convenient at the time fuel was needed. When the monthly statements arrived, it was easy to let them slide in lieu of more pressing expenses, such as salaries, motel bills, and equipment payments, since no one gas bill was that large. The following month the same procedure was repeated. After eight months, even though small payments had been made, the group realized they had a major bill confronting them. The group had been partially financing itself by using its gas credit cards. After a short period of time, the gas companies started revoking their cards and began instigating legal proceedings to collect the amounts due. This situation made it exceedingly difficult to get a bank loan to pay the accumulated debt.

Credit-card debt is fine for short-term financial help, but it's not a permanent or long-run solution. The artists could have avoided this embarrassing situation by seeking financial help from their banker in the beginning instead of waiting till their credit was nearly destroyed. Beware of credit-card debt.

The artist must also be cautious about the use of long-term bank debt or mortgage debt, both from a business and personal standpoint. The advice of an accountant, business advisor, or manager well-versed in business practices can be extremely useful in restraining the artist from overloading his debt position.

For the young artist, usually the reverse is true. He can't get enough financing to help develop his act due to the risky nature of the business. Here, too, the advice of a professional can be useful in helping the artist acquire the financing necessary to develop his career.

INVESTMENTS

The next major area of money management is investments. Almost everyone has some preconceived idea of what they'd like to do if they suddenly were wealthy. It might be oil investments, land, or stocks or bonds. The successful artist must realize that entertainment, by its very nature, is a feast-or-famine business that won't last forever. With this thought in mind, the artist would be wise to construct an investment portfolio to counteract the uncertainty of his career in entertainment. Of course, this is relative, depending on just how successful the artist has been and the amount of wealth he's accumulated.

Needless to say, the artist would be well advised to consider the assistance of an investment counselor. There are investment firms specializing in stock and bonds, real estate, or almost any other area of interest. The large lending institutions and insurance companies offer investment counseling to their customers. Whatever the choice, the artist should know what he wants from the investment: Guaranteed earnings? Diversification? Is he a risk averter or risk taker? What does the artist want his investments to do for him? Once those priorities are set, it is recommended that professional advice be sought, leading to a balanced investment portfolio.

TAX PLANNING

Closely linked to investments is tax planning. For artists in the high-income brackets, their investments are greatly influenced by their tax exposure. Investments that shelter income from taxes may be more attractive to some artists, even though the rate of return or potential profit margin is less than others.

Probably the greatest enemy of the successful artist is the Internal Revenue Service. However, this formidable adversary can be minimized by professional tax planning and money management. The advice of a certified public accountant or professional tax planner is absolutely necessary because of the ongoing and very technical changes in the tax laws.

Because most artists' income is concentrated in a limited time period, their potential for tax exposure is much greater than that of the normal individual. It's therefore imperative that as much of the earnings as possible be shielded from income-tax liability.

Tax avoidance is not tax evasion. In order to know exactly where the artist stands with the Internal Revenue Service, the services of an accountant should be used during all phases of the artist's career.

One of the most unfortunate situations that can occur is for an artist to finally achieve success, only to receive a visit from the IRS for back taxes due to filing improper income tax returns, or in some instances, failure to file any return. The artist and manager who bury their heads in the sand hoping that the IRS will go away are taking a foolhardy approach. No matter what amount of income the artist makes, he should file the proper tax returns. All supporting documents necessary to substantiate the tax return should be preserved. The importance of accurate record-keeping is magnified in light of a tax audit. The artist who maintains a good accounting system watched over by professionals is less likely to encounter problems with the tax authorities than the artist who disregards record-keeping and accounting altogether.

PLANNING FOR RETIREMENT

Also linked with investments, but extremely specialized in nature and serving a specific purpose, is a retirement plan for the artist. The investment portfolio can be constructed in such a way that certain investments will mature at a desired time, namely at retirement. On the other hand, investing with the primary purpose of retirement in mind would tend to limit investment opportunities. The artist should think of retirement as a specific part of his overall financial plan. Again, the advice of the accountant or investment counselor can be helpful in determining what can be expected from social security, union pension funds, or investments made specifically for retirement purposes. In addition, the artist's standard of living, dependents, and overall economic retirement needs should be analyzed. Based on these findings, a determination can be made regarding which course of action is necessary to provide the artist with an adequate retirement fund.

ESTATE PLANNING

Estate planning is the last major area of money management to be discussed. This area is concerned with the distribution of the artist's assets (after payment of all liabilities) to designated heirs. Unless an estate plan is implemented, the laws of the state in which the artist dies or where his property is located will dictate who will inherit his assets. The will is the legal instrument used to convey instructions regarding the distribution of the deceased party's assets. Failure to leave a will or write one properly can sometimes work terrible hardship on loved ones or cause serious economic consequences. By the use of the marital deduction, trusts, and other legal devices, sizeable amounts of money can be diverted from federal and state taxing authorities to family and friends. In addition to economic provisions, a properly drawn will can make provisions for guardianship of minor children, specific bequests, and other extraordinary transactions, such as gifts to charities.

The attorney drafting the artist's will should consult with the accountant and investment advisor in order to accumulate a complete set of facts about his client's economic picture and any special bequests. The will should be reviewed annually to determine if any modifications should be made due to changed circumstances. If the artist is married, it's advisable that the spouse also execute a will. Certain investments also can influence the estate plan. For instance, life insurance is frequently used to add liquidity to an estate. Joint ownership of properties, charitable donations, and gifts are a few of the other avenues available to the financial planner in structuring the estate.

SUCCESSFUL MONEY MANAGEMENT

The artist and manager should approach the financial or money management part of the overall plan with caution. This includes an awareness of the necessity of debt, its proper use and control, and keeping a watchful eye on the amount of debt and spending habits of the artist. The manager must maintain control over income and expense through "roadsheets," budgets, profit-and-loss statement, and balance sheet. It's also the manager's job to help the artist accumulate wealth. This is done by using the control devices just mentioned.

Once money is earned, the next concern of the artist and manager is to preserve it. Here the emphasis is on tax planning and sheltering.

Through investments, the artist's wealth should grow. The result should be sufficient funds to maintain a chosen lifestyle as well as an adequate retirement fund and a sizeable estate to help provide for loved ones. Accomplishing all of this is successful money management.

Superstardom:
What's Next?

The ultimate objective of every artist is to reach the status of "superstar." Many aspire to superstardom with mega-hit singles, streaks of hyper-popularity, and bursts of press and media attention, but in the end, few ever actually make it. A multitude of traps and barriers, along with the unpredictability of the public, can spell a sudden career stall despite the best efforts of an artist and manager to make the right moves up the career ladder. Superstardom is reserved only for the fortunate few who possess the rare combination of unique talent, artistic and business vision, single-minded drive, willingness to adapt and grow, and most importantly, blind luck.

To illustrate these points, we have selected a handful of consensus superstars who have put together careers that span at least a decade. With each name consider the early artistic years, the respective periods of dominance, the various phases their careers have gone through, their ability to diversify appeal and move into new areas, and their common ability to sustain that most elusive quality in show business—longevity. Just as business schools and law schools teach by the case method, so should managers and artists study the careers of superstars for patterns and examples that could be adapted for their own benefit. What qualities do Bruce Springsteen, Diana Ross, Donna Summer, Elton John, Kenny Rogers, Paul McCartney, Dolly Parton, Tom Petty, Michael Jackson, Rod Stewart, Cher, Aretha Franklin, and Madonna all share? Despite widely divergent styles and career paths, each has demonstrated the traits of vision, judgement, tenacity, and a willingness to change that matches the undeniable talent each possesses.

For those who have raw ability and choose to make a full-time commitment to persevering in the brutally competitive music world, we offer words of encouragement tempered by blunt pragmatism. Nobody has to be told that the dropout rate is high. However, we suspect that many people romanticize the business or underestimate the stress of irregular hours, constant traveling, seemingly endless rejection, and the fact that the entertainment business is no get-rich-quick proposition. Even for artists and managers with the talent and ability to do all the right things, there is still fierce competition for the available slots on record company and booking agency rosters. There is still an unending search for the hit song and the right publicity spin. Unfortunately, only a few artists ever get to experience a major record release or concert tour, much less sustain long-term superstardom.

Even after an artist convinces a record company, agent, publisher, and manager that his talents have the potential for being profitably marketed, success is still far from guaranteed. The artist and his team must still face the judgement of the public. And even then, a measure of public acclaim is not necessarily sufficient. To everyone but the hard-core fan, the artist is only as good as what he does today. Yesterdays seldom count. There's constant pressure to continue writing quality songs and keep producing hit records. Many can't stand up to the test and eventually fade back into obscurity.

Even for those who can meet the creative challenge, there are other barriers. While exceptions abound, age is still an ever-present adversary to the aspiring superstar. In many instances, the entertainment industry places a premium on youth: "You'd better make it today; tomorrow might be too late." The changing taste of the public is yet another trap that has ended many a search for superstardom. Then, as we've seen in an earlier chapter, success itself can be an artist's undoing. Too much glamour, fame, and money in too short a time can destroy the artist unable to cope with these elements of a "success crisis."

For those few fortunate artists who have achieved the artistic and financial fulfillment which accompanies superstardom, can there be any challenges remaining? Believe it or not, this can be a troubling question to one who's "done it all." In order to "make it," the superstar artist must have a special drive that allows him to keep going when others would give up. He must be a dreamer who seeks the unobtainable goal and is not afraid of attempting the impossible. Once the impossible is attained, there's a void. He has never been programmed to slow down or lay back. At this point, he needs new goals, new projects, and new directions for his life. The superstar artist's manager can play an important role in helping the artist begin this new stage. While such a situation can potentially present problems, it doesn't have to. The successful artist should appreciate that aspect of his life shared by only a few in this world: he has achieved total financial security. This, along with fame, maturity, and personal contacts, allows him to take his life in whatever direction he chooses. The best advice any manager could give to a client in this situation is simply, "Enjoy whatever you decide to do."

The alternatives available to the superstar are limitless. Many choose to keep on performing, recording, and writing. Their status gives them the freedom to expand artistically. They can choose the dates they want to play without giving primary emphasis to the money involved. They have more freedom of choice in the records they'll release and the songs they'll make and the songs they'll write. They can pace their careers to get more enjoyment out of the things they do rather than be controlled by the pressures of having to "make it."

Superstardom affords the artist the capability of getting involved as an entertainment entrepreneur. Many stars have successfully launched new record labels, motion picture productions, recording studios, publishing firms, booking agencies, and management companies. Others have used their fame and fortune in non-show-business ventures, including real estate and other investments. An artist's stature and financial stability also allow him to get involved in charities by giving benefit concerts or acting as a spokesman for a particular cause.

Many superstars use their financial security to develop themselves through other endeavors such as writing, lecturing, and travel. This also allows them the time to develop closer bonds with their families without the pressures of having to leave home for a tour or a recording date.

SUPERSTAR MANAGERS

We've seen how superstardom affects an artist and his career. We've also seen how the artist's success affects another very important person, his manager. The superstar success of the artist-client also translates into superstar status for the manager in business circles of the industry. Beyond financial rewards and respect for the manager by others in the entertainment industry, the superstar's manager can count on his client being a sure-fire drawing card for other promising artists seeking quality management. The old adage that "nothing succeeds like success" is certainly applicable to the career of the superstar manager.

Throughout the book we've stressed that entertainment is a business as sophisticated and complex as any other potentially lucrative endeavor. The artist striving to be tomorrow's superstar should never forget this. Apart from the financial reward and satisfaction that goes with achievement, the entertainment industry offers its participants a certain indefinable feeling that makes people do whatever is necessary just to experience it. Call it "Sawdust in Your Shoes" or the "Smell of Greasepaint and the Roar of the Crowd," but whatever it is, it gets in your blood, quickens your pulse, and makes all the headaches seem bearable. As any artist, manager, or other industry professional will undoubtedly tell you, "There's no business like show business."

APPENDIXES

APPENDIX I

American Federation of Musicians (AF of M) Agent-Musician Agreement

(Three Years or Less)

NOT FOR USE IN STATE OF CALIFORNIA

Name of Agent

Legal Name of Musician

Address of Agent

Professional Name of Musician

A.F.M. Booking Agent Number

Name of Musician's Orchestra or Group

Musician's A.F.M. Locals

This Agreement Begins on _____, 19____, and Ends on _____, 19____.

1. Scope of Agreement

Musician hereby employs Agent and Agent hereby accepts employment as Musician's exclusive booking agent, manager and representative throughout the world with respect to musician's services, appearances and endeavors as a musician. As used in this agreement "Musician" refers to the undersigned musician and to musicians performing with any orchestra or group which Musician leads or conducts and whom Musician shall make subject to the terms of this agreement; "A.F.M." refers to the American Federation of Musicians of the United States and Canada.

2. Duties of Agent

(a) Agent agrees to use reasonable efforts in the performance of the following duties: assist Musician in obtaining, obtain offers of, and negotiate, engagements for Musician; advise, aid, counsel and guide Musician with respect to Musician's professional career; promote and publicize Musician's name and talents; carry on business correspondence in Musician's behalf relating to Musician's professional career; cooperate with duly constituted and authorized representatives of Musician in the performance of such duties.

(b) Agent will maintain office, staff and facilities reasonably adequate for the rendition of such services.

(c) Agent will not accept any engagements for Musician without Musician's prior approval which shall not be unreasonably withheld.

(d) Agent shall fully comply with all applicable laws, rules and regulations of governmental authorities and secure such licenses as may be required for the rendition of services hereunder.

3. Rights of Agent

(a) Agent may render similar services to others and may engage in other businesses and ventures, subject, however, to the limitations imposed by 8 below.

(b) Musician will promptly refer to Agent all communications, written or oral, received by or on behalf of Musician relating to the services and appearances by Musician.

(c) Without Agent's written consent, Musician will not engage any other person, firm or corporation to perform the services to be performed by Agent hereunder (except that Musician may employ a personal manager) nor will Musician perform or appear professionally or offer so to do except through Agent.

(d) Agent may publicize the fact that Agent is the exclusive booking agent and representative for Musician.

(e) Agent shall have the right to use or to permit others to use Musician's name and likeness in advertising or publicity relating to Musician's services and appearances but without cost or expense to Musician unless Musician shall otherwise specifically agree in writing.

(f) In the event of Musician's breach of this agreement, Agent's sole right and remedy for such breach shall be the receipt from Musician of the commissions specified in this agreement, but only if, as, and when, Musician receives moneys or other consideration on which such commissions are payable hereunder.

4. Compensation of Agent

(a) In consideration of the services to be rendered by Agent hereunder, Musician agrees to pay to Agent commissions equal to the percentages, set forth below, of the gross moneys received by Musician, directly or indirectly, for each engagement on which commissions are payable hereunder:

(i) **Fifteen** per cent (15%) if the duration of the engagement is two (2) or more consecutive days per week.

(ii) **Twenty** per cent (20%) for Single Miscellaneous Engagements of one (1) day duration — each for a different employer in a different location.

(iii) In no event, however, shall the payment of any such commissions result in the retention by Musician for any engagement of net moneys or other consideration in an amount less than the applicable minimum scale of the A.F.M. or of any local thereof having jurisdiction over such engagement.

(iv) In no event shall the payment of any such commissions result in the receipt by Agent for any engagement of commissions, fees or other consideration, directly, or indirectly, from any person or persons, including the Musician, which in aggregate exceed the commissions provided for in this agreement. Any commission, fee, or other consideration received by Agent from any source other than Musician, directly or indirectly, on account of, as a result of, or in connection with supplying the services of Musician shall be reported to Musician and the amount thereof shall be deducted from the commissions payable by the Musician hereunder.

(b) Commissions shall become due and payable to Agent immediately following the receipt thereof by Musician or by anyone else in Musician's behalf.

(c) No commissions shall be payable on any engagement if Musician is not paid for such engagement irrespective of the reasons for such non-payment to Musician, including but not limited to non-payment by reason of the fault of Musician. This shall not preclude the awarding of damages by the International Executive Board to a booking agent to compensate him for actual expenses incurred as the direct result of the cancellation of an engagement when such cancellation was the fault of the member.

(d) Agent's commissions shall be payable on all moneys or other considerations received by Musician pursuant to contracts for engagements negotiated or entered into during the term of this agreement; **if specifically agreed to by Musician by initialing the margin hereof,** to contracts for engagements in existence at the commencement of the term hereof (excluding, however, any engagements as to which Musician is under prior obligation to pay commissions to another agent); and to any modifications, extensions and renewals thereof or substitutions therefor regardless of when Musician shall receive such moneys or other considerations.

(e) As used in this paragraph and elsewhere in this agreement the term "gross earnings" shall mean the gross amounts received by Musician for each engagement less costs and expenses incurred in collecting amounts due for any engagement, including costs of arbitration, litigation and attorney's fees.

(f) **If specifically agreed to by Musician by initialing the margin hereof, the following shall apply:**

(i) Musician shall advance to Agent against Agent's final commissions an amount not exceeding the following percentages of the gross amounts received for each engagement 15% on engagements of three (3) days or less; 10% on all other engagements.

(ii) If Musician shall so request and shall simultaneously furnish Agent with the data relating to deductions, the Agent within 45 days following the end of each 12 months period during the term of this agreement and within 45 days following the termination of this Agreement, shall account to and furnish Musician with a detailed statement itemizing the gross amounts received for all engagements during the period to which such accounting relates, the moneys or other considerations upon which Agent's commissions are based, and the amount of Agent's commissions resulting from such computations. Upon request, a copy of such statement shall be furnished promptly to the Office of the President of the A.F.M.

(iii) Any balances owed by or to the parties shall be paid as follows: by the Agent at the time of rendering such statement; by the Musician within 30 days after receipt of such statement.

5. Duration and Termination of Agreement

(a) The term of this agreement shall be as stated in the opening heading hereof, subject to termination as provided in 5 (b), 6 and 10 below.

(b) In addition to termination pursuant to other provisions of this agreement, this agreement may be terminated by either party, by notice as provided below, if Musician

(i) is unemployed for four (4) consecutive weeks at any time during the term hereof; or

(ii) does not obtain employment for at least twenty (20) cumulative weeks of engagements to be performed during each of the first and second six (6) months periods during the term hereof; or

(iii) does not obtain employment for at least forty (40) cumulative weeks of engagements to be performed during each subsequent year of the term hereof.

(c) Notice of such termination shall be given by certified mail addressed to the addressee at his last known address and a copy thereof shall be sent to the A.F.M. Such termination shall be effective as of the date of mailing of such notice if and when approved by the A.F.M. Such notice shall be mailed no later than two (2) weeks following the occurrence of any event described in (i) above: two (2) weeks following a period in excess of thirteen (13) of the cumulative weeks of unemployment specified in (ii) above; and two (2) weeks following a period in excess of twenty-six (26) of the cumulative weeks of unemployment specified in (iii) above. Failure to give notice as aforesaid shall constitute a waiver of the right to terminate based upon the happening of such prior events.

(d) Musician's disability resulting in failure to perform engagements and Musician's unreasonable refusal to accept and perform engagements shall not by themselves either deprive Agent of its right to or give Musician the right to terminate (as provided in (b) above).

(e) As used in this agreement, a "week" shall commence on Sunday and terminate on Saturday. A "week of engagements" shall mean any one of the following:

(i) a week during which Musician is to perform on at least four (4) days; or

(ii) a week during which Musician's gross earnings equals or exceeds the lowest such gross earnings obtained by Musician for performances rendered during any one of the immediately preceding six (6) weeks; or

(iii) a week during which Musician is to perform engagements on commercial television or radio or in concert for compensation equal at least to three (3) times the minimum scales of the A.F.M. or of any local thereof having jurisdiction applicable to such engagements.

6. Agent's Maintenance of A.F.M. Booking Agent Agreement

Agent represents that Agent is presently a party to an A.F.M. Booking Agent Agreement which is in full force and effect. If such A.F.M. Booking Agent Agreement shall terminate, the rights of the parties hereunder shall be governed by the terms and conditions of said Booking Agent Agreement relating to the effect of termination of such agreements which are incorporated herein by reference.

7. No other Agreements

This is the only and the complete agreement between the parties relating to all or any part of the subject matter covered by this agreement.* There is no other agreement, arrangement or participation between the parties, nor do the parties stand in any relationship to each other which is not created by this agreement,* whereby the terms and conditions of this agreement are avoided or evaded, directly or indirectly, such as, by way of example but not limitation, contracts, arrangements, relationships or participations relating to publicity services, business management, personal management, music publishing, or instruction.

* (A.F.M. Personal Management Agreement Excepted.)

8. Incorporation of A.F.M. Bylaws, etc.

There are incorporated into and made part of this agreement, as though fully set forth herein, the present and future provisions of the Bylaws, Rules, Regulations and Resolutions of the A.F.M. and those of its locals which do not conflict therewith. The parties acknowledge their responsibility to be fully acquainted, now and for the duration of this agreement, with the contents thereof.

9. Submission and Determination of Disputes

Every claim, dispute, controversy or difference arising out of, dealing with, relating to, or affecting the interpretation or application of this agreement, or the violation or breach, or the threatened violation or breach thereof shall be submitted, heard and determined by the International Executive Board of the A.F.M., in accordance with the rules of such Board (regardless of the termination or purported termination of this agreement or of the Agent's A.F.M. Booking Agent Agreement), and such determination shall be conclusive, final and binding on the parties.

10. No Assignment of this Agreement

This agreement shall be personal to the parties and shall not be transferable or assignable by operation of law or otherwise without the prior consent of the Musician and of the A.F.M. The obligations imposed by this agreement shall be binding upon the parties. The Musician may terminate this agreement at any time within ninety (90) days after the transfer of a controlling interest in the Agent.

11. Negotiation for Renewal

Neither party shall enter into negotiations for or agree to the renewal or extension of this agreement prior to the beginning of the final year of the term hereof.

12. Approval by A.F.M.

This agreement shall not become effective unless, within thirty (30) days following its execution, an executed copy thereof is filed with and is thereafter approved in writing by the A.F.M.

IN WITNESS WHEREOF, the parties hereto have executed this agreement the_____day of_____,
19_____.

_____	_____
Agent	Musician
By _____	_____
Title or Capacity	Residence Address
	_____
	City State Zip Code

Agent Representing No More Than Two Clients

If specifically agreed to by the parties by signing below:

(a) Agent warrants and represents that Agent presently serves, and Agent agrees that during the term hereof Agent will restrict its activities to serving, as booking agent, or manager, or representative, no more than one other musical soloist, orchestra, band or performing group. If such warranty and representation is untrue, this agreement is null and void. If such agreement is broken, this agreement shall automatically terminate.

(b) In consideration thereof, the parties agree that the provisions of 4(a) (i) and (ii) and 4(f) above shall be inapplicable and that the compensation of Agent shall be as set forth in Schedule 1 attached. In no event, however, shall the payment of any commission result in the retention by Musician for any engagement of net moneys or other consideration in an amount less than the applicable minimum scale of the A.F.M. or of any local thereof.

_____	_____
Agent	Musician
By _____	
Title or Capacity	

APPENDIX 2

AF of M Performance Contract (Local Engagements)

FOR LOCAL ENGAGEMENTS ONLY
(NOT FOR USE IN CANADA)

Whenever The Term "The Local Union" Is Used In This Contract, It Shall Mean Local Union No. _____ Of The Federation.

THIS CONTRACT for the personal services of musicians on the engagement described below is made this _____ day of _____, 19___, between the undersigned purchaser of music (herein called "Purchaser") and the undersigned musician or musicians.

1. Name and Address of Place of Engagement: _____

   Name of Band or Group: _____

   Number of Musicians: _____ Number of Vocalists: _____

2. Date(s) of Engagement; daily or weekly schedule and daily clock hours: _____

3. Type of Engagement (specify whether dance, stage show, banquet, etc.): _____

4. Compensation Agreed Upon: $_____
   (Amount and Terms)

5. Purchaser Will Make Payments As Follows: _____
   (Specify when payments are to be made)

6. No performance on the engagement shall be recorded, reproduced or transmitted from the place of performance, in any manner or by any means whatsoever, in the absence of a specific written agreement with the Federation relating to and permitting such recording, reproduction or transmission. This prohibition shall not be subject to the arbitration provisions set forth in 8 below and the Federation may enforce this prohibition in any court of competent jurisdiction.

7. This contract, and the terms and conditions contained herein, may be enforced by the Purchaser, and its agents, and by each musician who is a party to this contract or whose name appears on the contract or who has, in fact, performed the engagement contracted for (herein called "participating musician(s)"), and by the agent or agent(s) of each participating musician, including the Local Union. It is expressly understood by the Purchaser and the musician(s) who are parties to this contract that neither the Federation nor the Local Union are parties to this contract in any capacity except as expressly provided in 6 above and, therefore, that neither the Federation nor the Local Union shall be liable for the performance or breach of any provision hereof.

8. A representative of the Local Union shall have access to the place of engagement covered by this contract for purposes of communicating with the musician(s) performing the engagement and the Purchaser.

9. Resolution of controversies or claims: Any controversy or claim arising out of or relating to this contract, or breach thereof, shall be submitted to arbitration under one of the following procedures to be selected by the purchaser at the time that this contract is signed, by placing his or her initials in the box adjacent to the procedure selected. In the event that neither box is initialed, it will be presumed that the purchaser has chosen the procedures set forth in "B":

(Continued on reverse side)

IN WITNESS WHEREOF, the parties hereto have hereunto set their names and seals on the day and year first above written.

| Print Purchaser's Full and Correct Name (If Purchaser is Corporation, Full and Correct Corporate Name) | Print Name of Signatory Musician | Home Local Union No. |

X _____ **X** _____
Signature of Purchaser (or Agent thereof)   Signature of Signatory Musician

_____   _____
Street Address   Musician's Home Address

City   State   Zip Code   City   State   Zip Code

_____   _____
Telephone   Telephone

Booking Agent   Agreement No.   Address

A. **(American Arbitration Association)** Any controversy or claim arising out of or relating to this contract, or breach thereof, shall be settled by arbitration in accordance with the Commercial Arbitration Rules of the American Arbitration Association, and judgment upon the Award rendered may be entered in any court having jurisdiction thereof. The cost of the arbitration proceeding, except those costs personally incurred by the parties hereto for the presentation of their own case, shall be shared equally by the Purchaser and the Signatory Musician(s).

B. **(Local Union)** Any controversy or claim arising out of or relating to this contract, or the breach thereof, shall be settled by arbitration by the Executive Board or other body of the Local Union charged with the responsibility of settling such controversy or claim. All rulings and awards made by the Local Union in arbitration hereunder may be appealed to the International Executive Board of the Federation (herein called "IEB") by any party who was a participant therein. Appeals from such proceedings shall be perfected in the manner provided in the Rules of Practice and Procedure of the IEB in effect at the time of such appeal. All rulings and awards made by the Local Union in arbitration which are not appealed to the IEB shall be final and binding upon the Purchaser and participating musician(s) and all rulings and awards made by the IEB on appeal shall be final and binding upon the Purchaser and participating musician(s). Any party to an arbitration proceeding before the Local Union or to an arbitration appeal to the IEB may bring an action to confirm or enforce a final determination and award of the Local Union or, if appealed, of the IEB in the courts of the jurisdiction in which the office of the Local Union is located; and the Purchaser and participating musician(s) agree to submit to the jurisdiction of such court or courts for that purpose.

10. ADDITIONAL PROVISIONS: _____

_____
_____
_____
_____

Names of All Musicians	Local Union No.	U.S. Social Security Numbers	Direct Pay
			$

(IF ADDITIONAL SPACE IS NEEDED, ADD SEPARATE SHEET(S).)   (Form L-1)

APPENDIX 3

AF of M Performance Contract (Touring)

FOR TRAVELING ENGAGEMENTS ONLY

Whenever The Term "The Local Union" Is Used In This Contract, It Shall Mean Local Union No. _____ Of The Federation With Jurisdiction Over The Territory In Which The Engagement Covered Is To Be Performed.

THIS CONTRACT for the personal services of musicians on the engagement described below is made this _____ day of _____, 19 _____, between the undersigned purchaser of music (herein called "Purchaser") and the undersigned musician or musicians.

1. Name and Address of Place of Engagement: _____

   Name of Band or Group: _____

   Number of Musicians: _____   Number of Vocalists: _____

2. Date(s) of Engagement; daily or weekly schedule and daily clock hours:

   _____

3. Type of Engagement (specify whether dance, stage show, banquet, etc.): _____

4. Compensation Agreed Upon: $ _____
   (Amount and Terms)

5. Purchaser Will Make Payments As Follows: _____
   (Specify when payments are to be made)

_____ (Continued on reverse side) _____

IN WITNESS WHEREOF, the parties hereto have hereunto set their names and seals on the day and year first above written.

| Print Purchaser's Full and Correct Name (If Purchaser is Corporation, Full and Correct Corporate Name) | Print Name of Signatory Musician | Home Local Union No. |

X _____   **X** _____

| Signature of Purchaser (or Agent thereof) | Signature of Signatory Musician |

| Street Address | Musician's Home Address |

| City | State | Zip Code | City | State | Zip Code |

| Telephone | Telephone |

| Booking Agent | Agreement No. | Address to Which Official Communications Should Be Sent to Signatory Musician |

| Address | |

Names of All Musicians	Local Union No.	U.S. Social Security Nos.	Direct Pay
			$

6. No performance on the engagement shall be recorded, reproduced or transmitted from the place of performance, in any manner or by any means whatsoever, in the absence of a specific written agreement with the Federation relating to and permitting such recording, reproduction or transmission.

7. It is expressly understood by the Purchaser and the musician(s) who are parties to this contract that neither the Federation nor the Local Union are parties to this contract in any capacity except as expressly provided in 6 above and, therefore, that neither the Federation nor the Local Union shall be liable for the performance or breach of any provision hereof.

8. A representative of the Local Union, or the Federation, shall have access to the place of engagement covered by this contract for purposes of communicating with the musician(s) performing the engagement and the Purchaser.

Appendixes

9. The agreement of the musicians to perform is subject to proven detention by sickness, accidents, riots, strikes, epidemics, acts of God, or any other legitimate conditions beyond their control.

10. ADDITIONAL PROVISIONS:_____

Names of All Musicians	Local Union No.	U.S. Social Security Nos.	Direct Pay
			$

(IF ADDITIONAL SPACE IS NEEDED, ADD SEPARATE SHEET (S).)   (Form T-2)

APPENDIX 4

American Society of Composers, Authors and Publishers (ASCAP) Writer Agreement

AGREEMENT made between the Undersigned (for brevity called *"Owner"*) and the AMERICAN SOCIETY OF COMPOSERS, AUTHORS AND PUBLISHERS (for brevity called *"Society"*), in consideration of the premises and of the mutual covenants hereinafter contained, as follows:

1. The *Owner* grants to the *Society* for the term hereof, the right to license non-dramatic public performances (as hereinafter defined), of each musical work:

Of which the *Owner* is a copyright proprietor; or

Which the *Owner*, alone, or jointly, or in collaboration with others, wrote, composed, published, acquired or owned; or

In which the *Owner* now has any right, title, interest or control whatsoever, in whole or in part; or

Which hereafter, during the term hereof, may be written, composed, acquired, owned, published or copyrighted by the *Owner*, alone, jointly or in collaboration with others; or

In which the *Owner* may hereafter, during the term hereof, have any right, title, interest or control, whatsoever, in whole or in part.

The right to license the public performance of every such musical work shall be deemed granted to the *Society* by this instrument for the term hereof, immediately upon the work being written, composed, acquired, owned, published or copyrighted.

The rights hereby granted shall include:

(a) All the rights and remedies for enforcing the copyright or copyrights of such musical works, whether such copyrights are in the name of the *Owner* and/or others, as well as the right to sue under such copyrights in the name of the *Society* and/or in the name of the *Owner* and/or others, to the end that the *Society* may effectively protect and be assured of all the rights hereby granted.

(b) The non-exclusive right of public performance of the separate numbers, songs, fragments or arrangements, melodies or selections forming part or parts of musical plays and dramatico-musical compositions, the *Owner* reserving and excepting from this grant the right of performance of musical plays and dramatico-musical compositions in their entirety, or any part of such plays or dramatico-musical compositions on the legitimate stage.

(c) The non-exclusive right of public performance by means of radio broadcasting, telephony, "wired wireless," all forms of synchronism with motion pictures, and/or any method of transmitting sound other than television broadcasting.

(d) The non-exclusive right of public performance by television broadcasting; provided, however, that:

(i) This grant does not extend to or include the right to license the public performance by television broadcasting or otherwise of any rendition or performance of (a) any opera, operetta, musical comedy, play or like production, as such, in whole or in part, or (b) any composition from any opera, operetta, musical comedy, play or like production (whether or not such opera, operetta, musical comedy, play or like production was presented on the stage or in motion picture form) in a manner which recreates the performance of such composition with substantially such distinctive scenery or costume as was used in the presentation of such opera, operetta, musical comedy, play or like production (whether or not such opera, operetta, musical comedy, play or like production was presented on the stage or in motion picture form): provided, however, that the rights hereby granted shall be deemed to include a grant of the right to license non-dramatic performances of compositions by television broadcasting of a motion picture containing such composition if the rights in such motion picture other than those granted hereby have been obtained from the parties in interest.

(ii) Nothing herein contained shall be deemed to grant the right to license the public performance by television broadcasting of dramatic performances. Any performance of a separate musical composition which is not a dramatic performance, as defined herein, shall be deemed to be a non-dramatic performance. For the purposes of this agreement, a dramatic performance shall mean a performance of a musical composition on a television program in which there is a definite plot depicted by action and where the performance of the musical composition is woven into and carries forward the plot and its accompanying action. The use of dialogue to establish a mere program format or the use of any non-dramatic device merely to introduce a performance of a composition shall not be deemed to make such performance dramatic.

(iii) The definition of the terms "dramatic" and "non-dramatic" performances contain.d herein are purely for the purposes of this agreement and for the term thereof and shall not be binding upon or prejudicial to any position taken by either of us subsequent to the term hereof or for any purpose other than this agreement.

(e) The *Owner* may at any time and from time to time, in good faith, restrict the radio or television broadcasting of compositions from musical comedies, operas, operettas and motion pictures, or any other composition being excessively broadcast, only for the purpose of preventing harmful effect upon such musical comedies, operas, operettas, motion pictures or compositions, in respect of other interests under the copyrights thereof; provided, however, that the right to grant limited licenses will be given, upon application, as to restricted compositions, if and when the *Owner* is unable to show reasonable hazards to his or its major interests likely to result from such radio or television broadcasting; and provided further that such right to restrict any such composition shall not be exercised for the purpose of permitting the fixing or regulating of fees for the recording or transcribing of such composition, and provided further that in no case shall any charges, "free plugs", or other consideration be required in respect of any permission granted to perform a restricted composition; and provided further that in no event shall any composition, after the initial radio or television broadcast thereof, be restricted for the purpose of confining further radio or television broadcasts thereof to a particular artist, station, network or program. The *Owner* may also at any time and from time to time, in good faith, restrict the radio or television broadcasting of any composition, as to which any suit has been brought or threatened on a claim that such composition infringes a composition not contained in the repertory of *Society* or on a claim by a non-member of *Society* that *Society* does not have the right to license the public performance of such composition by radio or television broadcasting.

2. The term of this agreement shall be for a period commencing on the date hereof and expiring on the 31st day of December, 1995.

3. The *Society* agrees, during the term hereof, in good faith to use its best endeavors to promote and carry out the objects for which it was organized, and to hold and apply all royalties, profits, benefits and advantages arising from the exploitation of the rights assigned to it by its several members, including the *Owner*, to the uses and purposes as provided in its Articles of Association (which are hereby incorporated by reference), as now in force or as hereafter amended

4. The *Owner* hereby irrevocably, during the term hereof, authorizes, empowers and vests in the *Society* the right to enforce and protect such rights of public performance under any and all copyrights, whether standing in the name of the *Owner* and/or others, in any and all works copyrighted by the *Owner*, and/or by others; to prevent the infringement thereof, to litigate, collect and receipt for damages arising from infringement, and in its sole judgment to join the *Owner* and/or others in whose names the copyright may stand, as parties plaintiff or defendants in suits or proceedings; to bring suit in the name of the *Owner* and/or in the name of the *Society*, or others in whose name the copyright may stand, or otherwise, and to release, compromise, or refer to arbitration any actions, in the same manner and to the same extent and to all intents and purposes as the *Owner* might or could do, had this instrument not been made.

5. The *Owner* hereby makes, constitutes and appoints the *Society*, or its successor, the *Owner's* true and lawful attorney, irrevocably during the term hereof, and in the name of the *Society* or its successor, or in the name of the *Owner*, or otherwise, to do all acts, take all proceedings, execute, acknowledge and deliver any and all instruments, papers, documents, process and pleadings that may be necessary, proper or expedient to restrain infringements and recover damages in respect to or for the infringement or other violation of the rights of public performance in such works, and to discontinue, compromise or refer to arbitration any such proceedings or actions, or to make any other disposition of the differences in relation to the premises.

6. The *Owner* agrees from time to time, to execute, acknowledge and deliver to the *Society*, such assurances, powers of attorney or other authorizations or instruments as the *Society* may deem necessary or expedient to enable it to exercise, enjoy and enforce, in its own name or otherwise, all rights and remedies aforesaid.

7. It is mutually agreed that during the term hereof the Board of Directors of the *Society* shall be composed of an equal number of writers and publishers respectively, and that the royalties distributed by the Board of Directors shall be divided into two (2) equal sums, and one (1) each of such sums credited respectively to and for division amongst (a) the writer members, and (b) the publisher members, in accordance with the system of distribution and classification as determined by the Classification Committee of each group, in accordance with the Articles of Association as they may be amended from time to time, except that the classification of the *Owner* within his class may be changed.

8. The *Owner* agrees that his classification in the *Society* as determined from time to time by the Classification Committee of his group and/or The Board of Directors of the *Society*, in case of appeal by him, shall be final, conclusive and binding upon him.

The *Society* shall have the right to transfer the right of review of any classification from the Board of Directors to any other agency or instrumentality that in its discretion and good judgment it deems best adapted to assuring to the *Society's* membership a just, fair, equitable and accurate classification.

The *Society* shall have the right to adopt from time to time such systems, means, methods and formulae for the establishment of a member's status in respect of classification as will assure a fair, just and equitable distribution of royalties among the membership.

9. **"Public Performance" Defined.** The term *"public performance"* shall be construed to mean vocal, instrumental and/or mechanical renditions and representations in any manner or by any method whatsoever, including transmissions by radio and television broadcasting stations, transmission by telephony and/or "wired wireless"; and/or reproductions of performances and renditions by means of devices for reproducing sound recorded in synchronism or timed relation with the taking of motion pictures.

10. **"Musical Works" Defined.** The phrase *"musical works"* shall be construed to mean musical compositions and dramatico-musical compositions, the words and music thereof, and the respective arrangements thereof, and the selections therefrom.

11. The powers, rights, authorities and privileges by this instrument vested in the *Society*, are deemed to include the World, provided, however, that such grant of rights for foreign countries shall be subject to any agreements now in effect, a list of which are noted on the reverse side hereof.

12. The grant made herein by the owner is modified by and subject to the provisions of (a) the Amended Final Judgment (Civil Action No. 13-95) dated March 14, 1950 in U. S. A. v. ASCAP as further amended by Order dated January 7, 1960, (b) the Final Judgment (Civil Action No. 42-245) in U. S. A. v. ASCAP, dated March 14, 1950, and (c) the provisions of the Articles of Association and resolutions of the Board of Directors adopted pursuant to such judgments and order.

SIGNED, SEALED AND DELIVERED, on this.....................day of.., 19........

Owner $\left\{ \begin{array}{l} \text{..} \\ \text{..} \end{array} \right.$

Society $\left\{ \begin{array}{l} \text{AMERICAN SOCIETY OF COMPOSERS,} \\ \text{AUTHORS AND PUBLISHERS,} \\ \\ \text{By ....} \\ \text{President} \end{array} \right.$

APPENDIX 5

Broadcast Music, Inc. (BMI) Writer Agreement

Dear

The following shall constitute the agreement between us:

1. As used in this agreement:

(a) The word "period" shall mean the term from _____ to _____ , and continuing thereafter for additional terms of two years each unless terminated by either party at the end of said initial term or any additional term, upon notice by registered or certified mail not more than six months or less than sixty (60) days prior to the end of any such term.

(b) The word "works" shall mean:

(i) All musical compositions (including the musical segments and individual compositions written for a dramatic or dramatico-musical work) composed by you alone or with one or more collaborators during the period; and

(ii) All musical compositions (including the musical segments and individual compositions written for a dramatic or dramatico-musical work) composed by you alone or with one or more collaborators prior to the period, except those in which there is an outstanding grant of the right of public performance to a person other than a publisher affiliated with BMI.

2. You agree that:

(a) Within ten (10) days after the execution of this agreement you will furnish to us two copies of a completed clearance sheet in the form supplied by us with respect to each work heretofore composed by you which has been published in printed copies or recorded commercially or which is being currently performed or which you consider as likely to be performed.

(b) In each instance that a work for which clearance sheets have not been submitted to us pursuant to sub-paragraph (a) hereof is published in printed copies or recorded commercially or in synchronization with film or tape or is considered by you as likely to be performed, whether such work is composed prior to the execution of this agreement or hereafter during the period, you will promptly furnish to us two copies of a completed clearance sheet in the form supplied by us with respect to each such work.

(c) If requested by us in writing, you will promptly furnish to us a legible lead sheet or other written or printed copy of a work.

3. The submission of clearance sheets pursuant to paragraph 2 hereof shall constitute a warranty by you that all of the information contained thereon is true and correct and that no performing rights in such work have been granted to or reserved by others except as specifically set forth therein in connection with works heretofore written or co-written by you.

4. Except as otherwise provided herein, you hereby grant to us for the period:

(a) All the rights that you own or acquire publicly to perform, and to license others to perform, anywhere in the world, any part or all of the works.

(b) The non-exclusive right to record, and to license others to record, any part or all of any of the works on electrical transcriptions, wire, tape, film or otherwise, but only for the purpose of performing such work publicly by means of radio and television or for archive or audition purposes and not for sale to the public or for synchronization (i) with motion pictures intended primarily for theatrical exhibition or (ii) with programs distributed by means of syndication to broadcasting stations.

(c) The non-exclusive right to adapt or arrange any part or all of any of the works for performance purposes, and to license others to do so.

5. (a) The rights granted to us by sub-paragraph (a) of paragraph 4 hereof shall not include the right to perform or license the performance of more than one song or aria from a dramatic or dramatico-musical work which is an opera, operetta, or musical show or more than five minutes from a dramatic or dramatico-musical work which is a ballet if such performance is accompanied by the dramatic action, costumes or scenery of that dramatic or dramatico-musical work.

(b) You, together with the publisher and your collaborators, if any, shall have the right jointly, by written notice to us, to exclude from the grant made by sub-paragraph (a) of paragraph 4 hereof performances of works comprising more than thirty minutes of a dramatic or dramatico-musical work, but this right shall not apply to such performances from (i) a score originally written for and performed as part of a theatrical or television film, (ii) a score originally written for and performed as part of a radio or television program, or (iii) the original cast, sound track or similar album of a dramatic or dramatico-musical work.

✫ 245 ✫

(c) You retain the right to issue non-exclusive licenses for performances of a work or works (other than to another performing rights licensing organization), provided that within ten (10) days of the issuance of such license we are given written notice of the titles of the works and the nature of the performances so licensed by you.

6. (a) As full consideration for all rights granted to us hereunder and as security therefor, we agree to pay to you, with respect to each of the works in which we obtain and retain performing rights during the period:

(i) For performances of a work on broadcasting stations in the United States, its territories and possessions, amounts calculated pursuant to our then current standard practices upon the basis of the then current performance rates generally paid by us to our affiliated writers for similar performances of similar compositions. The number of performances for which you shall be entitled to payment shall be estimated by us in accordance with our then current system of computing the number of such performances.

It is acknowledged that we license the works of our affiliates for performance by non-broadcasting means, but that unless and until such time as feasible methods can be devised for tabulation of and payment for such performances, payment will be based solely on broadcast performances. In the event that during the period we shall establish a system of separate payment for non-broadcasting performances, we shall pay you upon the basis of the then current performance rates generally paid by us to our other affiliated writers for similar performances of similar compositions.

(ii) In the case of a work composed by you with one or more collaborators, the sum payable to you hereunder shall be a pro rata share, determined on the basis of the number of collaborators, unless you shall have transmitted to us a copy of an agreement between you and your collaborators providing for a different division of payment.

(iii) All monies received by us from any performing rights licensing organization outside of the United States, its territories and possessions, which are designated by such performing rights licensing organization as the author's share of foreign performance royalties earned by your works after the deduction of our then current handling charge applicable to our affiliated writers.

(b) We shall have no obligation to make payment hereunder with respect to (i) any performance of a work which occurs prior to the date on which we have received from you all of the information and material with respect to such work which is referred to in paragraphs 2 and 3 hereof, or (ii) any performance as to which a direct license as described in sub-paragraph (c) of paragraph 5 hereof has been granted by you, your collaborator or publisher.

7. We will furnish statements to you at least twice during each year of the period showing the number of performances as computed pursuant to sub-paragraph (a) (i) of paragraph 6 hereof and at least once during each year of the period showing the monies due pursuant to sub-paragraph (a) (iii) of paragraph 6 hereof. Each statement shall be accompanied by payment to you, subject to all proper deductions for advances, if any, of the sum thereby shown to be due for such performances.

8. (a) Nothing in this agreement requires us to continue to license the works subsequent to the termination of this agreement. In the event that we continue to license any or all of the works, however, we shall continue to make payments to you for so long as you do not make or purport to make directly or indirectly any grant of performing rights in such works to any other licensing organization. The amounts of such payments shall be calculated pursuant to our then current standard practices upon the basis of the then current performance rates generally paid by us to our affiliated writers for similar performances of similar compositions. You agree to notify us by registered or certified mail of any grant or purported grant by you directly or indirectly of performing rights to any other performing rights organization within ten (10) days from the making of such grant or purported grant and if you fail so to inform us thereof and we make payments to you for any period after the making of any such grant or purported grant, you agree to repay to us all amounts so paid by us promptly on demand. In addition, if we inquire of you by registered or certified mail, addressed to your last known address, whether you have made any such grant or purported grant and you fail to confirm to us by registered or certified mail within thirty (30) days of the mailing of such inquiry that you have not made any such grant or purported grant, we may, from and after such date, discontinue making any payments to you.

(b) Our obligation to continue payment to you after the termination of this agreement for performances outside of the United States, its territories and possessions shall be dependent upon our receipt in the United States of payments designated by foreign performing rights organizations as the author's share of foreign performance royalties earned by your works. Payment of such foreign royalties shall be subject to deduction of our then current handling charge applicable to our affiliated writers.

(c) In the event that we have reason to believe that you will receive or are receiving payment from a performing rights licensing organization other than BMI for or based on United States performances of one or more of your works during a period when such works were licensed by us pursuant to this agreement, we shall have the right to withhold payment for such performances from you until receipt of evidence satisfactory to us of the amount so paid to you by such other organization or that you have not been so paid. In the event that you have been so paid, the monies payable by us to you for such performances during such period shall be reduced by the amount of the payment from such other organization. In the event that you do not supply such evidence within eighteen (18) months from the date of our request therefor, we shall be under no obligation to make any payment to you for performances of such works during such period.

9. In the event that this agreement shall terminate at a time when, after crediting all earnings reflected by statements rendered to you prior to the effective date of such termination, there remains an unearned balance of

advances paid to you by us, such termination shall not be effective until the close of the calendar quarterly period during which (a) you shall repay such unearned balance of advances, or (b) you shall notify us by registered or certified mail that you have received a statement rendered by us at our normal accounting time showing that such unearned balance of advances has been fully recouped by us.

10. You warrant and represent that you have the right to enter into this agreement; that you are not bound by any prior commitments which conflict with your commitments hereunder; that each of the works, composed by you alone or with one or more collaborators, is original; and that exercise of the rights granted by you herein will not constitute an infringement of copyright or violation of any other right of, or unfair competition with, any person, firm or corporation. You agree to indemnify and hold harmless us and our licensees from and against any and all loss or damage resulting from any claim of whatever nature arising from or in connection with the exercise of any of the rights granted by you in this agreement. Upon notification to us or any of our licensees of a claim with respect to any of the works, we shall have the right to exclude such work from this agreement and/or to withhold payment of all sums which become due pursuant to this agreement or any modification thereof until receipt of satisfactory written evidence that such claim has been withdrawn, settled or adjudicated.

11. (a) We shall have the right, upon written notice to you, to exclude from this agreement, at any time, any work which in our opinion (i) is similar to a previously existing composition and might constitute a copyright infringement, or (ii) has a title or music or lyric similar to that of a previously existing composition and might lead to a claim of unfair competition, or (iii) is offensive, in bad taste or against public morals, or (iv) is not reasonably suitable for performance.

(b) In the case of works which in our opinion are based on compositions in the public domain, we shall have the right, upon written notice to you, either (i) to exclude any such work from this agreement, or (ii) to classify any such work as entitled to receive only a fraction of the full credit that would otherwise be given for performances thereof.

(c) In the event that any work is excluded from this agreement pursuant to paragraph 10 or sub-paragraph (a) or (b) of this paragraph 11, all rights in such work shall automatically revert to you ten (10) days after the date of our notice to you of such exclusion. In the event that a work is classified for less than full credit under sub-paragraph (b) (ii) of this paragraph 11, you shall have the right, by giving notice to us, within ten (10) days after the date of our letter advising you of the credit allocated to the work, to terminate our rights therein, and all rights in such work shall thereupon revert to you.

12. In each instance that you write, or are employed or commissioned by a motion picture producer to write, during the period, all or part of the score of a motion picture intended primarily for exhibition in theaters, or by the producer of a musical show or revue for the legitimate stage to write, during the period, all or part of the musical compositions contained therein, we agree to advise the producer of the film that such part of the score as is written by you may be performed as part of the exhibition of said film in theaters in the United States, its territories and possessions, without compensation to us, or to the producer of the musical show or revue that your compositions embodied therein may be performed on the stage with living artists as part of such musical show or revue, without compensation to us. In the event that we notify you that we have established a system for the collection of royalties for performance of the scores of motion picture films in theaters in the United States, its territories and possessions, we shall no longer be obligated to take such action with respect to motion picture scores.

13. You make, constitute and appoint us, or our nominee, your true and lawful attorney, irrevocably during the term hereof, in our name or that of our nominee, or in your name, or otherwise, to do all acts, take all proceedings, execute, acknowledge and deliver any and all instruments, papers, documents, process or pleadings that may be necessary, proper or expedient to restrain infringement of and/or to enforce and protect the rights granted by you hereunder, and to recover damages in respect to or for the infringement or other violation of the said rights, and in our sole judgment to join you and/or others in whose names the copyrights to any of the works may stand; to discontinue, compromise or refer to arbitration, any such actions or proceedings or to make any other disposition of the disputes in relation to the works, provided that any action or proceeding commenced by us pursuant to the provisions of this paragraph shall be at our sole expense and for our sole benefit.

14. You agree that you, your agents, employees or representatives will not, directly or indirectly, solicit or accept payment from writers for composing music for lyrics or writing lyrics to music or for reviewing, publishing, promoting, recording or rendering other services connected with the exploitation of any composition, or permit use of your name or your affiliation with us in connection with any of the foregoing. In the event of a violation of any of the provisions of this paragraph 14, we shall have the right, in our sole discretion, by giving you at least thirty (30) days' notice by registered or certified mail, to terminate this agreement. In the event of such termination no payments shall be due to you pursuant to paragraph 8 hereof.

15. No monies due or to become due to you shall be assignable, whether by way of assignment, sale or power granted to an attorney-in-fact, without our prior written consent. If any assignment of such monies is made by you without such prior written consent, no rights of any kind against us will be acquired by the assignee, purchaser or attorney-in-fact.

16. In the event that during the period (a) mail addressed to you at the last address furnished by you pursuant to paragraph 19 hereof shall be returned by the post office, or (b) monies shall not have been earned by you pursuant to paragraph 6 hereof for a period of two consecutive years or more, or (c) you shall die, BMI shall have the right to terminate this agreement on at least thirty (30) days' notice by registered or certified mail addressed to the last address furnished by you pursuant to paragraph 19 hereof and, in the case of your death, to the representative of your estate, if known to BMI. In the event of such termination no payments shall be due you pursuant to paragraph 8 hereof.

17. You acknowledge that the rights obtained by you pursuant to this agreement constitute rights to payment of money and that during the period we shall hold absolute title to the performing rights granted to us hereunder. In the event that during the period you shall file a petition in bankruptcy, such a petition shall be filed against you, you shall make an assignment for the benefit of creditors, you shall consent to the appointment of a receiver or trustee for all or part of your property, or you shall institute or shall have instituted against you any other insolvency proceeding under the United States bankruptcy laws or any other applicable law, we shall retain title to the performing rights in all works for which clearance sheets shall have theretofore been submitted to us and shall subrogate your trustee in bankruptcy or receiver and any subsequent purchasers from them to your right to payment of money for said works in accordance with the terms and conditions of this agreement.

18. Any controversy or claim arising out of, or relating to, this agreement or the breach thereof, shall be settled by arbitration in the City of New York, in accordance with the Rules of the American Arbitration Association, and judgment upon the award of the arbitrator may be entered in any Court having jurisdiction thereof. Such award shall include the fixing of the expenses of the arbitration, including reasonable attorney's fees, which shall be borne by the unsuccessful party.

19. You agree to notify our Department of Performing Rights Administration promptly in writing of any change in your address. Any notice sent to you pursuant to the terms of this agreement shall be valid if addressed to you at the last address so furnished by you.

20. This agreement cannot be changed orally and shall be governed and construed pursuant to the laws of the State of New York.

21. In the event that any part or parts of this agreement are found to be void by a court of competent jurisdiction, the remaining part or parts shall nevertheless be binding with the same force and effect as if the void part or parts were deleted from this agreement.

Very truly yours,

BROADCAST MUSIC, INC.

ACCEPTED AND AGREED TO:

By ....

....

Assistant Vice President

APPENDIX 6

Songwriters Guild of America Writer-Publisher Contract

NOTE TO SONGWRITERS: (A) DO NOT SIGN THIS CONTRACT IF IT HAS ANY CHANGES UNLESS YOU HAVE FIRST DISCUSSED SUCH CHANGES WITH THE GUILD; (B) FOR YOUR PROTECTION PLEASE SEND A FULLY EXECUTED COPY OF THIS CONTRACT TO THE GUILD.

POPULAR SONGWRITERS CONTRACT
© Copyright 1978 AGAC

AGREEMENT made this   day of   . 19   . between

....

(hereinafter called "Publisher") and ....

....

(Jointly and/or severally hereinafter collectively called "Writer"):

WITNESSETH:

Composition 1. The Writer hereby assigns, transfers and delivers to the Publisher a certain heretofore unpublished original musical composi-
(Insert title tion, written and/or composed by the above-named Writer now entitled ....
of composition→
here) ....
(hereinafter referred to as "the composition"), including the title, words and music thereof, and the right to secure copyright therein throughout the entire world, and to have and to hold the said copyright and all rights of whatsoever nature thereunder existing, for
(Insert number→ .... years from the date of this contract or 35 years from the date of the first release of a
of years here) *not more than 40*
commercial sound recording of the composition, whichever term ends earlier, unless this contract is sooner terminated in accordance with the provisions hereof.

Performing 2. In all respects this contract shall be subject to any existing agreements between the parties hereto and the following small
Rights Affiliation performing rights licensing organization with which Writer and Publisher are affiliated:
(Delete Two) ——→ (ASCAP, BMI, SESAC). Nothing contained herein shall, or shall be deemed to, alter, vary or modify the rights of Writer and Publisher to share in, receive and retain the proceeds distributed to them by such small performing rights licensing organization pursuant to their respective agreement with it.

Warranty 3. The Writer hereby warrants that the composition is his sole, exclusive and original work, that he has full right and power to make this contract, and that there exists no adverse claim to or in the composition, except as aforesaid in Paragraph 2 hereof and except such rights as are specifically set forth in Paragraph 23 hereof.

Royalties 4. In consideration of this contract, the Publisher agrees to pay the Writer as follows:
(Insert amount
of advance here) ——→ (a) $..................as an advance against royalties, receipt of which is hereby acknowledged, which sum shall remain the property of the Writer and shall be deductible only from payments hereafter becoming due the Writer under this contract.

Piano Copies (b) In respect of regular piano copies sold and paid for in the United States and Canada, the following royalties per copy:

Sliding Scale ....% (in no case, however, less than 10%) of the wholesale selling price of the first 200,000 copies or less; plus
(Insert percentage here)< ....% (in no case, however, less than 12%) of the wholesale selling price of copies in excess of 200,000 and not exceeding 500,000; plus
..........% (in no case, however, less than 15%) of the wholesale selling price of copies in excess of 500,000.

Foreign Royalties (c) ....% (in no case, however, less than 50%) of all net sums received by the Publisher in respect of regular piano
(Insert percentage here) copies, orchestrations, band arrangements, octavos, quartets, arrangements for combinations of voices and/or instru-
ments, and/or other copies of the composition sold in any country other than the United States and Canada, provided, however, that if the Publisher should sell such copies through, or cause them to be sold by, a subsidiary or affiliate which is actually doing business in a foreign country, then in respect of such sales, the Publisher shall pay to the Writer not less than 5% of the marked retail selling price in respect of each such copy sold and paid for.

Orchestrations and (d) In respect of each copy sold and paid for in the United States and Canada, or for export from the United States and
Other Arrangements, Canada, of orchestrations, band arrangements, octavos, quartets, arrangements for combinations of voices and/or instruments,
etc. and/or other copies of the composition (other than regular piano copies) the following royalties on the wholesale selling price (after trade discounts, if any):
(Insert percentage here)< ....% (in no case, however, less than 10%) on the first 200,000 copies or less; plus
..........% (in no case, however, less than 12%) on all copies in excess of 200,000 and not exceeding 500,000; plus
..........% (in no case, however, less than 15%) on all copies in excess of 500,000.

Publisher's (e) (i) If the composition, or any part thereof, is included in any song book, folio or similar publication issued by the
Song Book, Publisher containing at least four, but not more than twenty-five musical compositions, the royalty to be paid by the
Folio, etc. Publisher to the Writer shall be an amount determined by dividing 10% of the wholesale selling price (after trade discounts, if any) of the copies sold, among the total number of the Publisher's copyrighted musical compositions included in such publication. If such publication contains more than twenty-five musical compositions, the said 10% shall be increased by an additional ½% for each additional musical composition.

Licensee's (ii) If, pursuant to a license granted by the Publisher to a licensee not controlled by or affiliated with it, the composi-
Song Book, tion, or any part thereof, is included in any song book, folio or similar publication, containing at least four musical
Folio, etc. compositions, the royalty to be paid by the Publisher to the Writer shall be that proportion of 50% of the gross amount received by it from the licensee, as the number of uses of the composition under the license and during the license period, bears to the total number of uses of the Publisher's copyrighted musical compositions under the license and during the license period.

(iii) In computing the number of the Publisher's copyrighted musical compositions under subdivisions (i) and (ii) hereof, there shall be excluded musical compositions in the public domain and arrangements thereof and those with respect to which the Publisher does not currently publish and offer for sale regular piano copies.

(iv) Royalties on publications containing less than four musical compositions shall be payable at regular piano copy rates.

Professional (f) As to "professional material" not sold or resold, no royalty shall be payable. Free copies of the lyrics of the composition
Material and shall not be distributed except under the following conditions: (i) with the Writer's written consent; or (ii) when printed
Free Copies without music in limited numbers for charitable, religious or governmental purposes, or for similar public purposes, if no profit is derived, directly or indirectly; or (iii) when authorized for printing in a book, magazine or periodical, where such use is incidental to a novel or story (as distinguished from use in a book of lyrics or a lyric magazine or folio), provided that any such use shall bear the Writer's name and the proper copyright notice; or (iv) when distributed solely for the purpose of exploiting the composition, provided, that such exploitation is restricted to the distribution of limited numbers of such copies for the purpose of influencing the sale of the composition, that the distribution is independent of the sale of any other musical compositions, services, goods, wares or merchandise, and that no profit is made, directly or indirectly, in connection therewith.

Mechanicals, Electrical Transcription, Synchronization, All Other Rights	(g) ....% (in no case, however, less than 50%) of: **(Insert percentage here)** All gross receipts of the Publisher in respect of any licenses (including statutory royalties) authorizing the manufacture of parts of instruments serving to mechanically reproduce the composition, or to use the composition in synchronization with sound motion pictures, or to reproduce it upon electrical transcription for broadcasting purposes; and of any and all gross receipts of the Publisher from any other source or right now known or which may hereafter come into existence, except as provided in paragraph 2.
Licensing Agent's Charges	(h) If the Publisher administers licenses authorizing the manufacture of parts of instruments serving to mechanically reproduce said composition, or the use of said composition in synchronization or in timed relation with sound motion pictures or its reproduction upon electrical transcriptions, or any of them, through an agent, trustee or other administrator acting for a substantial part of the industry and not under the exclusive control of the Publisher (hereinafter sometimes referred to as licensing agent), the Publisher, in determining his receipts, shall be entitled to deduct from gross license fees paid by the Licensees, a sum equal to the charges paid by the Publisher to said licensing agent, provided, however, that in respect to synchronization or timed relation with sound motion pictures, said deduction shall in no event exceed $150.00 or 10% of said gross license fee, whichever is less; in connection with the manufacture of parts of instruments serving to mechanically reproduce said composition, said deductions shall not exceed 5% of said gross license fee; and in connection with electrical transcriptions, said deduction shall not exceed 10% of said gross license fee.
Block Licenses	(i) The Publisher agrees that the use of the composition will not be included in any bulk or block license heretofore or hereafter granted, and that it will not grant any bulk or block license to include the same, without the written consent of the Writer in each instance, except (i) that the Publisher may grant such licenses with respect to electrical transcription for broadcasting purposes, but in such event, the Publisher shall pay to the Writer that proportion of 50% of the gross amount received by it under each such license as the number of uses of the composition under each such license during each such license period bears to the total number of uses of the Publisher's copyrighted musical compositions under each such license during each such license period; in computing the number of the Publisher's copyrighted musical compositions for this purpose, there shall be excluded musical compositions in the public domain and arrangements thereof and those with respect to which the Publisher does not currently publish and offer for sale regular piano copies; (ii) that the Publisher may appoint agents or representatives in countries outside of the United States and Canada to use and to grant licenses for the use of the composition on the customary royalty fee basis under which the Publisher shall receive not less than 10% of the marked retail selling price in respect of regular piano copies, and 50% of all other revenue; if, in connection with any such bulk or block license, the Publisher shall have received any advance, the Writer shall not be entitled to share therein, but no part of said advance shall be deducted in computing the composition's earnings under said bulk or block license. A bulk or block license shall be deemed to mean any license or agreement, domestic or foreign, whereby rights are granted in respect of two or more musical compositions.
Television and New Uses	(j) Except to the extent that the Publisher and Writer have heretofore or may hereafter assign to or vest in the small performing rights licensing organization with which Writer and Publisher are affiliated, the said rights or the right to grant licenses therefor, it is agreed that no licenses shall be granted without the written consent, in each instance, of the Writer for the use of the composition by means of television, or by any means, or for any purposes not commercially established, or for which licenses were not granted by the Publisher on musical compositions prior to June 1, 1937.
Writer's Consent to Licenses	(k) The Publisher shall not, without the written consent of the Writer in each case, give or grant any right or license (i) to use the title of the composition, or (ii) for the exclusive use of the composition in any form or for any purpose, or for any period of time, or for any territory, other than its customary arrangements with foreign publishers, or (iii) to give a dramatic representation of the composition or to dramatize the plot or story thereof, or (iv) for a vocal rendition of the composition in synchronization with sound motion pictures, or (v) for any synchronization use thereof, or (vi) for the use of the composition or a quotation or excerpt therefrom in any article, book, periodical, advertisement or other similar publication. If, however, the Publisher shall give to the Writer written notice by certified mail, return receipt requested, or telegram, specifying the right or license to be given or granted, the name of the licensee and the terms and conditions thereof, including the price or other compensation to be received therefor, then, unless the Writer (or any one or more of them) shall, within five business days after the delivery of such notice to the address of the Writer hereinafter designated, object thereto, the Publisher may grant such right or license in accordance with the said notice without first obtaining the consent of the Writer. Such notice shall be deemed sufficient if sent to the Writer at the address or addresses hereinafter designated or at the address or addresses last furnished to the Publisher in writing by the Writer.
Trust for Writer	(l) Any portion of the receipts which may become due to the Writer from license fees (in excess of offsets), whether received directly from the licensee or from any licensing agent of the Publisher, shall, if not paid immediately on the receipt thereof by the Publisher, belong to the Writer and shall be held in trust for the Writer until payment is made; the ownership of said trust fund by the Writer shall not be questioned whether the monies are physically segregated or not.
Writer Participation	(m) The Publisher agrees that it will not issue any license as a result of which it will receive any financial benefit in which the Writer does not participate.
Writer Credit	(n) On all regular piano copies, orchestrations, band or other arrangements, octavos, quartets, commercial sound recordings and other reproductions of the composition or parts thereof, in whatever form and however produced, Publisher shall include or cause to be included, in addition to the copyright notice, the name of the Writer, and Publisher shall include a similar requirement in every license or authorization issued by it with respect to the composition.
Writers' Respective Shares	5. Whenever the term "Writer" is used herein, it shall be deemed to mean all of the persons herein defined as "Writer" and any and all royalties herein provided to be paid to the Writer shall be paid equally to such persons if there be more than one, unless otherwise provided in Paragraph 23.
Release of Commercial Sound Recording **(Insert period not exceeding 12 months)**	6. (a) (i) The Publisher shall, within....................months from the date of this contract (the "initial period"), cause a commercial sound recording of the composition to be made and released in the customary form and through the customary commercial channels. If at the end of such initial period a sound recording has not been made and released, as above provided, then, subject to the provisions of the next succeeding subdivision, this contract shall terminate.
(Insert amount to be not less than $250) **(Insert period not exceeding six months)**	(ii) If, prior to the expiration of the initial period, Publisher pays the Writer the sum of $........(which shall not be charged against or recoupable out of any advances, royalties or other monies theretofor paid, then due, or which thereafter may become due the Writer from the Publisher pursuant to this contract or otherwise), Publisher shall have an additional............months (the "additional period") commencing with the end of the initial period, within which to cause such commercial sound recording to be made and released as provided in subdivision (i) above. If at the end of the additional period a commercial sound recording has not been made and released, as above provided, then this contract shall terminate.
	(iii) Upon termination pursuant to this Paragraph 6(a), all rights of any and every nature in and to the composition and in and to any and all copyrights secured thereon in the United States and throughout the world shall automatically re-vest in and become the property of the Writer and shall be reassigned to him by the Publisher. The Writer shall not be obligated to return or pay to the Publisher any advance or indebtedness as a condition of such re-assignment; the said re-assignment shall be in accordance with and subject to the provisions of Paragraph 8 hereof, and, in addition, the Publisher shall pay to the Writer all gross sums which it has theretofore or may thereafter receive in respect of the composition.

Writer's Copies

(b) The Publisher shall furnish, or cause to be furnished, to the Writer six copies of the commercial sound recording referred to in Paragraph 6(a).

Piano Copies, Piano Arrangement or Lead Sheet (Select (i) or (ii))

(c) The Publisher shall

☐ (i) within 30 days after the initial release of a commercial sound recording of the composition, make, publish and offer for sale regular piano copies of the composition in the form and through the channels customarily employed by it for that purpose;

☐ (ii) within 30 days after execution of this contract make a piano arrangement or lead sheet of the composition and furnish six copies thereof to the Writer.

In the event neither subdivision (i) nor (ii) of this subparagraph (c) is selected, the provisions of subdivision (ii) shall be automatically deemed to have been selected by the parties.

Foreign Copyright

7. (a) Each copyright on the composition in countries other than the United States shall be secured only in the name of the Publisher, and the Publisher shall not at any time divest itself of said foreign copyright directly or indirectly.

Foreign Publication

(b) No rights shall be granted by the Publisher in the composition to any foreign publisher or licensee inconsistent with the terms hereof, nor shall any foreign publication rights in the composition be given to a foreign publisher or licensee unless and until the Publisher shall have complied with the provisions of Paragraph 6 hereof.

Foreign Advance

(c) If foreign rights in the composition are separately conveyed, otherwise than as a part of the Publisher's current and/or future catalog, not less than 50% of any advance received in respect thereof shall be credited to the account of and paid to the Writer.

Foreign Percentage

(d) The percentage of the Writer on monies received from foreign sources shall be computed on the Publisher's net receipts, provided, however, that no deductions shall be made for offsets of monies due from the Publisher to said foreign sources; or for advances made by such foreign sources to the Publisher, unless the Writer shall have received at least 50% of said advances.

No Foreign Allocations

(e) In computing the receipts of the Publisher from licenses granted in respect of synchronization with sound motion pictures, or in respect of any world-wide licenses, or in respect of licenses granted by the Publisher for use of the composition in countries other than the United States, no amount shall be deducted for payments or allocations to publishers or licensees in such countries.

Termination or Expiration of Contract

8. Upon the termination or expiration of this contract, all rights of any and every nature in and to the composition and in and to any and all copyrights secured thereon in the United States and throughout the world, shall re-vest in and become the property of the Writer, and shall be re-assigned to the Writer by the Publisher free of any and all encumbrances of any nature whatsoever, provided that:

(a) If the Publisher, prior to such termination or expiration, shall have granted a domestic license for the use of the composition, not inconsistent with the terms and provisions of this contract, the re-assignment may be subject to the terms of such license.

(b) Publisher shall assign to the Writer all rights which it may have under any such agreement or license referred to in subdivision (a) in respect of the composition, including, but not limited to, the right to receive all royalties or other monies earned by the composition thereunder after the date of termination or expiration of this contract. Should the Publisher thereafter receive or be credited with any royalties or other monies so earned, it shall pay the same to the Writer.

(c) The Writer shall not be obligated to return or pay to the Publisher any advance or indebtedness as a condition of the re-assignment provided for in this Paragraph 8, and shall be entitled to receive the plates and copies of the composition in the possession of the Publisher.

(d) Publisher shall pay any and all royalties which may have accrued to the Writer prior to such termination or expiration.

(e) The Publisher shall execute any and all documents and do any and all acts or things necessary to effect any and all re-assignments to the Writer herein provided for.

Negotiations for New or Unspecified Uses

9. If the Publisher desires to exercise a right in and to the composition now known or which may hereafter become known, but for which no specific provision has been made herein, the Publisher shall give written notice to the Writer thereof. Negotiations respecting all the terms and conditions of any such disposition shall thereupon be entered into between the Publisher and the Writer and no such right shall be exercised until specific agreement has been made.

Royalty Statements and Payments

10. The Publisher shall render to the Writer, hereafter, royalty statements accompanied by remittance of the amount due at the times such statements and remittances are customarily rendered by the Publisher, provided, however, that such statements and remittances shall be rendered either semi-annually or quarterly and not more than forty-five days after the end of each such semi-annual or quarterly period, as the case may be. The Writer may at any time, or from time to time, make written request for a detailed royalty statement, and the Publisher shall, within sixty days, comply therewith. Such royalty statements shall set forth in detail the various items, foreign and domestic, for which royalties are payable thereunder and the amounts thereof, including, but not limited to, the number of copies sold and the number of uses made in each royalty category. If a use is made in a publication of the character provided in Paragraph 4, subdivision (e) hereof, there shall be included in said royalty statement the title of said publication, the publisher or issuer thereof, the date of and number of uses, the gross license fee received in connection with each publication, the share thereto of all the writers under contract with the Publisher, and the Writer's share thereof. There shall likewise be included in said statement a description of every other use of the composition, and if by a licensee or licensees their name or names, and if said use is upon a part of an instrument serving to reproduce the composition mechanically, the type of mechanical reproduction, the title of the label thereon, the name or names of the artists performing the same, together with the gross license fees received, and the Writer's share thereof.

Examination of Books

11. (a) The Publisher shall from time to time, upon written demand of the Writer or his representative, permit the Writer or his representative to inspect at the place of business of the Publisher, all books, records and documents relating to the composition and all licenses granted, uses had and payments made therefor, such right of inspection to include, but not by way of limitation, the right to examine all original accountings and records relating to uses and payments by manufacturers of commercial sound recordings and music rolls; and the Writer or his representative may appoint an accountant who shall at any time during usual business hours have access to all records of the Publisher relating to the composition for the purpose of verifying royalty statements rendered or which are delinquent under the terms hereof.

(b) The Publisher shall, upon written demand of the Writer or his representative, cause any licensing agent in the United States and Canada to furnish to the Writer or his representative, statements showing in detail all licenses granted, uses had and payments made in connection with the composition, which licenses or permits were granted, or payments were received, by or through said licensing agent, and to permit the Writer or his representative to inspect at the place of business of such licensing agent, all books, records and documents of such licensing agent, relating thereto. Any and all agreements made by the Publisher with any such licensing agent shall provide that any such licensing agent will comply with the terms and provisions hereof. In the event that the Publisher shall instruct such licensing agent to furnish to the Writer or his representative statements as provided for herein, and to permit the inspection of the books, records and documents as herein provided, then if such licensing agent should refuse to comply with the said instructions, or any of them, the Publisher agrees to institute and prosecute diligently and in good faith such action or proceedings as may be necessary to compel compliance with the said instructions.

(c) With respect to foreign licensing agents, the Publisher shall make available the books or records of said licensing agents in countries outside of the United States and Canada to the extent such books or records are available to the Publisher, except that the Publisher may in lieu thereof make available any accountants' reports and audits which the Publisher is able to obtain.

(d) If as a result of any examination of books, records or documents pursuant to Paragraphs 11(a), 11(b) or 11(c) hereof, it is determined that, with respect to any royalty statement rendered by or on behalf of the Publisher to the Writer, the Writer is owed a sum equal to or greater than five percent of the sum shown on that royalty statement as being due to the Writer, then the Publisher shall pay to the Writer the entire cost of such examination, not to exceed 50% of the amount shown to be due the Writer.

(e) (i) In the event the Publisher administers its own licenses for the manufacture of parts of instruments serving to mechanically reproduce the composition rather than employing a licensing agent for that purpose, the Publisher shall include in each license agreement a provision permitting the Publisher, the Writer or their respective representatives to inspect, at the place of business of such licensee, all books, records and documents of such licensee relating to such license. Within 30 days after written demand by the Writer, the Publisher shall commence to inspect such licensee's books, records and documents and shall furnish a written report of such inspection to the Writer within 90 days following such demand. If the Publisher fails, after written demand by the Writer, to so inspect the licensee's books, records and documents, or fails to furnish such report, the Writer or his representative may inspect such licensee's books, records and documents at his own expense.

(ii) In the further event that the Publisher and the licensee referred to in subdivision (i) above are subsidiaries or affiliates of the same entity or one is a subsidiary or affiliate of the other, then, unless the Publisher employs a licensing agent to administer the licenses referred to in subdivision (i) above, the Writer shall have the right to make the inspection referred to in subdivision (i) above without the necessity of making written demand on the Publisher as provided in subdivision (i) above.

(iii) If as a result of any inspection by the Writer pursuant to subdivisions (i) and (ii) of this subparagraph (e) the Writer recovers additional monies from the licensee, the Publisher and the Writer shall share equally in the cost of such inspection.

Default in Payment or Prevention of Examination

12. If the Publisher shall fail or refuse, within sixty days after written demand, to furnish or cause to be furnished, such statements, books, records or documents, or to permit inspection thereof, as provided for in Paragraphs 10 and 11 hereof, or within thirty days after written demand, to make the payment of any royalties due under this contract, then the Writer shall be entitled, upon ten days' written notice, to terminate this contract. However if the Publisher shall:

(a) Within the said ten-day period serve upon the Writer a written notice demanding arbitration; and

(b) Submit to arbitration its claim that it has complied with its obligation to furnish statements, books, records or documents, or permitted inspection thereof or to pay royalties, as the case may be, or both, and thereafter comply with any award of the arbitrator within ten days after such award or within such time as the artibrator may specify;

then this contract shall continue in full force and effect as if the Writer had not sent such notice of termination. If the Publisher shall fail to comply with the foregoing provisions, then this contract shall be deemed to have been terminated as of the date of the Writer's written notice of termination.

Derivative Works

13. No derivative work prepared under authority of Publisher during the term of this contract may be utilized by Publisher or any other party after termination or expiration of this contract.

Notices

14. All written demands and notices provided for herein shall be sent by certified mail, return receipt requested.

Suits for Infringement

15. Any legal action brought by the Publisher against any alleged infringer of the composition shall be initiated and prosecuted at its sole cost and expense, but if the Publisher should fail, within thirty days after written demand, to institute such action, the Writer shall be entitled to institute such suit at his cost and expense. All sums recovered as a result of any such action shall, after the deduction of the reasonable expense thereof, be divided equally between the Publisher and the Writer. No settlement of any such action may be made by either party without first notifying the other; in the event that either party should object to such settlement, then such settlement shall not be made if the party objecting assumes the prosecution of the action and all expenses thereof, except that any sums thereafter recovered shall be divided equally between the Publisher and the Writer after the deduction of the reasonable expenses thereof.

Infringement Claims

16. (a) If a claim is presented against the Publisher alleging that the composition is an infringement upon some other work or a violation of any other right of another, and because therof the Publisher is jeopardized, it shall forthwith serve a written notice upon the Writer setting forth the full details of such claim. The pendency of said claim shall not relieve the Publisher of the obligation to make payment of the royalties to the Writer hereunder, unless the Publisher shall deposit said royalties as and when they would otherwise be payable, in an account in the joint names of the Publisher and the Writer in a bank or trust company in New York, New York, if the Writer on the date of execution of this contract resides East of the Mississippi River, or in Los Angeles, California, if the Writer on the date of execution of this contract resides West of the Mississippi River. If no suit be filed within nine months after said written notice from the Publisher to the Writer, all monies deposited in said joint account shall be paid over to the Writer plus any interest which may have been earned thereon.

(b) Should an action be instituted against the Publisher claiming that the composition is an infringement upon some other work or a violation of any other right of another, the Publisher shall forthwith serve written notice upon the Writer containing the full details of such claim. Notwithstanding the commencement of such action, the Publisher shall continue to pay the royalties hereunder to the Writer unless it shall, from and after the date of the service of the summons, deposit said royalties as and when they would otherwise be payable, in an account in the joint names of the Publisher and the Writer in a bank or trust company in New York, New York, if the Writer on the date of execution of this contract resides East of the Mississippi River, or in Los Angeles, California, if the Writer on the date of execution of this contract resides West of the Mississippi River. If the said suit shall be finally adjudicated in favor of the Publisher or shall be settled, there shall be released and paid to the Writer all of such sums held in escrow less any amount paid out of the Writer's share with the Writer's written consent in settlement of said action. Should the said suit finally result adversely to the Publisher, the said amount on deposit shall be released to the Publisher to the extent of any expense or damage it incurs and the balance shall be paid over to the Writer.

(c) In any of the foregoing events, however, the Writer shall be entitled to payment of said royalties or the money so deposited at and after such time as he files with the Publisher a surety company bond, or a bond in other form acceptable to the Publisher, in the sum of such payments to secure the return thereof to the extent that the Publisher may be entitled to such return. The foregoing payments or deposits or the filing of a bond shall be without prejudice to the rights of the Publisher or Writer in the premises.

Arbitration

17. Any and all differences, disputes or controversies arising out of or in connection with this contract shall be submitted to arbitration before a sole arbitrator under the then prevailing rules of the American Arbitration Association. The location of the arbitration shall be New York, New York, if the Writer on the date of execution of this contract resides East of the Mississippi River, or Los Angeles, California, if the Writer on the date of execution of this contract resides West of the Mississippi River. The parties hereby individually and jointly agree to abide by and perform any award rendered in such arbitration. Judgment upon any such award rendered may be entered in any court having jurisdiction thereof.

Assignment

18. Except to the extent herein otherwise expressly provided, the Publisher shall not sell, transfer, assign, convey, encumber or otherwise dispose of the composition or the copyright or copyrights secured thereon without the prior written consent of the Writer. The Writer has been induced to enter into this contract in reliance upon the value to him of the personal service and ability of the Publisher in the exploitation of the composition, and by reason thereof it is the intention of the parties and the essence of the relationship between them that the rights herein granted to the Publisher shall remain with the Publisher and that the same shall not pass to any other person, including, without limitations, successors to or receivers or trustees of the property of the Publisher, either by act or deed of the Publisher or by operation of law, and in the event of the voluntary or involuntary bankruptcy of the Publisher, this contract shall terminate, provided, however, that the composition may be included by the Publisher in a bona fide voluntary sale of its music business or its entire catalog of musical compositions, or in a merger or consolidation of the Publisher with another corporation, in which event the Publisher shall immediately give written notice thereof to the Writer; and provided further that the composition and the copyright therein may be assigned by the Publisher to a subsidiary or affiliated company generally engaged in the music publishing business. If the Publisher is an individual, the composition may pass to a legatee or distributee as part of the inheritance of the Publisher's music business and entire catalog of musical compositions. Any such transfer or assignment shall, however, be conditioned upon the execution and delivery by the transferee or assignee to the Writer of an agreement to be bound by and to perform all of the terms and conditions of this contract to be performed on the part of the Publisher.

Subsidiary Defined
19. A subsidiary, affiliate, or any person, firm or corporation controlled by the Publisher or by such subsidiary or affiliate, as used in this contract, shall be deemed to include any person, firm or corporation, under common control with, or the majority of whose stock or capital contribution is owned or controlled by the Publisher or by any of its officers, directors, partners or associates, or whose policies and actions are subject to domination or control by the Publisher or any of its officers, directors, partners or associates.

Amounts
20. The amounts and percentages specified in this contract shall be deemed to be the amounts and percentages agreed upon by the parties hereto, unless other amounts or percentages are inserted in the blank spaces provided therefor.

Modifications
21. This contract is binding upon and shall enure to the benefit of the parties hereto and their respective successors in interest (as hereinbefore limited). If the Writer (or one or more of them) shall not be living, any notices may be given to, or consents given by, his or their successors in interest. No change or modification of this contract shall be effective unless reduced to writing and signed by the parties hereto.

The words in this contract shall be so construed that the singular shall include the plural and the plural shall include the singular where the context so requires and the masculine shall include the feminine and the feminine shall include the masculine where the context so requires.

Paragraph Headings
22. The paragraph headings are inserted only as a matter of convenience and for reference, and in no way define, limit or describe the scope or intent of this contract nor in any way affect this contract.

Special Provisions
23.

Witness: ....

....

Witness: ....

....

Witness: ....

....

Witness: ....

....

Publisher ....

By ....

Address ....

Writer ....(L.S.)

Address ....

Soc. Sec. # ....

Writer ....(L.S.)

Address ....

Soc. Sec. # ....

Writer ....(L.S.)

Address ....

Soc. Sec. # ....

FOR YOUR PROTECTION,
SEND A COPY OF THE FULLY SIGNED CONTRACT TO THE GUILD.

· · · · ·

Special Exceptions to apply only if filled in and initialed by the parties.
☐ The composition is part of an original score (not an interpolation) of
   ☐ Living Stage Production   ☐ Motion Picture   ☐ Night Club Revue
   ☐ Televised Musical Production
which is the subject of an agreement between the parties dated   , a copy of which is hereto annexed. Unless said agreement requires compliance with Paragraph 6 in respect of a greater number of musical compositions, the Publisher shall be deemed to have complied with said Paragraph 6 with respect to the composition if it fully performs the terms of said Paragraph 6 in respect of any one musical composition included in said score.

APPENDIX 7

Popular Songwriters Contract

AGREEMENT made this   day of   ,19   ,between

(hereinafter called "Publisher") and

jointly and/or severally, (hereinafter called "Writer(s)"):

WITNESSETH:

(1) The Writer(s) hereby sells, assigns, transfers and delivers to the Publisher, its successors and assigns, a certain heretofore unpublished original musical composition, written and/or composed by the Writer(s) now entitled:

Title   Year in which creation was completed

including the title, copyrights and/or words and music thereof, all of the rights therein, as well as the entire exclusive right to publicly perform and televise the same, the right to secure copyright therein, and renewals and extensions thereof, throughout the world, in its own name as proprietor or otherwise, and such copyrights, renewals and extensions; TO HAVE AND TO HOLD the said musical composition, all the rights therein, the copyrights therein, and renewals and extensions thereof for the full terms thereof. The Writer(s) hereby conveys an irrevocable power of attorney, authorizing the Publisher, its successors and assigns, to file applications for renewal and renew and extend the copyrights in his name, and upon the issuance of such renewals, to execute proper and formal assignments thereof in his name, so as to secure to the Publisher, its successors and assigns, the renewal copyrights and extensions thereof.

(2) In all respects this contract shall be subject to any existing agreements between all of the parties hereto and the American Society of Composers, Authors and Publishers.

(3) The Writer(s) hereby warrants that the said composition is his sole, exclusive and original work, and that he has full right and power to make the within agreement, and that there exists no adverse claim to or in the said composition, except as set forth in Clause 2 hereof.

(4) In consideration of this agreement, the Publisher agrees to pay the Writer(s) as follows:

(a) In respect of regular piano copies sold and paid for in the United States of America, a royalty of   cents per copy.

(b) A royalty of   % of all net sums received by the Publisher in respect of regular piano copies and/or orchestrations thereof sold and paid for in any foreign country, or sold and paid for in the United States pursuant to a print right granted by the Publisher.

(c) A royalty of   cents per copy of orchestrations thereof in any form sold and paid for in the United States of America.

(d) A royalty equal to that proportion of twelve and one-half (12½%) per cent of the wholesale selling price of each folio or book issued by the Publisher, and sold and paid for and not returned as the said composition bears to the total number of musical compositions in such folio or book.

(e) As to "professional material" — not sold or resold, no royalty shall be payable.

(f) An amount equal to   % of:

All receipts of the Publisher in respect of any licenses issued authorizing the manufacture and distribution of phono-records embodying in said composition, or the use of the said composition in synchronization with sound motion pictures, or the reproduction thereof upon so-called electrical transcription for broadcasting purposes; and of any and all receipts of the Publisher from any other source or right now known or which may hereafter come into existence, all such sums to be divided amongst the Writer(s) of said composition as provided in Paragraph 5 hereof; provided, however, that if the Publisher administers the said licenses, or any of them, through the agent, trustee or other administrator acting for a substantial part of the industry and not in the exclusive employ of the Publisher, the Publisher, in determining his receipts, shall be entitled to deduct from gross license fees paid by the licensees a sum equal to the charges paid by the said Publisher to said agent, trustee or administrator.

(g) The percentage of the Writer(s) on monies received from foreign sources shall be computed on the Publisher's net receipts in U.S. Dollar currency, and at the same rate of exchange as that received by the Publisher.

(h) The Writer(s) shall not be entitled to any share of the monies distributed to the Publisher by the American Society of Composers, Authors and Publishers or any other performing rights society throughout the world which makes a

 ★   254   ★

distribution to writers either directly or through the American Society of Composers, Authors and Publishers of an amount which, in the aggregate, is at least equal to the aggregate amount distributed to Publishers.

(5) It is understood and agreed by and between all of the parties hereto that all sums hereunder payable jointly to the Writer(s) shall be divided amongst them respectively as follows:

NAME   SHARE

_____   _____

_____   _____

_____   _____

(6) The Publisher shall render the Writer(s), as above, on or about each August 15th and February 15th covering the six months ending June 30th and December 31st hereafter, so long as he shall continue publication or the licensing of any rights in the said composition, royalty statements accompanied by remittance of the amount due.

(7) The Publisher shall have the right to alter, change, edit or translate the composition or any part thereof, in any way it may be necessary. In the event it be necessary for the Publisher to cause lyrics to be written in other languages for and as part of the composition, the Publisher shall in such event have the right to deduct from the heretofore agreed royalties payable to the Writer(s), the cost or obligation thereof, but in no event more than a sum equal to one-half.

(8) The Writer(s) hereby agrees to indemnify and save harmless the Publisher against any loss, expense or damage by reason of any adverse claims made by others with respect to the composition and agreed that all expenses incurred in defense of any such claims, including counsel fees, as well as any and all sums paid by the Publisher, pursuant to a judgment, arbitration or any settlement or adjustment which may be made in the discretion of the Publisher, or otherwise, shall at all times be borne by the Writer(s), and may be deducted by the Publisher from any money accruing to the Writer(s) under this agreement or otherwise.

(9) This agreement is binding upon the parties hereto and their respective successors in interest.

If work has been recorded and released fill in:

Date and Place of First release: _____

Record Company: _____

Record Number: _____

SS #

Date of Birth:

Witness: Writer: _____ (L.S.)

_____   Address: _____

Publisher: _____

Witness: By: _____

_____   Address: _____

APPENDIX 8

Exclusive Songwriter Contract

AGREEMENT made this   day of   , 19   between,

hereinafter designated as Publisher and

. . . . of . . . .

hereinafter designated as Writer.

WITNESSETH:

For and in consideration of the mutual covenants and agreements hereinafter contained, and the further sum of One Dollar by each of the parties in hand paid to the other, receipt whereof is hereby acknowledged, it is mutually agreed as follows:

(1) The Writer agrees to compose and write music and/or lyrics exclusively for and during the period of this agreement and/or extension thereof, for and on behalf of the Publisher and/or any of its related or associated companies. The Writer agrees that he will not, as an author and/or composer of musical compositions, render his services for any other person, firm or corporation during the term of this agreement or any extension thereof, unless he first obtains the written consent of the Publisher.

(2) The term of this agreement shall be for a period of . . . . year(s)

commencing . . . . and terminating . . . .

(3) The Writer agrees to, and by these presents does hereby sell, assign, transfer and deliver to the Publisher, its successors and assigns, all rights whatsoever, including public performance, for the entire world, in and to all and every work that he has at any time heretofore written and now owns, as well as all and every work that he shall write, compose or create during the full term and/or extension hereof, either alone or in collaboration with others; together with the copyrights and/or the right to copyright the same as proprietor in its own name, or otherwise, as it may elect in all countries, and to obtain renewals of each and every such copyright, to the fullest extent. The Writer herein conveys an irrevocable power of attorney authorizing and empowering the Publisher, its successors and assigns, to file application and renew the copyrights in the name of the Writer, and upon such renewals to execute proper and formal assignments thereof, so as to secure to the Publisher, its successors and assigns, the renewal terms of, in and to the said copyrights, works and/or compositions.

(4) The Writer warrants that all of said compositions are and/or will be original works; that he has the right to make the within agreement, and that there exists and/or will exist no adverse claim to or in the said compositions, and that the Writer will indemnify and hold the Publisher harmless.

(5) The Publisher covenants that it is engaged in the music publishing industry and as such will make reasonable efforts to publish or exploit certain of the musical compositions composed and written by the Writer, wherein title has been vested unto the Publisher, as copyright owner, by virtue of the terms of this agreement.

(6) In consideration of this agreement, the Publisher agrees to pay to the Writer, jointly, only the following royalties:

(a) . . . . . . ¢ per copy, in respect of regular piano copies and/or orchestrations, sold in the United States and for which the Publisher received payment; a royalty equal to that proportion of twelve and one-half (12½%) per cent of the wholesale selling price of each folio or book issued by the Publisher, and sold and paid for and not returned as the said composition bears to the total number of musical compositions in such folio or book.

(b) . . . . . . % of the net amount received by the Publisher, in respect of regular piano copies and/or orchestrations sold and paid for in any foreign country, or sold and paid for in the United States pursuant to a print right granted by the Publisher.

(c) . . . . . . % of the net amount received by the Publisher, in respect of any licenses issued authorizing the manufacture and distribution of phonorecords and/or electrical transcriptions embodying said work, or the use of said work in synchronization with sound motion pictures.

(d) The share of performing fees allocated to the Writer and designated as the Writer Share, if and when such Writer Share is received by the Publisher.

In the event that a composition has not been wholly written by the Writer, the above royalties shall be paid jointly and in equal shares to all writers, and in the event lyrics are written for a composition, other than in the original language, the Publisher shall have the right to deduct from the above royalties, the cost or obligation therefore, but in no event more than a sum equal to one-half (½) thereof. The Publisher shall have the right to alter, change, edit or translate the work(s) or any part thereof, in any way it may be necessary, and to cause new lyrics to be written in other languages.

(7) Heretofore agreed royalties shall be payable to the Writer with respect to net amounts received by the Publisher from foreign countries, only when such net amounts are received by the Publisher in United States dollar currency; and at the same rate of exchange as that received by the Publisher.

(8) Statements shall be rendered on February 15th and August 15th of each year, or as soon as possible thereafter, for the periods ending December 31st and June 30th of each year.

(9) In addition hereto, the Writer sells, assigns, transfers and delivers to the Publisher, its successors and assigns, any and all works acquired and to be acquired hereunder, all of the rights therein, the right to secure copyrights, renewals and extensions thereof throughout the world, and the copyrights, renewals and extensions thereof; TO HAVE AND TO HOLD the said works, copyrights, renewals and extensions thereof and all rights of whatsoever nature thereunder existing, for the full terms thereof. The Writer hereby conveys an irrevocable power of attorney, authorizing the Publisher, its successors and

assigns, to file applications for renewal and renew and extend the copyrights in his name, and upon the issuance of such renewals, to execute proper and formal assignments thereof in his name, so as to secure to the Publisher, its successors and assigns, the renewal copyrights and extensions thereof. The Writer hereby also conveys an irrevocable power of attorney authorizing the Publisher, its successors and assigns to execute proper and separate assignments in his name, in favor of the Publisher, its successors and assigns so as to secure to it the said copyrights, and all the rights therein throughout the world for the full life of such copyrights.

(10) It is agreed between the parties that the Publisher shall have the option and right to renew and extend this agreement upon the same terms for an additional period of _____ year(s) by giving written notice by registered mail to the Writer not later than Thirty (30) days prior to the termination.

(11) This agreement is to be construed and its validity determined according to the laws of the State of New York, and shall apply to, bind and be for the benefit of the heirs, executors, administrators, successors and assigns of the parties hereto.

IN WITNESS WHEREOF the parties hereto have hereunto set their hands and affixed their seals the day and year first above written.

WITNESS:　　　　　　　　　　　SS #
　　　　　　　　　　　　　　　　Date of Birth _____
　　　　　　　　　　　　　　　　　　　　WRITER

WITNESS:　　　　　　　　　　　PUBLISHER:
　　　　　　　　　　　　　　　　By _____

APPENDIX 9

Management Agreement A

AGREEMENT made this _____ day of _____, 19__, by and between
_____ whose address is _____, (hereinafter
referred to as "Manager", and _____ whose address is
_____ (hereinafter referred to as "Artist").

WITNESSETH:

WHEREAS, Artist desires to obtain advice, guidance and counseling in the development and furtherance of his career, individually and as a member of any group with which he later becomes associated as a performer and entertainer, musician, composer, arranger, publisher, recording artist, actor, and in such new and different areas as can be developed and exploited, and

WHEREAS, Manager, by reason of his contacts, experience and background, is qualified to render such advice, guidance and counsel to Artist;

NOW THEREFORE, in consideration of the premises and mutual promises herein contained, the parties do hereby agree as follows:

1.   Artist hereby engages Manager and Manager agrees to render his services as a personal manager to provide such advice, guidance, counsel and direction as Artist may reasonably require to further his career as a performer and entertainer, musician, composer, arranger, publisher, recording artist, actor, and in such new and different areas as can be developed and exploited, including but not limited to the following services:

a.   to supervise and direct Artist in his professional activities and, in Artist's behalf, to consult with others so as to ensure the proper use and marketing of Artist's talent; and

b.   to be available at reasonable times and places to confer with Artist in connection with all matters concerning his professional career, interests, services and publicity; and

c.   to provide advice and counsel regarding the exploitation of Artist's personality in the media and, in connection therewith and for the purpose of trade, advertising and publicity, to approve and permit the use, dissemination, reproduction and publication of Artist's name, likeness and voice; and

d.   to represent Artist in all dealings with any union.

2.   a.   The initial term of this Agreement shall be for a period of one (1) year from the date hereof.

b.   Manager shall have four (4) irrevocable option periods in which to renew this Agreement for additional one (1) year terms, which options shall be automatically exercised by the passage of time unless and until Manager gives Artist written notification within thirty (30) days prior to the end of the original term or preceding option term, whichever is applicable, of his desire and intent not to exercise said option.

3.   a.   As compensation for services to be rendered hereunder, Manager shall receive from Artist a sum of money equal to _____ percent (00%) of Artist's gross monthly earnings during the term of this Agreement, as well as _____ percent (00%) of all monies earned and received by Artist following the termination or expiration of this Agreement, which monies were received by Artist as a result of Manager's services rendered during the term of this Agreement.

b.   The term "Gross Monthly Earnings" as used herein refers to the total of all earnings and receipts, whether in the form of salary, bonus, mechanical and performance royalties, artist royalties, interest, advances against royalties or any other type of income which is reasonably related to Artist's career in the entertainment, amusement, music, recording, motion picture, television, radio and advertising fields, whether now known or hereafter devised, in which Artist's artistic talents are exploited, which monies are received during any calendar month by Artist or by any of his heirs, executors, administrators, assigns or by any person, firm or corporation on his behalf.

      c. In the event Artist forms a corporation during the term hereof for the purpose of furnishing and exploiting his artistic talents, Artist agrees that said corporation will be subject to the terms of this Agreement, and that the gross monthly receipts of such corporation shall be included in Artist's gross monthly earnings as defined in this Agreement for the purpose of determining the compensation due Manager.

      d. Artist agrees that all gross monthly earnings as herein defined shall be paid directly to Manager by all persons, firms or corporations, and shall not be paid to Artist, and that Manager may withhold Manager's compensation therefrom as well as expenses incurred by Manager on Artist's behalf as defined herein. In the event that Artist nevertheless receives gross monthly earnings directly, Artist shall be deemed to hold in trust for Manager that portion of Artist's gross monthly earnings considered Manager's compensation.

      4. Artist agrees to exert his best efforts in the furtherance of his career during the term of this Agreement, and to cooperate with Manager to the fullest extent possible in the interest of promoting Artist's career.

      5. Artist understands that Manager is not a talent agency, but that Manager has been engaged solely as a personal manager and therefore will not be responsible for obtaining and procuring employment for Artist.

      6. Manager is not required to render his exclusive services to Artist, or to devote his entire time to Artist's affairs. Nothing herein shall be construed as limiting Manager's rights to represent other individuals whose talents may be similar to or who may be in competition with Artist, or to have and pursue business interests which may be similar to or may compete with those of Artist. It is further understood and agreed that Manager shall have the right to delegate management powers and responsibilities to others under his supervision and control.

      7. Artist hereby appoints Manager as his sole and exclusive personal manager throughout the entire world to render services set forth in this Agreement and Artist agrees to seek such services from Manager solely and exclusively and further agrees not to engage any other agent, representative or manager to render similar services and Artist agrees not to perform said services on his own behalf and will not negotiate, accept or execute any agreement concerning his career without Manager's express prior consent. Furthermore, Artist agrees to devote his full time and attention to the development and enhancement of his artistic career.

      8.   **a.** Artist hereby irrevocably appoints Manager for the term of this Agreement as his true and lawful attorney-in-fact to sign, execute and deliver any and all contracts in Artist's name, to make, execute, endorse, accept, collect and deliver any and all checks and notes as Artist's said attorney, to demand, sue, collect, recover and receive goods, claims, money, interest or other items that may be due to Artist or belongs to Artist; and to make, execute and deliver receipts, releases and other discharges therefor under sale or otherwise; and to defend, settle, adjust, compound, submit to arbitration and compromise, all actions, suits, accounts, claims and demands whatsoever that are or shall be pending in such manner and in all respects as Manager in his sole discretion shall deem advisable; and without in any way limiting the foregoing generally to do, execute and perform any other act, deed or thing whatsoever that reasonably ought to be done, executed and performed of any and every nature as fully and effectively as Artist could do if personally present; and Artist hereby ratifies and affirms all acts performed by Manager by virtue of this power of attorney.

b. Artist expressly agrees that he will not exert any of the powers herein granted to Manager without express prior written consent of Manager.

c. It is expressly understood that the foregoing power of attorney is limited to matters reasonably related to Artist's career in the entertainment industry.

d. Artist agrees and understands that the grant of power of attorney to Manager is coupled with an interest, which Artist irrevocably grants to Manager, in Artist's career, artistic talents and the products of said career and talents.

9. Artist shall be solely responsible for payment of all booking agency fees, union dues, publicity costs, promotional costs, accounting and legal fees, telephone, telex and telefax fees, copying, postage, printing, tape copying, photos, and any and all out-of-pocket expenses incurred by Manager arising out of the performance of his services hereunder. Artist further agrees to be responsible for any traveling expenses, including meals, travel and accommodations associated with Manager's performance of his services to Artist, but subject to approval by Artist prior to being incurred.

10. Artist warrants that he is under no disability, restriction or prohibition with respect to his right to execute this Agreement and perform its terms and conditions. Artist warrants and represents that no act or omission by Artist hereunder will violate any right or interest of any person or firm or will subject Manager to any liability to any person or firm. Artist further agrees to indemnify Manager and hold him harmless against any damages, costs, expenses, fees (including all attorneys fees) incurred by Manager in any claim, suit or proceedings instituted against Manager and arising out of any breach or claimed breach by Artist of any warranty, representation or covenant of Artist. Artist authorizes Manager to withhold any and all sums due Artist to satisfy any claims or judgments rendered, on any fees incurred during the pendency of any legal proceeding brought against Artist and/or Manager.

11. Manager agrees to maintain accurate books and records of all transactions concerning Artist, which books and records may be inspected during normal business hours by a Certified Public Accountant designated by Artist upon twenty (20) business days notice to Manager, but in no event shall Artist examine said books and records more than once per calendar year.

12. Artist acknowledges and agrees that (a) Manager's right to represent Artist, as Artist's sole and exclusive personal manager, and Artist's obligation to solely and exclusively use Manager in such capacity, is unique, irreplaceable and extraordinary, and (b) any breach or threatened breach by Artist thereof may be material and shall cause Manager immediate and irreparable damage which cannot be adequately compensated for by money judgment. Accordingly, should Artist breach any of the terms and conditions of this Agreement, Manager will be entitled to seek and obtain, in addition to all other forms of relief which may be available, injunctive relief prohibiting and preventing Artist from engaging the services and abilities of any other person or firm in the capacity of personal manager, until and unless all of the terms and conditions of this Agreement have been satisfied.

13. This Agreement does not and shall not be construed to create a partnership or joint venture between the parties hereto, it being specifically understood and agreed that Manager is an independent contractor.

14. All written correspondence and notification shall be sent by Certified Mail, return receipt requested, to the respective addresses set forth above, and shall be considered received by said other party upon deposit in the United States Mail.

15. This Agreement shall terminate upon the happening of one of the following events:

a. natural expiration of the original term and/or option periods;

b. death of Manager;

c. death or medically diagnosed disability of Artist, in which event Manager will continue to receive all sums due Manager from exploitation of Artist's career in the entertainment industry prior to Artist's death or disability;

d. written consent of both parties.

16. Artist acknowledges that Manager has an insurable interest in the life of Artist, and therefore Artist agrees that should Manager, at Manager's own expense, elect to secure a life insurance policy on Artist with Manager as beneficiary, Artist will assist Manager in obtaining such a policy, including by submitting to a physical examination.

17. Manager shall have the right to assign this Agreement or any part hereof. Artist may not assign any of his rights and/or obligations hereunder without the express written permission of Manager.

18. **a.** This Agreement and all amendments or modifications hereof shall be governed by and interpreted in accordance with the laws of the state of Tennessee applicable to contracts executed and to be fully performed in said state. The invalidity of any clause, part or provision of this Agreement shall be restrictive in effect to said clause, part or provision, and shall not be deemed to affect the validity of the entire Agreement.

b. This Agreement embodies all the representations, terms and conditions of the parties' agreement, and there is no other collateral agreement, oral or written, between us in any manner relating to the subject matter hereof.

c. No alteration, amendment or modification hereof shall be binding unless set forth in a writing signed by all fo the parties hereto.

d. This Agreement shall not take effect until fully executed by all of the parties hereto.

e. Any reference herein to the singular shall be deemed to include the plural if the contest so requires, and any reference to the masculine pronoun shall be deemed to include the feminine if the context so requires.

f. Artist hereby acknowledges that Artist was permitted the opportunity to consult an attorney of his own choosing and has either consulted with such attorney prior to executing this Agreement or has voluntarily waived such right and entered into this Agreement freely, without coercion or any duress.

g. No breach of this Agreement on the part of Manager or Artist shall be deemed material, unless the party alleging such breach shall have given the other party notice of such breach, and said other party shall fail to discontinue the practice complained of or otherwise cure such breach, within thirty (30) days after receipt of such notice, if such breach is reasonably capable of being fully cured within such thirty (30) day period, or, if such breach is not reasonably capable of being fully cured within such thirty (30) day period, if Manager or Artist commences to cure such breach within such thirty (30) day period and proceeds with reasonable diligence to complete the curing of such breach. However, the provisions of this Paragraph 18(g) shall in no way limit or postpone the implementation or exercise of either party's rights under Paragraphs 7, 8, 10, and 12 hereof.

IN WITNESS WHEREOF, the parties have hereunto placed their seals the day and year first written above.

MANAGER:

_____

ARTIST:

_____

ACKNOWLEDGMENT

STATE OF _____

COUNTY OF _____

Before me, a Notary Public of the State and County aforesaid, personally appeared _____ the within named Artist, with whom I am personally acquainted, and who acknowledged that he executed the foregoing Management Agreement for the purposes therein contained.

WITNESS my hand and official seal on this _____ day of _____, 19___.

_____
Notary Public

My Commission Expires:

_____

APPENDIX 10

Management Agreement B
(with changes negotiated by artist's attorney)

AGREEMENT made as of this ___ day of _____, 19__, by and between _____, pka _____ whose address is _____ (hereinafter referred to as "Artist"), and _____ whose address is _____ (hereinafter referred to as "Manager)."

<u>W I T N E S S E T H</u>:

WHEREAS, Artist wishes to obtain advice, guidance, counsel and direction in the development and furtherance of Artist's career as a musician, composer, arranger, publisher and performing Artist, and in such new and different areas as Artist's artistic talents can be developed and exploited, and

WHEREAS, Manager, by reason of Manager's contacts, experience and background, is qualified to render such advice, guidance, counsel and direction to Artist;

NOW THEREFORE, in consideration of the mutual promises herein contained, it is agreed and understood as follows:

1.   Manager agrees to render such advice, guidance, counsel and other services as Artist may reasonably require to further Artist's career as a musician, composer, arranger, publisher, actor, writer and performing Artist, and to develop new and different areas within which Artist's artistic talents can be developed and exploited, including but not limited to the following services:

a.   to represent Artist and act as Artist's negotiator, to fix the terms governing all manner of disposition, use, employment or exploitation of Artist's talents and the products thereof; and

b.   to supervise Artist's professional employment and, on Artist's behalf, to consult with employers and prospective employers so as to assure the proper use and continued demand for Artist's services; and

c.   to be available at reasonable times and places to confer with Artist in connection with all matters concerning Artist's professional career, business interests, employment and publicity; and

d.   to exploit Artist's personality in all media and, in connection therewith to approve and permit, for the purpose of trade, advertising and publicity, the use, dissemination, reproduction or publication of Artist's name, photographic likeness, voice and artistic and musical materials; and

e.   to engage, discharge and/or direct such theatrical agents, booking agencies, and employment agencies as well as other firms, persons or corporations who may be retained for the purpose of securing contracts, engagements or employment for Artist. It is understood, however, that Manager is not a booking agent but rather shall represent Artist with all such agencies. Manager is not obligated to and shall not render any services or advice which would require Manager to be licensed as an employment agency in any jurisdiction; and

f.   to represent Artist in all dealings with any union; and

g.   to exercise all powers granted to Manager pursuant to paragraph "4" hereof.

2.   Manager is not required to render exclusive services to Artist, or to devote the entire time of Manager or the entire time of any of Manager's employees to Artist's affairs. Nothing

herein shall be construed as limiting Manager's rights to represent other persons whose talents may be similar to or who may be in competition with Artist, or to have and pursue business interests which may be similar to or may compete with those of Artist. This Agreement is entered into based upon the unique and personal qualifications of Manager, and accordingly Manager's duties may be delegated to others under the supervision of Manager, but Manager shall be ultimately responsible to Artist for the proper delivery of Manager's services as described herein. This Agreement shall not be assignable, except by written approval by Artist.

3.   Artist hereby appoints Manager as Artist's sole and exclusive personal manager in all matters usually and normally within the jurisdiction and authority of personal managers, including but not limited to the advice, guidance, counsel and direction specifically referred to in paragraph "1" hereof. Artist agrees to seek such advice, guidance, counsel and direction from Manager solely and exclusively, and agrees that Artist will not engage any other agent, representative or manager to render similar services, and that Artist will not negotiate, accept or execute any agreement, understanding or undertaking concerning Artist's career without prior consultation with Manager.

4.   a.   Artist hereby irrevocably appoints Manager for the term of this Agreement and any extensions hereof as Artist's true and lawful attorney-in-fact to sign, make, execute and deliver any and all contracts in Artist's name; to make, execute, endorse, accept, collect and deliver any and all bills of exchange, checks and notes as Artist's said attorney; to demand, sue for, collect, recover and receive goods, claims, money, interest or other items that may be due to Artist or belong to Artist; and to make, execute and deliver receipts, releases or other discharges therefor under sale or otherwise; and to defend, settle, adjust, compound, submit to arbitration and compromise, all actions, suits, accounts, reckonings, claims and demands whatsoever that are or shall be pending in such manner and in all respects as Manager in Manager's sole discretion shall deem advisable; and without in any way limiting the foregoing, generally to do, execute and perform any other act, deed or thing whatsoever that reasonably ought to be done, executed and performed of any and every nature and kind as fully and effectively as Artist could do if personally present; and Artist hereby ratifies and affirms all acts performed by Manager by virtue of this power of attorney.

b.   On any occasion which Manager accepts money or payment on behalf of Artist, Manager agrees to accept said funds or payment as a fiduciary on behalf of Artist, and to deposit said funds into a trust account from which all disbursements to Manager, third parties or to Artist shall be made. Manager further agrees to account quarterly to Artist for all funds so accepted by Manager and the disposition of said funds during the previous calendar quarter within thirty (30) days of the end of the calendar quarter. Manager shall maintain books and records of all trust fund transactions, and said books and records shall be available to Artist or Artist's representative upon reasonable notice to Manager. In the event that Artist receives payment for Artist's entertainment services, on which Manager's commission is due to Manager, Artist agrees to accept said portion of said funds which represents Manager's commission as a fiduciary and to promptly pay over Manager's portion of said funds to Manager or to account to Manager for said commission.

c.   Notwithstanding the foregoing, Manager agrees that he shall not exercise the powers-of attorney described in this paragraph 4, without first disclosing to Artist the material terms of the transaction in which Manager plans to act on behalf of Artist, and after such disclosure Manager obtains Artist's consent. In the event Artist is not available to Manager to discuss the material terms of the transaction and to provide Artist's consent, and the exigent circumstances and the best interests of the Artist demand that Manager act immediately by exercising said powers, Manager agrees to notify Artist as soon as possible as to the action taken by Manager and all material terms of the transaction. In so acting, Manager agrees to act as a reasonably prudent person under similar circumstances, and Manager agrees to be diligent in communicating promptly with the Artist as to the action taken.

d.   It is expressly understood that the foregoing power of attorney is limited to matters reasonably related to Artist's career as musician, composer, arranger, publisher and performing artist and such new and different areas within which Artist's artistic talents can be developed and exploited.

e.   Artist agrees and understands that the grant of power of attorney to Manager is coupled with an interest, which Artist irrevocably grants to Manager, in Artist's career, artistic talents and the products of said career and talents, and in Artist's earnings arising by reason of such career, talents and products.

5.   a.   As compensation for services to be rendered hereunder, Manager shall receive from Artist (or shall retain from Artist's gross monthly earnings) at the end of each calendar month during the term hereof, a sum of money equal to ___ percent (00%) of Artist's gross monthly earnings from entertainment industry sources only as provided herein. Artist hereby assigns to Manager an interest in such earnings to the extent of ___ percent (00%) thereof. Said assignment is intended by Artist to create an assignment coupled with an interest.

b.   The term "gross monthly earnings" as used herein, refers to the total of all earnings, which shall not be accumulated or averaged (whether in the form of salary, bonuses, royalties (or advances against royalties), interests, percentages, shares of profits, merchandise, shares in ventures, products, properties, or any other kind or type of income which is reasonably related to Artist's career in the entertainment, amusement, music, recording, motion picture, television, radio, literary, theatrical and advertising fields and all similar areas whether now known or hereafter devised, in which Artist's artistic talents are developed and exploited), received during any calendar month by Artist or by any of Artist's heirs, executors, administrators, assigns, or by any person, firm or corporation (including Manager) on Artist's behalf. It is understood that, for the purpose hereof, no expense, cost or disbursement incurred by Artist in connection with the receipt of "gross monthly earnings" shall be deducted therefrom prior to the calculation of Manager's compensation hereunder.

c.   The compensation agreed to be paid to Manager shall be based upon gross monthly earnings (as herein defined) of Artist accruing to or received by Artist during the term of this Agreement or subsequent to the termination of this Agreement as a result of: (i) any services performed by Artist during or prior to the term hereof, or (ii) any contract negotiated during or prior to the term hereof and any renewal, extension or modification of such contract, or (iii) any product of Artist's services or talents or of any property created by Artist in whole or in part during or prior to the term hereof. Artist'S obligation to pay commission to Manager beyond the term of this Agreement shall be subject to Manager'S rights as defined by this Paragraph 5(c) hereof, and in no event shall Artist have any obligation to pay commission to Manager on any income received by Artist after the expiration of twenty-four (24) months following the expiration or termination of the this Agreement, unless otherwise agreed by Artist in a written agreement.

d.   In the event that Artist forms a corporation during the term hereof for the purpose of furnishing and exploiting Artist's artistic talents, Artist agrees that said corporation shall offer to enter into a management contract with Manager identical in all respects to this Agreement (except as to the parties thereto.)

(i)   In the event that Manager accepts such offer, then the gross monthly earnings of such corporation prior to the deduction of any corporate income taxes and of any corporate expenses or other deductions shall be included as part of Artist's gross monthly earnings as herein defined, and any salary paid to Artist by such corporation shall be excluded from Artist's gross monthly earnings for the purpose of calculating the compensation due to Manager hereunder.

(ii)   In the event that Manager refuse such offer, then the gross monthly earnings of such corporation prior to deduction of any corporate income taxes and any other corporate expenses or deduction shall be excluded from Artist's gross monthly earnings as defined hereunder, and such salary as is paid to Artist by such corporation shall be included as part of Artist's gross monthly earnings as herein defined.

e.   In the event that Artist forms a corporation or enters into a contract with a corporation during the term hereof for the purpose of exploiting or furnishing Artist's artistic talents, then in addition to any and all other considerations to be paid Manager hereunder, Manager shall be entitled to purchase at least ____ Percent (00%) of the capital stock of such corporation at the price of One Dollar ($1.00) per share. Artist agrees expressly not to enter into any contract with a corporation or to create any corporation for such purpose unless said option is made available to Manager.

f.   Artist agrees that all gross monthly earnings as herein defined shall be paid directly to Manager by all persons, firms or corporations, and shall not be paid by such persons, firms or corporations to Artist, and that Manager may withhold Manager's compensation therefrom and may reimburse itself therefrom for any fees, costs or expenses advanced or incurred by Manager pursuant to paragraph "6" hereof. In the event that Artist nevertheless receives gross monthly earnings directly, Artist shall be deemed to hold in trust for Manager that portion of Artist's gross monthly earnings which equals Manager's compensation hereunder and such disbursements incurred by Manager on behalf of Artist.

6.   Artist shall be solely responsible for payment of all booking agency fees, union dues, publicity costs, promotional or exploitation costs, travelling expenses and/or wardrobe expenses and all other expenses, fees and costs incurred by Artist. In the event that Manager advances any of the foregoing fees, costs or expenses on behalf of Artist, or incurs any other reasonable costs, fees or expenses in direct connection with Artist's professional career or with the performance of Manager's services hereunder, Artist shall promptly reimburse Manager for such fees, costs and expenses. Without limiting the foregoing, such direct expenses, costs or fees incurred by Manager shall include direct long distance phone calls, promotion and publicity expenses and first-class travel and living expenses and costs whenever Manager, in Manager's opinion, shall deem it advisable to accompany Artist outside of Nashville. No legal fees, accounting fees or bookkeeping fees of Manager shall be reimbursable by Artist, unless Artist expressly approves such expenses in advance.
Notwithstanding the foregoing, in order for Manager to be reimbursed by Artist for expenses, Manager agrees to adhere to the following requirements:

a.   Manager will not incur any expenses over $____ per month without Artist's prior express approval.

b.   Manager will not be reimbursed by Artist for travel expenses in excess of $_____ per month, unless approved by Artist in advance.

c.   Manager will not travel at a higher class than Artist or stay at more expensive accomodations than Artist.

d.   If Manager travels on behalf of more than one client including Artist, expenses will be prorated between (among) the clients.

e.   In order to be reimbursed, Manager must present valid receipts or other evidence of expenditures incurred.

7.   a.   Artist warrants that Artist is under no disability, restriction or prohibition with respect to Artist's right to execute this Agreement and perform its terms and conditions. Artist warrants and represents that no act or omission by Artist hereunder will violate any right or interest of any person or firm or will subject Manager to any liability, or claim of liability to any person. Artist agrees to indemnify Manager and to hold Manager harmless against any damages, costs, expenses, fees (including attorneys' fees) incurred by Manager in any claim, suit or proceeding instituted by or against Manager in which any assertion is made which is inconsistent with any warranty, representation or covenant of Artist.

b.   Manager warrants that he is under no disability, restriction or prohibition with respect to Manager's right to execute this agreement and perform its terms and conditions. Manager warrants and represents that no act or omission by Manager hereunder will violate any right or interest of any person or firm or will subject Artist to any liability, or claim of liability to any person. Manager agrees to indemnify Artist and to hold Artist harmless against any damages, costs, expenses, fees (including attorneys' fees) incurred by Artist in any claim, suit or proceeding instituted by or against Artist in which any assertion is made which is made which is inconsistent with any warranty, representation or covenant of Manager

8.   a.   The initial term of this Agreement shall be for a period of ___ (0) years from the date hereof.

b.   Manager shall have the irrevocable option to renew this Agreement for ___ (0) additional period of one (1) year by written notice mailed to Artist no less than sixty (60) days prior to the expiration of the initial term.

c.   In the event that Artist shall fail for any reason to fulfill any obligation assumed by Artist hereunder (all of which obligations are agreed to be "of the essence" and material), Manager shall be entitled (by written notice mailed to Artist at any time) to extend the duration of the initial term (or of the option period in the event that such notice is mailed by Manager during the option period) for a period of time equal to the duration of such failure by Artist and until Artist shall fully cure any such failure. It is understood that no failure or delay of Manager to enforce the rights of Manager under this subparagraph shall be deemed a waiver of Manager's subsequent right to exert the rights granted to Manager hereunder.

9.   Manager agrees to maintain accurate books and records of all transactions concerning Artist, which books and records may be inspected by a Certified Public Accountant or attorney designated by Artist, at Artist's expense, upon reasonable written notice to Manager, at Manager's office in Nashville and during normal business hours.

10.   There shall be no change, amendment or modification of this Agreement unless it is reduced to writing and signed by all parties hereto. No waiver of any breach of this Agreement shall be construed as a continuing waiver or consent to any subsequent breach hereof.

11.   It is agreed that as a condition precedent to any assertion by either party that the other party is in default in performing any obligation contained herein, the party claiming such default must advise the other party in writing of the specific facts upon which it is claimed that such party is in default and of the specific obligation which it is claimed has been breached, and the breaching party shall be allowed a period of thirty (30) days after receipt of such written notice, within which to cure such default. It is agreed that in the event that the alleged breach is cured within such thirty (30) day period, that the alleged breach shall then be deemed to have never occurred.

12.   Artist acknowledges and agrees that Manager's right to represent Artist, as Artist's sole and exclusive personal Manager, and Artist's obligation to solely and exclusively use Manager in such capacity, are unique, irreplaceable and extraordinary rights and obligations, and that any breach or threatened breach by Artist thereof shall be material and shall cause Manager immediate and irreparable damages which cannot be adequately compensated for by money judgment. Accordingly, Artist agrees that, in addition to all other forms of relief and all other remedies which may be available to Manager in the event of any such breach or threatened breach by Artist, Manager (subject to the notice provision contained in paragraph "11") shall be entitled to seek and obtain injunctive relief against Artist, and Artist agrees that in seeking such injunctive relief, Manager shall not be obligated to secure any bond or relief.

13.   This Agreement does not and shall not be construed to create a partnership or joint venture between the parties hereto.

14.   This Agreement shall be construed in accordance with the laws of the State of Tennessee governing contracts wholly executed and performed therein, and shall be binding upon and inure to the benefit of the parties, their respective heirs, executors, administrators and successors.

15.   In the event any provision hereof shall be for any reason illegal or unenforceable, the same shall not affect the validity or enforceability of the remaining provisions hereof.

16.   All written correspondence and notification shall be sent by Certified Mail, Return Receipt Requested, to the respective addresses set forth above, and shall be considered received by said other party upon deposit in the United States Mail.

[Signatures follow as on p. 262]

APPENDIX II

Recording Contract (excerpts)

AGREEMENT made as of the _____ day of _____, 19____ by and between ARISTA RECORDS, INC., 6 West 57th Street, New York, New York 10019 ("Company") and _____, f/s/o _____.
              ("Producer")   ("Artist")

In consideration of the representations and warranties and the mutual promises hereinafter set forth, it is agreed as follows:

1. For the purposes of this agreement, the following terms shall have the following meanings:

(a) "Master" means a recording of one (1) Composition embodying the recorded performances of Artist.

(b) (i) "Seven-inch Single" means a phonograph record embodying thereon one (1) or two (2) Masters; "Twelve-inch Single" means a phonograph record embodying thereon not less than one (1) Master and not more than four (4) Masters; Seven-inch Singles and Twelve-inch Singles are herein sometimes collectively referred to as "Singles."

(ii) "EP" means a phonograph record embodying thereon not less than five (5) Masters and not more than seven (7) Masters.

(iii) "LP" means a phonograph record embodying thereon not less than eight (8) Masters and not more than ten (10) Masters, containing a minimum of thirty-six (36) minutes of Artist's performances.

(c) Notwithstanding paragraph 1(b) above, if a particular record is marketed by Company or its Licensees as a particular configuration of record (e.g., Seven-inch Single, Twelve-inch Single, EP, etc.), then such record shall be deemed to be such form of configuration.

(d) "Records" and "phonograph records", mean all forms of reproductions, now or hereafter known, including new technologies, embodying audio alone, and/or audio coupled with visual images.

(e) "Retail list price" means the suggested retail list price in, at Company's election, the country of manufacture or sale of records sold in the United States and in any other country where Company manufactures and sells records for its own account as opposed to licensing such rights to third parties and, for records sold elsewhere, the suggested retail list price, or a constructed price, whichever is the basis used by a particular Licensee of Company to report to Company. Notwithstanding anything to the contrary contained in this agreement, Company may change the method by which it computes royalties (for some or all of the Territory) from one of the above methods to some other method (the "New Method"). If Company adopts a New Method, such New Method shall be deemed incorporated herein in lieu of the present method of computing royalties with respect to all records derived from the Masters thereafter sold, an appropriate reference in respect of the New Method shall replace the current references to the retail list price, and the royalty rates provided for herein shall be adjusted to the appropriate royalty which would be applied to the New Method so that upon the first change to the New Method, the dollars-and-cents royalty amounts payable with respect to the top-line LPs in any configuration being sold by Company would be identical to that which was payable immediately prior to such change. All other royalty rates shall be proportionately adjusted. The royalty adjustments to be made pursuant to this paragraph shall be based on net dollars-and-cents royalty amounts and shall take into account any factors (including, without limitation, Company's regular "free goods" policies before and after Company's adoption of the New Method) affecting such net royalty amounts.

(f) "Composition" means a musical composition or medley consisting of music with or without words.

(g) "Recording Costs" means all costs incurred with respect to the production of Masters embodying Artist's performances. Recording Costs include, without limitation, union scale, the costs of all instruments, musicians, vocalists, conductors, arrangers, orchestrators, copyists, etc., payments to a trustee or fund based on wages to the extent required by any agreement between Company and any labor organization or trustee, all studio costs, tape, editing, mixing, mastering to tape, engineering, the costs of cutting references, travel, per diems, production fees and/or advances, rehearsal halls, costs of non-studio facilities and equipment, dubbing, transportation of instruments and other costs and expenses incurred in producing the Masters hereunder, which are customarily recognized as Recording Costs in the phonograph record industry.

(h) "Territory" means the world.

(i) "Deliver" or "Delivery" or "Delivered" (or any of said terms in lower case) when used with Masters means Company's receipt of newly-recorded satisfactory Masters to constitute the LP concerned (two-track stereo tapes, fully edited, mixed, leadered and equalized), together with one (1) reference therefor and all necessary licenses, approvals, consents and permissions, in accordance with the terms of this agreement.

(j) "Licensee" or "licensee" includes, without limitation, sublicensees, affiliates, subsidiaries, wholly or partly owned, and other divisions of Company.

(k) "Books and Records" or "books and records" means that portion of Company's books and records which specifically reports sales of records embodying the Masters produced hereunder and/or specifically reports net royalty receipts or the net amount received from any other exploitation of such Masters; provided that such defined term shall not be deemed to include any manufacturing records (e.g., inventory and/or production records) or any other of Company's records.

(l) "Initially released in the United States" means the initial date customarily used by Company as the release date for any configuration of a particular LP.

2. (a) Producer shall produce and deliver Masters embodying the performances of Artist exclusively to Company for a term consisting of an Initial Period and the Option Periods hereinafter set forth if Company exercises any one or more of its options. The Initial Period as the same may be extended is hereinafter called the "Term". Producer hereby irrevocably grants to Company the option to extend the Initial Period for four (4) further consecutive renewal periods ("Option Periods"). Each option shall be exercised, if at all, by written notice to Producer prior to or on the date that the Term would otherwise expire. Each period of the Term is sometimes hereinafter referred to as a "Contract Period".

(b) The first Contract Period shall commence on the date hereof and shall continue until the end of the ninth full month after the month in which there occurs the completion of Delivery of the recording obligation for the first Contract Period. Each Option Period shall commence upon the date following the last day of the immediately preceding Contract Period and shall continue until the end of the ninth full month after the month in which there occurs the completion of Delivery of the recording obligation for the Option Period concerned. Notwithstanding the two preceding sentences, if

Company exercises its Overcall Right for any Contract Period, then such Contract Period shall instead continue until the end of the ninth full month after the month in which there occurs the completion of Delivery of the Overcall LP for the Contract Period concerned.

3. (a) Producer warrants that, during the Term, Artist will record Masters exclusively for Producer and Company, in an approved recording studio, embodying Compositions not theretofore recorded by Artist, and Producer shall deliver to Company the number of Masters embodying the performances of Artist as herein provided. Company shall have the right and opportunity to have a representative attend each recording session.

(b) During each Contract Period, Producer shall produce and deliver to Company Masters to constitute one (1) LP embodying Artist's performances in accordance with the provisions of this agreement. The aforesaid Masters to be recorded during each Contract Period are herein sometimes referred to as the "recording obligation" or the "committed LPs" for the Contract Period concerned. Company shall have the right and option to require Producer to produce and deliver to Company Masters to constitute one (1) additional LP during each Contract Period. Said option is referred to herein as the "Overcall Right" and said additional Masters to be recorded during each Contract Period are herein referred to as the "Overcall LP." Company can exercise the Overcall Right at any time prior to or on the date the particular Contract Period would otherwise expire. The Overcall LP shall be subject to the terms and conditions of this agreement.

(c) Company and Producer shall jointly select the Compositions to be recorded and each Master shall be subject to Company's approval as satisfactory for the manufacture and sale of phonograph records. Upon Company's request, Producer shall cause Artist to record additional Compositions and/or re-record any Composition recorded hereunder, as necessary, until a Master which in Company's sole judgment is satisfactory for the manufacture and sale of phonograph records shall have been obtained.

(d) Company can release so-called "Greatest Hits" or "Best Of" LPs without Producer's consent, and no such LP shall be deemed to be in partial or complete fulfillment of any of Producer's obligations hereunder. Producer shall not deliver Masters to constitute two or more LPs intended to be marketed as a single package ("Multiple Record Set") to satisfy Producer's obligation to deliver Masters to constitute one (1) LP without Company's prior written consent, which consent may be withheld for any reason. If Producer delivers and Company accepts Masters to constitute a Multiple Record Set, it shall be deemed to be a single LP for the purposes of this agreement. No Masters consisting of "live" or instrumental recordings shall be delivered or shall be deemed to be in partial or complete fulfillment of any of Producer's obligations hereunder.

(e) Producer's submission of Masters to Company shall constitute Producer's representation that it has obtained all necessary licenses, approvals, consents and permissions. Company's payment of any monies due in respect of the delivery of Masters hereunder shall not be deemed to be a waiver of Producer's obligation to obtain and furnish all such licenses, approvals, consents and permissions and shall not be deemed to be a waiver of Producer's obligation to make delivery.

4. (a) Producer warrants that, during the Term, Artist will not perform or authorize or knowingly permit to be recorded any performance, for or by anyone other than Company, without in each case taking measures to prevent the exploitation of phonograph records embodying such performances. Producer further warrants that, during the Term, Producer and Artist will not license or consent to the use of Artist's name, likeness, voice, biographical material or other identification ("Artist's Identification"), in connection with the recording or exploitation of phonograph records by anyone other than Company.

(b) Producer warrants that neither it nor Artist will produce or perform in connection with the production of any record embodying any Composition recorded by Artist under this agreement prior to the later of five (5) years subsequent to the date of Delivery to Company of a Master embodying that Composition or two (2) years subsequent to the expiration of the Term of this agreement. Should Producer or Artist so produce or perform in connection with any such Composition during the period referred to above, then, without limiting any of Company's other rights or remedies, Company shall have no further obligation to pay royalties to Producer which otherwise would accrue to Producer hereunder on records which contain Artist's performance of such Composition.

5. Each Master produced during the Term shall, from the inception of its creation, be considered a "work made for hire" for Company within the meaning of the U.S. Copyright Law. If it is determined that a Master does not so qualify, then such Master, together with all rights in it, shall be deemed transferred to Company by this agreement. All such Masters shall be recorded by Producer and performed by Artist on Company's behalf and all records made therefrom, together with the performances embodied therein, shall, from the inception of their creation, be entirely the property of Company in perpetuity, throughout the Territory, free of any claim whatsoever by Producer or by Artist, or by any persons deriving any rights or interests therefrom; and Company shall have the right to secure the sound recording (P) copyright in and to the Masters in Company's name as the owner and author thereof and to secure any and all renewals of such copyright. Producer and Artist shall execute and deliver to Company such instruments of transfer and other documents regarding the rights of Company in the Masters as Company may reasonably request to carry out the purposes of this agreement, and Company may sign such documents in Producer's or Artist's name and make appropriate disposition of them. Company (and its Licensees) shall have the exclusive right to use the Masters in perpetuity and throughout the Territory or any part thereof in any manner it sees fit, including, without limitation, the exclusive right:

(a) To manufacture, distribute and exploit the Masters and records embodying the Masters, in any or all fields of use, by any method now or hereafter known, upon such terms and conditions as Company (and its Licensees) may elect or, in its sole discretion, to refrain therefrom;

(b) To release records embodying the Masters under any name, and trademark or label which Company (and its Licensees) may from time to time elect;

(c) To use (including publish) the names (including all professional, group and assumed or fictitious names), likenesses, photographs and biographical material of any party, including Artist, rendering services in connection with the Masters for the purpose of publicizing or exploiting the rights granted hereunder; and

(d) To publicly perform or to permit the public performance of the Masters by means of radio broadcast, television broadcast or any other method now or hereafter known including new technologies.

6. Company shall pay to Producer the following royalties for the use by Company or its Licensees of the Masters against which all advances paid to or on behalf of Producer, including, without limitation, the sums referred to in paragraphs 8 and 9 shall be chargeable:

(a) (i) A royalty of the following percent of the retail list price for the following records derived from the Masters recorded during the following Contract Periods and sold by Company for distribution in the United States and not returned (the "basic royalty rate" for the United States):

TYPE OF RECORD	CONTRACT PERIOD	RATE
(A) LPs	1st	
(B) LPs	2nd	

(C) LPs	3rd, 4th and 5th	_____
(D) Seven-inch Singles	1st and 2nd	_____
(E) Seven-inch Singles	3rd, 4th and 5th	_____
(F) Twelve-inch Singles	1st and 2nd	_____
(G) Twelve-inch Singles	3rd, 4th and 5th	_____

(ii) As to EPs derived from the Masters, sold by Company for distribution in the United States and not returned, the royalty rate shall be two-thirds (2/3) of the otherwise applicable LP royalty rate provided for above.

(iii) As to Multiple Record Sets derived from the Masters, sold by Company for distribution in the United States and not returned, the royalty rate shall be one-half (1/2) of the otherwise applicable LP royalty rate provided for above.

(iv) Notwithstanding the royalty rates contained in subparagraph 6(a) (i) above, with respect to net sales of a particular LP through normal retail channels in the United States, for which royalties are payable pursuant to such subparagraph, in excess of the following number of units, the applicable royalty rate for such excess sales shall be the applicable rate set forth below:

LP	UNITS	RATES
First or second LP	250,000	
in first Contract Period:	500,000	_____
First or Second LP	250,000	
in second Contract Period:	500,000	_____

(b) (i) A royalty of the following percent of the retail list price for all LPs derived from the Masters recorded during the following Contract Periods and sold by Company or its regular foreign distributors for distribution outside of the United States, as to which Company receives payment (the "basic royalty rate" for outside of the United States):

Territory	Contract Period	Rate

(ii) As to EPs, Singles and Multiple Record Sets derived from the Masters sold by Company or its regular foreign distributors for distribution outside of the United States, as to which Company receives payment, the royalty rate shall be one-half (1/2) of the otherwise applicable LP royalty rate provided for in this paragraph 6(b).

(iii) As to sales of such records released by Company's Licensees (other than its regular foreign distributors), Company shall credit Producer's royalty account with fifty (50%) percent of Company's net royalty receipts from such sales.

(c) Notwithstanding anything to the contrary contained in paragraphs 6(a) and 6(b) above:

(i) As to records derived from the Masters and sold by Company or its regular foreign distributors in the "compact disc" format or the digital audio format (or any other format not specifically provided for in this paragraph 6), the retail list price of the record shall be deemed to be no greater than the retail list price for Company's or Company's regular foreign distributors' (as applicable) then-current similar vinyl disc record or analog tape equivalent (whichever is lower).

(ii) Notwithstanding anything to the contrary contained in subparagraph 6(c) (i) above, for the purpose of calculating the royalty payable for sales in the "compact disc" format in the United States of the _____ LP for the _____ Contract Period and such sales of each subsequent LP Delivered hereunder in such format(s), the retail list price for the particular LPs concerned shall be deemed to be eighty (80%) percent of the actual retail list price for the particular record concerned.

(d) As to sales of records not consisting entirely of Masters delivered hereunder, Producer's royalties otherwise payable hereunder shall be prorated based upon the number of such Masters which are on such records compared to the total number of recordings on such records.

(e) Royalties shall be calculated based upon the retail list price after deducting all taxes and duties and Company's customary container charges. At the present time, Company's customary container charges are as follows for the following records: ten (10%) percent of the retail list price for disc records (other than Seven-inch Singles released in standard generic sleeves and other than those LPs listed below); twelve and one-half (12-1/2%) percent of the retail list price for a single disc LP released in a double-fold album jacket or in an album jacket which contains an insert; twenty (20%) percent of the retail list price for a non-disc record for Multiple Record Sets, for audio-visual records and for a double-disc LP released in a double-fold album jacket; twenty-five (25%) percent of the retail list price for a record accounted for pursuant to subparagraph 6(c) (ii) above; and five (5%) percent of the retail list price in addition to the container charges set forth in this paragraph for records in oversized cardboard containers (e.g., 3″ × 12″, 4″ × 12″ cardboard containers).

(f) As to LPs derived from the Masters, which have a retail list price that is at least Two ($2.00) Dollars (or its foreign equivalent) less than the retail list price used for top line phonograph records released by Company or its regular foreign distributors in the particular country, the royalty rate shall be one-half (1/2) of the otherwise applicable basic royalty rate provided for in paragraphs 6(a) and 6(b) above. As to such records released by Company's Licensees (other than its regular foreign distributors), Company shall credit Producer's royalty account with fifty (50%) percent of Company's net royalty receipts from such sales.

(g) As to records derived from the Masters sold through record clubs or similar sales plans or devices by Company's Licensees, Company shall credit Producer's royalty account with fifty (50%) percent of Company's net royalty receipts from such sales.

(h) In computing the number of records sold hereunder, Company shall have the right to deduct returns and credits of any nature. Company shall have the right to withhold a portion of Producer's royalties as a reserve in accordance with normal company policies, which for LPs in any configuration are as follows:

(i) Thirty (30%) percent of the royalties otherwise earned during a given accounting period, except that, if an LP is released during the last sixty (60) days of an accounting period, then the reserve for such accounting period shall be forty (40%) percent.

(ii) Over each of the four (4) accounting periods immediately following the accounting period in which the applicable reserve was established,

Company shall credit Producer's royalty account with one-fourth of the royalty reserve amount originally withheld with respect to a given accounting period.

(i)   No royalties shall be payable for promotional records designed for distribution without charge or for sale at a substantially lower price than the regular price of Company's equivalent records.

(j)   As to flat fee licenses of the Masters to third parties for phonograph records use and all other types of use, Company shall credit Producer's royalty account with fifty (50%) percent of the net amount received by Company and attributable to the Masters under each such license.

(k)   For each eighty-five (85) disc LPs or tapes (or EPs) that Company ships to its distributors for which royalties shall be payable hereunder, Company shall have the right to ship to its distributors on a no-charge basis or at a cost which is fifty (50%) percent or less of Company's regular wholesale price fifteen (15) disc LPs or tapes (or EPs) for which royalties shall not be payable; for each eighty (80) compact disc records that Company ships to its distributors for which royalties shall be payable hereunder, Company shall have the right to ship to its distributors on a no charge basis or at a cost which is fifty (50%) percent or less of Company's regular wholesale price twenty (20) compact disc records for which royalties shall not be payable; and for each one hundred (100) Singles that Company ships to its distributors for which royalties shall be payable hereunder, Company shall have the right to ship to its distributors on a no-charge basis or at a cost which is fifty (50%) percent or less of Company's regular wholesale price thirty (30) Singles for which royalties shall not be payable. No royalties shall be payable for records used for the purpose of publicity or advertising, for records distributed to radio stations, television stations, motion picture companies, publishers or others, for records used on transportation facilities or as in-store play samplers, for records sold as cutouts or overstock, or for records sold as scrap. Notwithstanding anything to the contrary hereinabove set forth, if Company changes its overall policy with respect to records shipped to distributors on a no-charge basis or at a cost which is fifty (50%) percent or less of Company's regular wholesale price on which royalties are not payable, then Company shall have the right to change the limitations hereinabove set forth in accordance with such new policy. If records derived from the Masters are sold to distributors or others for less than Company's regular wholesale price, or at a discount therefrom, but for more than fifty (50%) percent of such regular wholesale price, then, for purposes of this paragraph, a percentage of such records shall be deemed non-royalty bearing records, which percentage shall be an amount equal to the percentage amount of the applicable discount; provided, however, that the aggregate number of records deemed to have been shipped on a non-royalty bearing basis pursuant to this sentence and the number of records so shipped pursuant to the preceding sentences of this paragraph 6(k), shall be subject to the limitations set forth above in this paragraph 6(k) or otherwise herein. Company shall have the right to exceed any of the limitations described in this paragraph for promotions, including short term and catalog programs, without Producer's consent. Records returned shall be prorated between royalty free records and records on which royalties are payable in the same proportion as such returned records are credited to distributors.

(l)   For the sale by Company's Licensees of records which include Masters delivered hereunder through "key outlet marketing" and/or direct mail or mail order, and/or audiophile or other specialty markets, and for the sale by Company's Licensees of records not consisting entirely of Masters delivered hereunder through normal retail channels, Company shall credit Producer's royalty account with fifty (50%) percent of Company's net royalty receipts attributable to the Masters from such sales.

(m)   The royalty rate for records derived from the Masters and sold for sale in Armed Forces Post Exchanges shall be one-half (1/2) of the otherwise applicable basic royalty rate provided for in paragraphs 6(a) and 6(b) above.

(n)   The royalty rate payable hereunder for records derived from the Masters and sold by Company as "premiums", and for records derived from the Masters and sold by Company or its Licensees in conjunction with a major television or radio promotion campaign, shall be one-half (1/2) of the otherwise applicable basic royalty rate provided for in paragraphs 6(a) and 6(b) above and the retail list price for such records shall be deemed to be Company's or its Licensees' actual sales price. As to such records sold as "premiums" by Company's Licensees, Company shall credit Producer's royalty account with fifty (50%) percent of Company's net royalty receipts from such sales. Company shall be entitled to use and publish, and to license or permit others to use and publish, Artist's Identification with respect to the products or services in connection with which such "premium" records are sold or distributed.

(o)   With respect to any Master embodying Artist's performances hereunder together with the performance of another artist or artists to whom Company is or becomes obligated to pay royalties in respect of phonograph records embodying the joint performances contained on such Master: (i) the royalty rate to be used in determining the royalties payable to Producer in respect of such Master shall be computed by multipying the royalty rate otherwise applicable thereto by a fraction, the numerator of which shall be one and the denominator of which shall be the total number of royalty artists whose performances are embodied on such Master; and (ii) in determining the portion of Recording Costs applicable to such Master which shall be charged against Producer's royalties, such proportion shall be computed by multiplying the aggregate amount of such Recording Costs by the same fraction used in determining the royalties payable to Producer in respect of such Master. No such joint recording shall be counted toward the fulfillment of the recording obligation hereunder unless Company shall specifically consent, in writing, to count such joint recording toward the fulfillment of such recording obligation.

(p)   Royalties for phonograph records derived from the Masters and sold for distribution outside of the United States shall be paid at the same rate of exchange as Company is paid, provided, however, that such royalties shall not be payable until payment has been received by Company in the United States in United States Dollars. If Company shall not receive payment in the United States or in United States Dollars and shall elect to accept payment in a foreign currency or in a foreign country, Company may deposit to the credit of Producer (and at the expense of Producer) in such country in a depository selected by Company payments so received applicable to royalties hereunder, and shall notify Producer promptly thereof. Deposit as aforesaid shall fulfill the obligations of Company as to phonograph record sales to which such royalty payments are applicable.

7.   (a)   Company shall account to Producer on or before the first day of October for the period ending the preceding June 30th, and on or before the first day of April for the period ending the preceding December 31st, together with the payment of any royalties accrued during such preceding half-year. Royalties payable or credited to Producer hereunder shall be less whatever taxes the laws of any applicable jurisdiction require be withheld in connection with such royalties. All statements shall be binding upon Producer unless specific written objection, stating the basis thereof, is given to Company within one (1) year from the date rendered. Producer shall be foreclosed from maintaining any action, claim or proceeding against Company in any forum or tribunal with respect to any statement or accounting due hereunder unless Producer commences such action, claim or proceeding in a court of competent jurisdiction within two (2) years after the date such statement or accounting is rendered. Producer shall have the right to appoint a Certified Public Accountant, who is not then currently engaged in an outstanding audit of Company, to examine Company's books and records insofar as they pertain to this agreement provided such examination shall take place at Company's offices during normal business hours, on reasonable written notice, not more than once in any calendar year during which Producer receives a statement and at Producer's sole expense. Such examination shall be conditioned upon the accountant's agreement to Company that he is not being compensated on a contingent fee basis. Producer acknowledges that Company's books and records contain confidential trade information and warrants and represents that neither Producer nor Artist nor their representatives will communicate to others or use on behalf of any other person any facts or information obtained as a result of such examination of Company's books and records.

(b) If Producer claims that additional monies are payable to Producer, Company shall not be deemed in material breach of this agreement unless such claim shall have been reduced to a final judgment by a court of competent jurisdiction and Company shall have failed to pay Producer the amount thereof within thirty (30) days after Company shall have received notice of the entry of such judgment.

8. (a) Company shall advance all Recording Costs incurred in connection with the production of the Masters in accordance with a written budget submitted by Producer and approved by Company prior to the recording session for such Masters. Company shall not withhold approval of a budget for the production of Masters to constitute an LP if the total recording budget submitted for the production of such Masters does not include any fees in excess of union scale or any other unusual expense and if the total recording budget for the production of such LP, including any fees to be paid to the individual producer, does not exceed ninety (90%) percent of the applicable minimum Recording Fund fixed in paragraph 9 below (as same may be reduced pursuant to the provisions of this agreement).

(b) If Recording Costs for the production of the Masters exceed the applicable approved budget, then Producer shall be solely responsible for and shall pay such excess costs, provided, however, that Company shall have the right to pay such excess and, without limiting its rights, to deduct the amount of such excess from any sums that may be payable to Producer hereunder.

9. Company shall advance to Producer the following sums to be charged against and recouped from royalties payable by Company to Producer:

10. In addition to delivering the Masters hereunder, Producer shall deliver to Company or, at Company's option, shall keep available for Company and subject to Company's control at the recording studios the following: each and every original session tape, each multi-track master, a non-equalized copy of the Masters and each and every mother, Master, acetate copy or other derivative of the Masters.

11. Company shall be responsible for the payment of mechanical copyright royalties directly to the copyright proprietors. Producer warrants that the Compositions embodied on the Masters shall be available for mechanical licensing and Producer shall assist Company in entering into mechanical licenses, which licenses (subject to the provisions outlined herein) shall be in the general form utilized by The Harry Fox Agency, Inc., or in a form that is otherwise acceptable to Company. The mechanical licenses for Compositions recorded pursuant to this agreement which are written, in whole or in part, by Artist or by an individual producer of Masters, or owned or controlled directly or indirectly, by Producer, Artist or such individual producer or by any party associated or affiliated with Producer, Artist or such individual producer ("Controlled Composition") shall be licensed to Company, for the Territory excluding the United States, at the rates set forth below and such mechanical licenses shall also provide that mechanical royalties shall only be payable on records for which royalties are payable pursuant to paragraph 6 hereof. In addition, each Controlled Composition is hereby licensed to Company, for the United States, at the rates set forth below and mechanical royalties for such uses of such Compositions shall only be payable on records for which royalties are payable pursuant to paragraph 6 hereof.

(a) Three-fourths (3/4) of the then-current minimum fixed statutory copyright royalty rate under the U.S. Copyright Law per Controlled Composition for the United States, determined as of the date the Masters embodying Controlled Compositions were initially recorded or the last date by which the Masters embodying such Controlled Compositions were originally scheduled to be recorded pursuant to paragraph 24(b), whichever is earlier; Two (2¢) cents per Controlled Composition for Canada; and the minimum statutory rate or, if there is no such minimum statutory rate, the standard industry rate per Controlled Composition for each other country in the Territory;

(b) Notwithstanding the rates specified in paragraph 11(a) above, it is specifically understood and agreed that the maximum copyright royalty rate which Company will be required to pay in respect of a record released hereunder in any configuration shall be equal to the number of Masters contained on such record times the applicable rate provided for in paragraph 11(a) (the "maximum mechanical rate"), but in no event shall the maximum mechanical rate for an LP in any configuration exceed ten times such applicable rate nor shall the maximum mechanical rate for a Single exceed two times such applicable rate. Notwithstanding the immediately preceding sentence, if the same version (i.e., the same mix) of a Master embodying a particular Composition is contained on both sides of a cassette tape, then Company shall be obligated to pay a mechanical royalty in respect of only one use of such Composition in connection with the particular tape concerned. If Company or any of its Licensees releases a Multiple Record Set, the maximum mechanical rate otherwise applicable by a fraction, the numerator of which is the retail list price for the Multiple Record Set in the configuration concerned and the denominator of which is the retail list price used for top line phonograph records in such configuration released by Company. Without limiting Company's rights pursuant to the foregoing, in the event the aggregate copyright royalty rate for a record shall exceed the maximum mechanical rate, it is specifically understood and agreed that such excess may be deducted from any and all sums due Producer hereunder including without limitation royalties payable for Controlled Compositions.

(c) Notwithstanding anything to the contrary contained in paragraph 11(b) hereof, Producer shall not be responsible for mechanical copyright royalty payments in excess of the maximum mechanical rate, which excess is due solely to the inclusion on an LP of a Composition which is not a Controlled Composition for which Company becomes obligated to pay a mechanical royalty at a rate in excess of the applicable rate set forth in paragraph 11(a) above, provided: (i) such Composition was initially submitted to Producer by Company; or (ii) Producer uses its reasonable efforts to obtain a license from the copyright proprietor at the rate set forth in paragraph 11(a) above, Producer notifies Company in writing prior to the recording of such Composition that it is unable to obtain such a rate, and Company nevertheless approves the recording of such Composition.

(d) Notwithstanding the rates specified in paragraph 11(a) above, the mechanical royalty rates for Controlled Compositions embodied on LPs sold with a reduced retail list price pursuant to paragraph 6(f) hereof shall be one-half (1/2) of the otherwise applicable rate set forth in paragraph 11(a) above.

(e) No mechanical copyright royalties shall be payable in respect of Controlled Compositions which are arrangements of selections in the public domain or in respect of any other instrumentations, orchestrations and arrangements owned or controlled, directly or indirectly, by Producer or by Artist or by an individual producer of Masters. Notwithstanding the foregoing, if any arrangement of a selection in the public domain is credited by ASCAP or BMI and Producer furnishes to Company a copy of the letter from ASCAP or BMI setting forth the percentage of credit which the publisher will receive for such public performances, then Company shall license such arrangement at a mechanical copyright royalty rate equal to the relevant rate specified in paragraph 11(a) above multiplied by the percentage utilized by ASCAP or BMI.

(f) With respect to Controlled Compositions licensed hereunder for the United States, Company shall render to Producer quarterly statements, and payments therefor, of all royalties payable hereunder, within sixty (60) days after March 31, June 30, September 30 and December 31, for each quarter for which any such royalties accrue pursuant to the terms hereof. Company shall have the right to withhold a portion of such royalties as a reserve in accordance with normal company policies. The provisions of paragraph 7 hereof (other than the first sentence of said paragraph) shall be applicable to accountings rendered by Company pursuant to this paragraph 11.

(g) The provisions of this paragraph 11 shall constitute and are accepted by Producer, on Producer's and Artist's behalf and on behalf of any other owner of any Controlled Compositions or any rights therein, as full compliance by Company with all of its obligations, under the compulsory license provisions of the Copyright Law, as the same may be amended, or otherwise, arising from or connected with Company's use of said Controlled Compositions.

12. Artist shall be available, from time to time during the Term, at Company's request and expense, whenever the same will not unreasonably interfere with other professional activities of Artist, to appear for photo sessions and interviews and to perform other reasonable promotional services.

13. Producer warrants and represents the following:

(a) Producer has the right to enter into this agreement and to grant to Company the rights granted hereunder. If Producer is a corporation, then Producer is and shall be a corporation in good standing in the jurisdiction of its incorporation.

(b) Producer has a valid and enforceable agreement with Artist under which Artist is required to perform exclusively for Producer as a recording artist during the Term of this agreement. During the Term of this agreement, Producer will take all steps necessary or desirable to keep the same in full force and effect so that Company shall have the benefits of Artist's services hereunder as if Artist had contracted directly with Company.

(c) During the Term, Producer and Artist shall not be bound by any agreement which will interfere in any manner with the complete performance of this agreement by Producer and by Artist. Producer and Artist are and shall be under no disability, restriction or prohibition with respect to their rights to sign and perform under this agreement, including without limitation, restrictions regarding Compositions Artist may record for Company.

(d) As of the date hereof, there are no prior recorded performances by Artist unreleased within the United States.

(e) The Masters and Videos shall be produced in accordance with the rules and regulations of the American Federation of Musicians, the American Federation of Television and Radio Artists and all other unions having jurisdiction, including without limitation paragraph 31 of the 1987 - 1990 AFTRA Code of Fair Practice for Phonograph Recordings (or the comparable provision of any successor agreement) and all persons rendering services in connection with the Masters shall fully comply with the provisions of the Immigration Reform Control Act of 1986.

(f) The Materials, as hereinafter defined, or any use thereof will not violate or infringe upon the rights of any third party. "Materials", as used in this paragraph, means (i) all Controlled Compositions, (ii) each name used by Producer, Artist and/or any individual producer in connection with the Masters delivered hereunder, and (iii) all other musical, dramatic, artistic, and literary materials, ideas and other intellectual properties (including, without limitation, publicity material), furnished or selected by Producer, Artist and/or any individual producer and contained in or used in connection with any Masters delivered hereunder or the packaging, sale, distribution, advertising, publicizing, or any other exploitation thereof. Company's acceptance and/or utilization of Masters or Materials hereunder shall not constitute a waiver of any of Producer's and/or Artist's representations, warranties or agreements in respect thereof.

(g) Producer shall be solely responsible for and shall pay all sums due Artist, the individual producer of the Masters (subject to paragraph 15 herein), and all other parties entitled to receive royalties in connection with the use of the Masters. The sums set forth in paragraphs 6 and 28 include all royalties due such parties and Company shall not be obligated to pay any advances or royalties in excess of those expressly provided herein.

(h) Producer does hereby indemnify, save and hold Company harmless of and from any and all loss and damage (including reasonable attorneys' fees) arising out of or connected with any claim by any third party or any act by Producer or Artist which is inconsistent with any of the warranties, representations or agreements made by Producer in this agreement, and agrees to reimburse Company on demand for any payment made or loss suffered with respect to any claim or act to which the foregoing indemnity applies. If the amount of any such claim or loss has not been determined, Company may withhold sums due Producer hereunder in an amount consistent with such claim or loss pending such determination. Company shall notify Producer in writing of any claim and Producer shall have the right to participate in the defense of any claim with counsel of Producer's own choice and at Producer's own expense; provided Company shall have the right at all times, in its sole discretion, to retain or resume control of the conduct thereof. Notwithstanding anything to the contrary contained in paragraph 25 hereof, solely for the purpose of enforcing the provisions of the foregoing indemnification, Producer and Artist shall submit to the personal jurisdiction of any court, tribunal or forum in which an action or proceeding is brought against Company involving a claim to which the foregoing indemnification applies.

14. (a) By notice to Producer, Company may suspend its obligations and/or extend the expiration date of the then-current Contract Period hereunder for the duration of any default or breach by Producer or Artist in the performance of any of Producer's or Artist's obligations, warranties or representations hereunder, or any labor disagreement, fire, catastrophe, shortage of materials or other event beyond Company's control that materially hampers or makes commercially impracticable Company's normal business operations. In addition, in the event of any breach or default by Producer or Artist in the performance of any obligations, warranties or representations hereunder, Company may terminate the Term by notice to Producer. Company may elect to exercise any or all of its rights pursuant to this paragraph in addition to any other rights or remedies it may have at law or otherwise.

(b) If, at any time during the Term hereof, Artist fails for a continuous period of 180 days or more to perform actively before audiences or on live television presentations, Company, by written notice to Producer, in addition to any other rights or remedies which it may have at law or otherwise, may terminate the Term hereof.

(c) Notwithstanding anything to the contrary contained herein, if Company advances any monies hereunder to Producer or on Producer's behalf with respect to Masters to constitute any LP to be produced hereunder and thereafter Producer fails to deliver such Masters in accordance with the terms of this agreement, then, in addition to any other rights or remedies which Company may have as a result thereof and upon Company's written demand therefor, Producer shall promptly repay to Company such theretofore paid monies.

15. (a) Company and Producer shall mutually select the individual producer of the Masters embodying Artist's performances. If the individual producer approved to produce Masters hereunder is not then on Company's staff, Producer, shall engage and pay for the services rendered by such individual producer, and Company shall be under no obligation in connection therewith. If the individual producer approved to produce Masters hereunder is then on Company's staff, Company shall furnish and pay for the services rendered by such individual producer, and in respect of records derived from Masters produced by such individual producer, four (4%) percent shall be deducted from the otherwise applicable royalty rate provided for in paragraph 6(a) hereof, plus appropriate deductions and apportionments for Singles, foreign, club and other ancillary sales, etc. Notwithstanding the above, Company may engage the approved individual producer directly; in such event, Producer hereby directs Company to deduct, from all monies payable or becoming payable to Producer, the royalties that Company is obligated to pay such individual producer in respect of records derived from Masters produced by such individual producer. If the individual producer is on Company's staff or is engaged directly by Company, all sums to be recouped by Company from royalties due Producer pursuant to the provisions of this agreement shall be recouped from royalties due Producer after deducting the royalties due such individual producer.

(b) All monies paid by Company or its Licensees for independent promotion for records derived from any of the Masters shall be charged against and recouped from royalties due Producer hereunder.

16. Company may require Producer to formally give or withhold any approval or consent hereunder by notifying Producer in writing requesting the same and furnishing Producer with the information or material in respect of which such approval or consent is sought. Producer shall notify Company in writing of approval or disapproval within three (3) business days after such notice is received by Producer. _____ shall be deemed an authorized agent of Producer to give such approval or disapproval. In the event of disapproval or no consent, the reasons therefor shall be stated. Failure to so notify Company within the aforesaid period shall be deemed to be consent or approval.

17. During the Term, neither Producer nor Artist shall endorse any blank tape or other blank recording media (except professional tape and professional recording equipment) or otherwise permit Artist's Identification to be used in connection with such products.

18. (a) Producer agrees that, in all of Artist's endeavors in the entertainment field, Producer and Artist will exert best efforts to cause Artist to be billed as an "Arista Records Exclusive Recording Artist".

(b) Producer agrees to furnish Company at no cost twenty (20) tickets for each of Artist's concert performances during the Term hereof.

19. This agreement has been entered into in the State of New York, and the validity, interpretation and legal effect of this agreement shall be governed by the laws of the State of New York applicable to contracts entered into and performed entirely within the State of New York, with respect to the determination of any claim, dispute or disagreement which may arise out of the interpretation, performance, or breach of this agreement. All claims, disputes or disagreements which may arise out of the interpretation, performance or breach of this agreement shall be submitted exclusively to the jurisdiction of the state courts of the State of New York or the Federal District courts located in New York City. Any process in any such action or proceeding may among other methods be served upon Producer by delivering or mailing the same pursuant to paragraph 23 hereof. Any such delivery or mail service shall be deemed to have the same force and effect as personal service within the State of New York. Producer hereby submits to the jurisdiction of the aforesaid courts.

20. This writing sets forth the entire understanding between the parties with respect to the subject matter hereof. No modification or waiver of any provision of or of any default under this agreement shall be binding upon Company or Producer unless confirmed in writing by an authorized officer of Company and Producer. No such waiver shall constitute a waiver by Company of compliance thereafter with the same or any other provision or of its right to enforce the same or any other provision thereafter.

21. (a) The term "Artist" or "Group" as used in this agreement, shall be deemed to refer jointly and severally to the individuals first mentioned herein as comprising Artist and to such other individual(s) who during the Term shall then comprise the Group. The substitution of any individuals in the Group and the adding to or subtracting from the individuals comprising the Group shall be done only with the written approval of Company. Any such substituted or added individual shall be deemed to have agreed to be bound by all of the terms and conditions of this agreement. Producer shall notify Company immediately in writing if any member of the Group leaves the Group or if any individual is added to the Group or if the Group disbands; in such case, Company shall have the right, to be exercised within ninety (90) days after Company's receipt of such written notice, to terminate the Term of this agreement by notifying Producer in writing. If Company so requests within said ninety (90) day period, Producer shall deliver to Company a "demo" tape embodying the performances of the members of the Group at that time or, at Company's election, shall hold a live audition by such members, and the ninety (90) day period in which Company may elect to terminate the Term of this agreement shall be deemed to commence upon the date of the delivery to Company of the demo tape or upon the date of the live audition, as the case may be.

(b) Each of the individuals comprising the Group agree that, if any of them leave the Group or if the Group disbands, Company shall have the irrevocable option to be exercised within ninety (90) days after Company receives written notice that an individual has left the Group (or, if within such ninety (90) day period Company so requests a demo tape or live audition by such leaving member, within ninety (90) days following the date of delivery to Company of the demo tape or of the live audition) to enter into an exclusive individual recording agreement with any one or more of such individuals (including for a Term equal to the initial Contract Period and any and all Option Periods provided for herein), except that: the royalties payable to such individual shall be two-thirds of the royalties provided for herein; the amount to be paid for Recording Costs shall be the amount provided for in the first sentence of paragraph 8(a); and there shall be no payments made pursuant to paragraph 9. If the Group has an unearned balance (i.e., unrecouped advances or other outstanding offsets against Producer's royalties hereunder), then Company shall have the right to apply sums payable to each such leaving member pursuant to any such exclusive individual recording agreement against the Group's unearned balance; provided, however, if the Group has not disbanded, Company shall not be entitled to recoup more than a prorata share of the Group's unearned balance (i.e., a ratio based on the number one (1) compared to the total number of Group members as of the date the leaving member concerned enters into an exclusive individual recording agreement with Company) from sums payable to such leaving member. Each such individual recording agreement shall remain in full force and effect whether or not Company exercises its right to any or all Option Periods with respect to the Group, or with respect to any of the other individuals comprising the Group.

22. (a) Company shall have the right, but not the obligation, to produce one (1) or more film(s) or videotape(s) ("Video(s)") based upon Artist's performance(s). Producer warrants and represents that Artist shall be available to perform for the production of each Video and that Producer and Artist shall fully cooperate with the producer, director and all other production personnel in the production of each Video. For each Video that Company so produces, Company will bear all of the production costs contained within a budget described in paragraph 28(b) below.

(b) Each such Video shall be produced in accordance with a written budget approved by Company prior to its production. If production costs for the production of a particular Video exceed those contained in the applicable approved budget, then Producer shall be solely responsible for and shall pay such excess costs if such excess costs are incurred as a result of Producer's and/or Artist's acts or omissions, provided, however, that Company shall have the right to pay such excess and, without limiting its rights, to deduct the amount of such excess from any sums which may be payable to Producer under this agreement. Each Video shall be shot on a date or dates and at a location to be approved by Company. Company and Producer shall mutually approve the Composition which is to be the subject of the Video, the concept and storyboard of the Video, the director and any other creative participants of the Video. A Composition embodied on a Single is hereby deemed approved by Producer.

(c) Company shall pay to Producer the following royalties for the sale by Company or its Licensees of Videos, against which all amounts incurred and/or paid by Company in respect of the production costs of Videos and all other advances paid to or on behalf of Producer shall be chargeable:

(i) A royalty of ten (10%) percent of the retail list price for all Videos sold by Company for distribution in the United States and not returned (rather than the royalty under paragraph 6(a) hereof).

(ii) A royalty of seven and one-half (7-1/2%) percent of the retail list price for all Videos sold by Company or its regular foreign distributors for distribution outside of the United States, as to which Company receives payment (rather than the royalty under paragraph 6(b) hereof).

(iii) A royalty of fifty (50%) percent of Company's net receipts for all other commercial exploitations of Videos.

(iv) The above amounts shall be inclusive of any payments required to be made to any third parties.

(v) Except as otherwise provided herein, the provisions of paragraphs 6 and 7 concerning the computation and payment of record royalties shall be applicable to the payment of Video royalties.

(d) With respect to records containing separate portions of audio alone and audio coupled with visual images (e.g., CDVs), Company shall pay to Producer the royalties set forth in paragraph 6 hereof, rather than the royalties set forth in paragraph 28(c) above; provided, however, Company shall be entitled to charge fifty (50%) percent of the royalties payable to Producer in respect of such records against the production costs of Videos.

(e) Company shall be entitled to recoup fifty (50%) percent of the production costs of Videos from the royalties payable to Producer under paragraph 6 hereof.

(f) Producer shall issue (or shall cause the music publishing companies having the right to do so to issue) (i) worldwide, perpetual synchronization licenses, and (ii) perpetual licenses for public performance in the United States (to the extent that ASCAP and BMI are unable to issue same) to Company at no cost for the promotional use and commercial exploitation of all Controlled Compositions in Videos effective as of the commencement of production of the applicable Video (and Producer's execution of this agreement shall constitute the issuance of such licenses by any music publishing company which is owned or controlled directly or indirectly by Producer, Artist or the individual producer of a Master embodied in a particular Video or by any party associated or affiliated with Producer, Artist or such individual producer). If Producer fails to cause any such music publishing company to issue any such license to Company, and if Company thereafter pays any fee to such music publishing company in order to obtain any such license, then Company shall have the right, without limiting its rights, to deduct the amount of such license fee from any sums payable to Producer under this agreement.

(g) Each Video shall be Company's exclusive property throughout the Territory and Company shall have the right to exploit each Video for promotional and commercial purposes in perpetuity throughout the Territory. Company shall have no obligation to pay Producer or Artist in connection with Company's distribution, exhibition and broadcast of each Video for promotional purposes throughout the Territory.

IN WITNESS WHEREOF, the parties hereto have executed this agreement the day and year hereinabove first written.

ARISTA RECORDS, INC.

By

_____

_____

By

_____

Federal Tax Identification Number

_____

APPENDIX 12
Organizations, Unions, and Guilds

American Federation of Musicians (AF of M), 1501 Broadway, Suite 600, New York, NY 10036. Tel: (212) 869-1330.

American Federation of Television and Radio Artists (AFTRA), 260 Madison Ave., New York, NY 10016. Tel: (212) 532-0800.

American Guild of Musical Artists (AGMA), 1727 Broadway, New York, NY 10019-5284. Tel: (212) 265-3687.

American Guild of Variety Artists (AGVA), 184 Fifth Ave., New York, NY 10010. Tel: (212) 675-1003.

American Society of Composers, Authors and Publishers (ASCAP), One Lincoln Plaza, New York, NY 10023. Tel: (212) 595-3050.

Broadcast Music, Inc. (BMI), 320 West 57th St., New York, NY 10019. Tel: (212) 586-2000. In Los Angeles: 8730 Sunset Boulevard, 3rd Floor West, Los Angeles, CA 90069. Tel: (213) 659-9109. In Nashville: 10 Music Square East, Nashville, TN 37203. Tel: (615) 259-3625.

Conference of Personal Managers, East, 1650 Broadway, Suite 705, New York, NY 10019. Tel: (212) 265-3366.

Conference of Personal Managers, West, 10707 Camarillo Street, Suite 308, North Hollywood, California 91602. Tel: (818) 762-6276.

Country Music Association (CMA), 7 Music Circle North, Nashville, TN 37203. Tel: (615) 244-2840.

Gospel Music Association, 39 Music Square West, Nashville, TN 37203. Tel: (615) 242-0303.

The Harry Fox Agency, Inc., 205 East 42nd St., New York, NY 10017. Tel: (212) 370-5330.

Music Performance Trust Funds, 1501 Broadway, Suite 315, New York, NY 10036-5503. Tel: (212) 391-3950.

National Academy of Recording Arts and Sciences (NARAS), 303 North Glenoaks Blvd., Burbank, CA 91502. Tel: (213) 849-1313. In New York: 157 West 57th St., Suite 902, New York, NY 10019. Tel: (212) 245-5440.

National Music Publishers Association, 205 East 42nd St., 18th fl., New York, NY 10017. Tel: (212) 370-5330.

Recording Industry Association of America, Inc. (RIAA), 1020 19th St., NW, Suite 3200, Washington, DC 20036. Tel: (202) 775-0101.

SESAC, 55 Music Square East, Nashville, TN 37203. Tel: (615) 320-0055.

The Songwriters Guild of America, 276 Fifth Ave., Suite 306, New York, NY 10001. Tel: (212) 686-6820. In Los Angeles: 6430 Sunset Boulevard, Hollywood, CA 90028. Tel: (213) 462-1108. In Nashville: 50 Music Square West, Nashville, TN 37203. Tel: (615) 329-1782.

APPENDIX 13
Suggested Further Reading

Books and Reference Works

The Billboard Guide to Music Publicity, by Jim Pettigrew, Billboard Books, 1989.

The Billboard International Buyer's Guide, Billboard Publications, published yearly.

The Encyclopedia of the Music Business, by Harvey Rachlin, Harper & Row, 1981.

Making It in the New Music Business, by James Riordan, Writer's Digest, 1988.

Making Money Making Music, by James W. Dearing, Writer's Digest, 1982.

More About This Business of Music, Fourth Edition, by Sidney Shemel and M. William Krasilovsky, Billboard Books, 1989.

Musician's Guide to Copyright, by J. Gunnar Erickson, Edward R. Hearn, and Mark E. Halloran, Charles Scribner's Sons, 1983.

A Musician's Guide to the Road, by Gary Burton, Billboard Books, 1981.

The One-Minute Manager, by Kenneth Blanchard and Spencer Johnson, Morrow, 1982.

This Business of Music, Fifth Edition, by Sidney Shemel and M. William Krasilovsky, Billboard Books, 1987.

Periodicals

Billboard, 1515 Broadway, New York, NY (weekly)

Musician, 31 Commercial St., Gloucester, MA (monthly)

Radio and Records, 1930 Century Park West, Los Angeles, CA (weekly)

Rolling Stone, 745 Fifth Ave., New York, NY (monthly)

Variety, 475 Park Avenue South, New York, NY (weekly)

Index

Accountants, 74–75
Accounting and trusts, 56
Accounting Department, 189
Adaptations, 176
Advertising, 164–71, 191
Advisors, business, 75–76
American Federation of Musicians, 160, 200
Appearances: foreign, 177; personal, 86–87, 152–62; television, 145–48
Appointment, getting the, 28–30
Appointment of authority, 46–48
Arrangements, 176
Artist: evaluation of, 78–81; finding an, 32–33; material, 207–8; as publisher, 138–39
Artist and Repertoire (A&R) Department, 190
Artist management: defined, 11–13; limited, 20; self-, 19–20; total, 21
Artist/manager relationship: establishing, 7–57; evaluating, 210
Artist Relations Department, 191, 199
Artist's development team, 105–10
Attorneys, 73–74

Balance sheet, 222–23
Banking, 66–67
Booking agency, 161–62
Booking agent, 209–10
Bookkeeping/tax planning, 69–70
Budgeting, 70–71
Business, types of, 61–65
Business Affairs Department, 189

Career: evaluating, 205–11; maintenance and control, 181–211; planning, 88–93
Career Development Department, 191–92

Clubs, 153–56
Commercials, 164–71
Concerts, 157–59
Contracts: management, 44–57; negotiating, 169–70; performance, 160–61; renewals and extensions, 50–51; recording, see Recording contracts; term, 125–26
Corporate sponsorship, 167–68
Corporation, 63–64
Credentials, 37
Credit, using, 223–24

Demo, multi-track, 113–14
Disputes, 54–55

Employment agency disclaimer, 48
Employment agreements, 65
Endorsements, 167
Estate planning, 226
Exclusive Personal Services Agreement, 115
Exclusivity, 52–53
Expense control, 222–24

Fame, coping with, 215–20
Foreign music publishing, 174–76
Foreign record sales, 173–74

Goals, 81–82, 89–91, 210–11

Hotels and club chains, 156

Image: enhancing, 207–11; formulation, 81–85; marketing, 85–87
Insurance: equipment, 68; liability, 68; life, 69; vehicle, 67–68
International markets, 172–77
Investments, 224

Joint ownership agreement, 139

Legal clauses, general, 56–57

Legal Department, 189

Listening room, 154–55

Lounge, 153–54

Manager: conflict of interest with, 38–39; contacts, 31; credentials, 10–11, 37; death of, 51; education of, 32; fees of, 37–38; finding a, 23–31; responsibilities of, 47, 140–41, 181–86; role of, 7–8

Manager/artist relationship. See Artist/manager relationship

Management: compensation, 48–52; contract, 44–57; of money, 221–27; self-, 19–20

Marketing, Sales, and Distribution Department, 190

Merchandising, 164

Money management, 221–27

Motion pictures, 150–51

Movie synchronization fees, 135

Multi-track demo, 113–14

Music publishing, 129–41; foreign, 174–76

Music videos, 143–44; costs, 144–45

Negotiating: commercials and endorsements, 169–70; record contracts, 122–23, 128

Parties, private, 156–57

Partnership, 62–63

Payment, time of, 49–50

Percentage base, establishing, 49

Performing rights, 135

Personal appearances, 86–87, 145–48, 152–62, 177

Personnel, finding, 116–17

Power of attorney, 47–48

Presentation kit, 30–31

Press kit, 86

Press, Publicity, and Advertising Department, 191, 199

Printed music, sale of, 135

Producer, finding a, 114–16

Profit-and-loss statement, 222–23

Promotion Department, 190–91

Promotions, 158–59

Proprietorship, 62

Public relations, 201

Publicity Department, 191, 199

Publisher, finding a, 136–38

Publishing, music, 129–41; foreign, 174–76

Radio, 148–50

Record company, 208; cooperating with, 192–94; operations of, 188–92

Record producer, 208

Record sales, foreign, 173–74

Recording contracts, 118–128

Recordings, making, 112–14

Rehearsals, 117–18

Retirement, planning for, 225

Road manager, responsibilities of, 196–204

Rock and show rooms, 154

Royalties: accounting of, 127; for recordings, 123–25, 134; on foreign record sales, 173; performance, 140; songwriters, 133

Sales kit, 30–31

Self-management, 19–20

Service mark, 66

Showcase, 154–55; artist-sponsored, 155–56

Show rooms, 154

Studio, finding a, 116–17

Success, 109–10, 215–31

Tax planning, 69–70, 224–25

Television, 145–48

Tour: after, 204; on the road, 203–4; preparations for, 197–200

Trade name. See Service mark

Translations, 176

Travel arrangements, 200. See also Tour

Trusts, 56

Videos. See Music videos

Warrantees, artist, 55–56